PRAISE

CRAFT AND CONSCIENCE

"*Craft and Conscience* is that rigorously researched and lushly written 'How-to' book that every single human who has dared to write needs in our lives. . . . Rarely do we get books that encourage readers to reconsider how we read and write. Intellectually and soulfully invigorating."

—KIESE LAYMON, author of *Heavy: An American Memoir*

"A gift to writers and justice seekers everywhere! *Craft and Conscience* is a handbook for how to wield words to shape culture and inspire change. Insightful, practical, and empowering. Thank you, Kavita Das!"

—VALARIE KAUR, civil rights leader and author of
See No Stranger: A Memoir and Manifesto of Revolutionary Love

"In *Craft and Conscience*, Kavita Das constructs a vocabulary, a methodology, and an ethics for socially engaged writing, while bringing together a staggering range of writers and issues. In the process, Das makes a profound and compelling argument for why this kind of writing matters and the radical, transformative power it holds. This book has restored my faith in the written word."

—LACY M. JOHNSON, author of *The Reckonings*

"Kavita Das has assembled a vital primer on writing with purpose, a guidebook that our turbulent times demand. In addition to her own insightful essays, she has compiled an impressive roster of dauntless thinkers who don't hesitate to share necessary and even troubling truths. These essays not only address the role of writing in exposing tyranny and injustice but also provide glimpses of a world where love and equality shape our lives."

—JABARI ASIM, author of *We Can't Breathe:
On Black Lives, White Lies, and the Art of Survival*

"Writing with conscience' is sometimes pitted against 'good writing' as though the two cannot mean the same thing. Das blows up this false equivalency. *Craft and Conscience* is so clear, accessible, and profound, I wondered how a book on these themes had not existed before. The answer: it needed Das, who combines her unique skills as reader and writer to demonstrate how great writing always sees deeply into the human heart. As a teacher, Das breaks down precisely how and why such writing—across race, gender, and class—reverberates, inspiring and challenging us to do our best and most intentional work. A book of phenomenal intelligence, generosity, and wisdom, and indispensable for the classroom and for anyone who wants to make words matter."

—MARIE MUTSUKI MOCKETT, author of
American Harvest: God, Country, and Farming in the Heartland

"Brilliant! A must-read for anyone who cares deeply about social and political issues and wants to make their own voice heard. Kavita Das's *Craft and Conscience* aims to bring out the inner activist in your writing—whether you're an emerging writer or an established one—by showing you how to articulate your motivations, by showcasing essays from masters of the genre, and by analyzing what forceful, well-thought arguments are made of."

—LAURIE GWEN SHAPIRO, author of *The Stowaway:*
A Young Man's Extraordinary Adventure to Antarctica

"This compendium is a brilliant and kaleidoscopic must-read for writers. Das gathers up a wide-ranging and whip-smart array of thinkers while serving us a feast of timely advocacy and learning."

—AIMEE NEZHUKUMATATHIL, author of *World of Wonders:*
In Praise of Fireflies, Whale Sharks, and Other Astonishments

"This is the book I wish I'd had when I was starting out! What a joy to have it now. Kavita Das orients us with great precision to the many contradictory considerations that nonfiction writers face, from how we enter the story to how we balance dramatic elements and historical context. I found myself reading and nodding in agreement, thinking: yes, that's exactly right!"

—DAISY HERNÁNDEZ, author of *The Kissing Bug: A True Story of a Family, an Insect, and a Nation's Neglect of a Deadly Disease*

"An instructive guide for writers hoping to move the needle, *Craft and Conscience* gathers some of our best contemporary writers, like Alexander Chee, Kaitlyn Greenidge, and Nicole Chung, while Kavita Das's steady voice introduces prospective writers to critical writing in our dystopian era."

—MATTHEW SALESSES, author of *Craft in the Real World: Rethinking Fiction Writing* and *Workshopping*

"For writers seeking guidance on how to write about social justice with compassion and insight, Das curates an eclectic mix of essays by authors who've long contemplated the immense struggles facing humanity, while proffering a thoughtful way of bearing witness to the world."

—TANAÏS, author of *In Sensorium: Notes for My People*

"A fascinating and forceful guide to stepping up and speaking out on the page."

—SUSAN SHAPIRO, author of *The Byline Bible: Get Published in 5 Weeks*

"Kavita Das's book is part how-to, part call to action. It is 100 percent lyrical and passionate and will resonate with anyone who is compelled to share and transform narratives that reflect the world. Filled with prose and practicality from some of the greatest writers and thinkers of our times, *Craft and Conscience* feels like the action plan we always intend to put in place after our fiery salons, dinner parties, and community gatherings. It is more needed than ever."

—S. MITRA KALITA, founder and publisher of Epicenter NYC and cofounder of URL Media

CRAFT
AND
CONSCIENCE

HOW TO WRITE ABOUT
SOCIAL ISSUES

KAVITA DAS

BEACON PRESS, BOSTON

BEACON PRESS
Boston, Massachusetts
www.beacon.org

Beacon Press books
are published under the auspices of
the Unitarian Universalist Association of Congregations.

25 24 23 22   8 7 6 5 4 3 2 1

This book is printed on acid-free paper that meets the uncoated paper
ANSI/NISO specifications for permanence as revised in 1992.

Text design and composition by Kim Arney

Excerpts from "Love the Masters," by Jericho Brown,
from *The Racial Imaginary: Writers on Race in the Life of the
Mind*, and from "Small Acts of Creation: On the Short Story and
the Novel," by Zeyn Joukhadar, from *Bird's Thumb: Write Here,
Write Now*, are printed here by permission.

Library of Congress Cataloging-in-Publication Data is available for this title.
Library of Congress Control Number: 2022017382
Paperback ISBN: 978-0-8070-4649-4
Ebook ISBN: 978-0-8070-4653-1

*To the social change agents,
who risk much to change the way we think and act,
by speaking out and marching forward,
and most importantly, by modeling a better society.*

*To the writers,
who take us on journeys,
within and without,
through their wondrous imaginations and words.*

*And to those, like me,
who straddle these two realms,
fervently believing that writing can, and has,
changed the world.*

Every poem is a love poem. Every poem is a political poem. So say the masters. Every love poem is political. Every political poem must fall in love.

JERICHO BROWN, from "Love the Masters," in *The Racial Imaginary: Writers on Race in the Life of the Mind*

Every act of creation begins with a first impulse that things could be different. Small acts catalyze movements and monuments, placing a single word or stone on another until a larger structure emerges. This, too, is how we write.

—ZEYN JOUKHADAR, from "Small Acts of Creation: On the Short Story and the Novel," in *Bird's Thumb: Write Here, Write Now*

CONTENTS

B efore we have the words for understanding the systems we live in, before we can track the relationship between social change and social justice, we have our own acutely observing bodies and our ever-present desire to be part of the group. Humans, we know, have evolved to be social animals, an early need to band together against predators and elements becoming the desire to build complex communities, hold collective grief, warm ourselves with shared laughter and stories. Our instinct to bond is so deep that, sometimes, observing what keeps us apart from the group can feel like paving the path to our own exile.

What will happen to us if we dare call attention to the parts of the system that benefit some at great cost to others? Will it be received as an act of sabotage, or selfishness, or fragility? Will we find ourselves discredited or, worse, banished, and if so, how will we face that wilderness alone?

The last decade in the US has been marked by fervent calls for change and equally fervent calls to squash, smear, and exile those seeking it. Systems that have long operated to benefit few at the expense of many—patriarchy, white supremacy, capitalism—are being named and shamed, which is to say recognized as deeply unfair and challenged to evolve. Along with calls for accountability have come a slew of insults targeting those who demand it. They've been labeled everything from traitors (sabotaging) to parasites (selfish) to snowflakes (fragile). While the accusations are unsurprising, they're also telling in what they seek to undermine, namely the growing compassion, clarity, and solidarity between so many disparate groups. It's easier to label someone a special snowflake and tell them to go home if they don't like it here. It's much harder to tell many equals, with lives every bit as precious and valuable as your own, to keep suffering in their own home so you can thrive. Doing it while calling it "life and liberty and the pursuit of happiness" for all? Impossible.

While it might seem silly to think that a well-written essay or an op-ed could possibly offer anything helpful in the face of all this, the power of words—to challenge, to illuminate, and, yes, to *help*—cannot be overstated. We can't fight against what we can't see, nor can we coalesce around a shared problem when we don't know how it touches and implicates each of us. And none of us can fix a broken system alone. Think of this book as a sure step toward understanding how words can become community and contribute to change. Each of the pieces contained within it have walked us toward a formerly murky corner of oppression and allowed us to clearly see all its working parts, including, in some cases, our own complicity. Through deft assessment, sound reasoning, and daring imagination, they show us not only what we have endured separately but how we might realign ourselves into collective thriving. It's a particular kind of help this book offers, then—a possible map through the wilderness as well as a revelation of how many of us already live here together, deep in the work of building a better home.

—Mira Jacob

INTRODUCTION

I came to writing gradually, yet all at once. I had been working in social change for several years, and during that time, two forces simultaneously pulled me to writing. I increasingly began to believe in the importance of writing about the issues I was working on in a way that reached hearts and minds, whether it was raising awareness of breast cancer, addressing challenges faced by returning veterans and their families, or pushing for greater racial justice and equity. In parallel, I became interested in creative writing, taking classes and joining a longtime writing group but held no aspirations to be a writer.

As I wrote more and more opinion editorials (op-eds) and letters to the editor about the issues I was dedicatedly working to address in my career, I was also writing, workshopping, and publishing stories, often inspired by my own experiences and my need to make sense of them. Even though I saw these two forms of writing as completely separate, with little overlap—one professional and one personal—they were both fed by my motivation and commitment to social change, as well as my desire to express myself artistically. And I now understand they were feeding each other.

Writing and social change work are both about transformation. Deeply affecting writing brings about personal transformation through subtle shifts in awareness, perspective, and empathy. Meanwhile, social change work, as its name suggests, is built around changing systems, policies, and culture to address injustices and improve lives. Writing about social issues, therefore, sits at the intersection of writing and social change work. When writing about social issues is effective, it has the power to spark a personal transformation that feeds into collective social and cultural transformation.

When I made the decision to leave my nearly fifteen-year career in social change because I felt compelled to write the life story of an overlooked woman of color artist, it seemed sudden and drastic. Although the worlds of social change and writing seemed far apart, I came to realize they are connected by writers like me, who view social issues as inextricably linked to their artistic endeavors. Since I jumped into writing full-time without an MFA in creative writing or an MA in journalism, intent on writing about issues I believed in deeply while also developing myself as a writer, I sought to connect with and study the work of writers who consistently engage social issues in their work.

I wrestled with the question *Is it possible to write about a social issue in a way that is compelling while doing it justice?* Writing about social issues for various outlets and reading and examining the work of other writers confirmed for me that it *is* possible to write compellingly yet with integrity. To do so requires that the writer be clear about their own motivations for writing about an issue as well as who they are trying to reach and what their hopes are for their work out in the world.

I created the class Writing About Social Issues several years ago because it was the class I wish I'd had as an emerging writer, a class where I teach key lessons, reflections, frameworks, and considerations for writing effectively about social issues. I've been so inspired by the work of my students, on and off the page. They come from a diverse array of identities and experiences but share a commitment to raising awareness and sparking change around social issues they care about.

We are living in challenging times fraught with complex issues, yet we are also more socially aware than ever before. Inequities and injustices that were long overlooked, hidden, or socially accepted have risen to the surface through concerted struggles to be questioned, challenged, and in the best cases, rectified. In teaching

Writing About Social Issues for several years across different venues, it's clear that these lessons are universal, as more writers are seeking to grapple with social issues in their work. So, now I've written the book I wish I'd had as an emerging writer.

Just as I had to clarify my own motivations and goals for writing about social issues when I transitioned to becoming a writer, any writer considering writing about a social issue should start with a clear understanding of why they are writing and what hopes they have for their writing. Through trial and error and reflection, I learned that I needed to find the right balance between focusing on my subject—the issue I was passionate about—and focusing on my readers—the people whom I was trying to reach and persuade. And to achieve the right balance, I had to determine how much context or background to provide and how much to be driven by the story and its narrative elements.

Should I tell the story from my perspective, as someone who has experienced the issue personally, or would the issue be better served told from the vantage point of a reported perspective? Perhaps I should use my topical expertise to write an opinion editorial piece to raise awareness and change minds?

I've found myself on both sides of ever-raging debates around cultural appropriation because, as a woman of color writer, I've watched with great frustration as writers engage issues of race and culture in ways that lack knowledge and sensitivity, often exoticizing or vilifying these issues. At the same time, I don't believe in censorship. I believe in a world where most anyone can write about most anything. Ultimately, I've tried to be culturally sensitive as a writer, especially when writing about issues outside of my experience and identity.

When some people consider writing about social issues, they naively presume they will write about an issue about which they care deeply and social change will follow soon after—minds changed, policies drafted, cultures shifted. One reason for this presumption might be because our media has a habit of focusing on the moment of change rather than the decades or centuries of struggle that preceded it. Those who work in social change movements know change is painfully slow, thwarted by major structural barriers and hostile resistance on the part of those invested in keeping things as they are because they benefit from the status quo. So, when we consider the implications of writing about social issues, we must consider not just the positive implications but the negative ones, both to ourselves and to others.

In *Craft and Conscience*, I share my own lessons and reflections, culled from close to a decade of writing about social issues and fifteen years of working in social change. I include twelve of my own essays on a range of issues, from racial injustice and inequity to the impact of cultural erasure and cultural appropriation to the perils of the anti-vaccine movement against the backdrop of perpetual health inequities, heightened by a pandemic, to misogyny and patriarchy here and abroad. I offer my writer's perspective, picking them apart and explaining my goals for each piece and the decisions I made. In some chapters where I discuss narrative choices, writing from reported perspective versus personal perspective, for example, I include essays I've written about the same issue but from differing perspectives and compare my approach to each one. I want to demonstrate that it is possible to write about the same topic in different ways, which allows us to reach different audiences and achieve different goals.

I'm especially thrilled to pull together in *Craft and Conscience* the work of some of the writers I most admire, for their consistently incisive, thoughtful, and compelling writing on a diverse range of crucial social issues. I offer my perspective as a reader on why and how each of their pieces is effective in illuminating an issue while keeping the reader engaged. What better way of contemplating and learning how to write with integrity and nuance about social issues than by examining the work of those who have done so by being attentive to both craft and conscience?

We start by examining the prescient words of two of the best-known writers of conscience of this past century—George Orwell and James Baldwin—who anchor us in the importance of knowing our own motivations and goals for writing about social issues, even if those motivations are complicated and evolving. Garnette Cadogan shares two pieces on the experiences of being a Black man in public spaces and the ways in which these experiences shape the person and the place. In the first, he focuses on the reader, emphasizing narrative elements, while in the second, he focuses on the subject, the lens that captures Black boys transforming public spaces through their love of soccer.

To understand how to balance context and narrative, we examine excerpts of Imani Perry's searing epistolary work, *Breathe: A Letter to My Sons*, and Roxanne Dunbar-Ortiz's groundbreaking *An Indigenous Peoples' History of the United States*, as well as a piece by Gaiutra Bahadur, reflecting on her experience writing *Coolie Woman: The Odyssey of Indenture*, which explores the journeys of migrant indentured servants through the story of her own great-grandmother's life journey.

Jaquira Díaz shares two pieces about the lives of marginalized Latina teenage girls that demonstrate how to mine life experiences and write with authority from both a personal perspective and a reported perspective. And through the work of visual artist and writer Crystal Z Campbell, we see that it is possible to creatively blend multiple elements and perspectives.

One of the ways our society engages in raising awareness and debating about the thorny social issues of our times is through opinion pieces (op-eds), where influential leaders, topical experts, and everyday citizens share their own opinions, expertise, and experiences to help us understand the true implications of these issues on human lives. We review thought-provoking op-eds from Nicole Chung, who refutes long-held problematic notions of transracial adoption by illuminating the experiences of transracial adoptees, and Yashica Dutt, who calls attention to how the harms of casteism persist not only in India but throughout the diaspora, even in the pioneering halls of Silicon Valley.

One of the most fraught and debated issues in recent years has been cultural appropriation. Some writers have accused others of cultural appropriation for writing outside of their sphere of identity and experience. In response, other writers have countered with their own accusations of censorship. These explosive binary conversations rarely explore what is lost through cultural appropriation and, just as importantly, what is gained by cultural sensitivity. To better understand the charged complexity of cultural appropriation, we start by getting a concrete definition of *cultural appropriation* and some background on the forces involved in contributing to it from Lauren Michele Jackson's incisive *White Negroes: When Cornrows Were In Vogue . . . and Other Thoughts on Cultural Appropriation*. Alexander Chee offers sage advice on the importance of pausing and revisiting our motivations by asking ourselves, why do *I* want to tell *this* story? Meanwhile, Kaitlyn Greenidge deftly untangles the importance of creative freedom, concerns around cultural sensitivity and appropriation, and accusations of censorship from writers who are bristling against being held accountable for their blatant cultural insensitivity.

When we talk about writing about social issues, we tend to focus on raising awareness, changing attitudes, and the potential for engendering social change. While this is certainly possible, I believe it is important for us to also be aware that writing about social issues can have potentially negative implications. Writing about fraught issues can provoke strong reactions from those who disagree with our perspective and, in this era of unfettered social media, unleash backlash against the writer or, even worse, vulnerable individuals or communities already impacted by the issue.

Beyond this, if a writer is writing about themselves or their own community, there are ripple effects on themselves and others that should be considered before their work goes out into the world. Alice Wong shares insights into what is involved and at stake, on and off the page, in her work as a writer and a disability rights advocate. And Gabrielle Bellot immerses us in the experience of navigating life as a transgender woman and writer of color.

We each have the ability to spark change on the page. Whether you are a seasoned writer who wants to engage more intentionally and responsibly with social issues in your writing, a social change agent who wants to bring to the page the passion and understanding you have from working on an issue, or an individual who has personally been impacted by an issue and wants to use your own story to offer powerful insights, my deepest hope is that this book invites more writers, emerging and established, to engage social issues in their work, because doing so compellingly yet with integrity is a critical first step in creating social change.

CHAPTER 1

WHY WE WRITE

*Interrogating Our Motivations for
Writing About Social Issues*

"Is all writing political?"

This is the first question I ask students in my Writing About Social Issues class, which I created and have taught for several years. We tend to associate political writing with certain types of nonfiction, such as journalistic investigations, exposés of a social issue, or opinion pieces (op-eds) weighing in on one side or another of the public debate over a fraught topic. In response to my question, some students point to recent novels revolving around pop culture themes or genres like romance novels or westerns as evidence that all writing is not political.

I prompt them to take a deeper look at these examples. When *Sex and the City*, a novel-turned-blockbuster TV series about four young professional women in New York City, features barely any major characters of color, that is a statement on the creators' perception of one of the most diverse cities in the world. Similarly, westerns and historical romance novels are now facing reckonings with how they've portrayed, or erased, characters of color—such as Bass Reeves, a storied Black cowboy lawman who some say is the true inspiration for the Lone Ranger—and also how their rosters have been filled overwhelmingly with white writers who have perpetuated an incomplete and biased perspective of history.[1]

Therefore, it becomes clear that all writing is political, whether the author or publisher intended it to be or not. Every piece of writing reflects a certain perspective or worldview that either directly or indirectly acknowledges social issues, or eschews them, which too is both an artistic choice and a political statement made by the writer.

When we turn our attention to the focus of this book, which is exploring the task of intentionally and explicitly writing about social issues, it seems fitting to start with a working definition of *social issue*. While it is hard to find a definition of the term *social issue*, *Merriam-Webster*'s dictionary defines *social* as "of or relating to human society, the interaction of the individual and the group, or the welfare of human beings as members of society" and defines *issue* as "a vital or unsettled matter."[2] This dictionary does, however, include a definition for *social conscience*: "caring or concern about important social issues." So, putting these together, we can say that writing about social issues encompasses writing conscientiously about vital or unsettled matters relating to human society and welfare.

I take an expansive view of social issues so I define them as any topics that pertain to how an individual or a group is impacted by societal conditions. Some examples of crucial social issues of the moment include racial justice, racial and class equity, gender disparities and misogyny, climate change, reproductive rights, transgender rights, and gun control. Social issues can be the result of restrictive formal laws and policies but can also manifest through long-held social conventions and practices, and often the two reinforce each other. Additionally, social issues can be compounded by other social considerations, including race, class, and gender. For example, a 2017 report by the United States Sentencing Commission noted that Black male offenders receive longer sentences than their white counterparts.[3] The social issues highlighted by this include racial justice and criminal justice reform, but also on a deeper level, economic inequities and the school-to-prison pipeline.

Most current social issues, from climate change to transgender rights, are urgent because of how they are impacting lives in the present moment. And then there's how we feel about them. If we're directly affected by a social issue or it resonates with our sense of justice, we feel passionate and called upon to address it through our actions, which can include protesting, engaging in public policy campaigns, lobbying, and of course, writing about them. Yet, before we rush into writing about social issues, it is crucial that we explore and clarify our own motivations for writing about an issue.

We should have a clear understanding of why we want to write about an issue and what we hope our work will accomplish. It is also vital that we reflect on who we are as storytellers and how we relate to the issue in terms of our identities. We should approach understanding our motivations not as a static process but as an evolving one by checking in with ourselves regularly about our motivations for writing about a social issue, taking note of how these motivations might shift and what factors contribute to those shifts, including events happening in our own lives or in the larger world.

Here are a few key questions we should ask ourselves before we begin writing about a social issue in order to understand our motivations:

- Which social issue do I want to write about?
- Why am I passionate about this issue, and why do I want to write about it?

As noted, it's important to revisit these questions periodically, ideally before embarking on each new writing project. Once you've fleshed out why you want to write about a specific social issue, do a deeper exploration by answering the following questions, which will help you understand and address the internal and external obstacles you face and guide the scope, tone, and reach of your writing:

- What are your goals and hopes for your writing about this issue?
- What are your fears when it comes to writing about this issue?
- What obstacles do you face in terms of writing, in general, and what obstacles do you face when it comes to writing about this specific issue?
- Who are you writing for? Who is your primary audience?
- What are the possible implications—positive and negative—of writing about this issue?

I have my students ask and answer these questions for themselves at the start of the course so that their work is anchored in the clarity of their motivations. Students cite a wide range of motivations for writing about social issues:

- to understand and clarify their own thoughts
- to raise awareness
- to connect and be in dialogue with those with similar views
- to change minds
- to change policies
- to change culture

The first motivation might seem like an obvious one because it resides within us, but it's crucial for us to clarify our own understanding of and relationship to an issue before we broach it with others. The late great writer Joan Didion, chronicler of key sociocultural moments of the turbulent 1960s, in her essay "Why I Write" (a title she borrowed from George Orwell, the late great writer of conscience, whose essay is included in this chapter), speaks to the importance of this first motivation: "I write entirely to find out what I'm thinking, what I'm looking at, what I see and what it means. What I want and what I fear."[4] Didion concludes her essay by observing how her motivation to understand acts as an engine powering her work: "Who was this narrator? Why was this narrator telling me this story? Let me tell you one thing about why writers write: had I known the answer to any of these questions I would never have needed to write a novel."[5]

Raising awareness is a fitting motivation because you are seeking to highlight the issue, which may be familiar to some and new or murky to others. Sometimes people who are passionate about an issue have a tendency to reach out only to those who think similarly, a phenomenon captured in the popular expression, "preaching to the choir." However, this rarely creates the groundswell of awareness and concern that engenders change. So, consider how your writing invites people to get to know the issue by making it compelling and accessible.

Similarly, when it comes to changing minds, it is crucial that you not only understand the issue inside and out but become familiar with oppositional views on the issue so that you can speak to and refute them. To the extent you can do so with facts, data, observations, and direct experiences rather than just opinions, you have a stronger chance to change people's minds or at least to have them acknowledge the possibility of your point of view. While, ultimately, we hope to spark changes in policies or cultural practices, these shifts usually take years. So, it's more realistic to view our writing as contributing to the larger body of work on an issue that will hopefully one day reach critical mass and tilt towards change in policies and attitudes.

Relatedly, as we interrogate our motivations and clarify our intentions for writing about a specific social issue, we should reflect on who we are as the storyteller and how we relate, directly or indirectly, to the issue. We should ask ourselves: How have our views on the issue been shaped by our identity and experience? Do our motivations for engaging this issue through our writing contribute to existing biased or stereotypical perspectives on that issue?

In her 2009 TED Talk, award-winning writer Chimamanda Ngozi Adichie warns of "the danger of a single story."[6] As writers and individuals, we are shaped by our identity, upbringing, and education, which, in turn, shape our views on the world and on issues. In 2012, the Pulitzer Prize–winning writer Junot Díaz gave a talk at the Facing Race conference, run by Race Forward, the racial justice organization for which I worked. Speaking to the impact of our perceptions on us, he noted that we each hold blind spots and biases shaped like ourselves, shaped by the layers of our identities and experiences.* I carry this observation with me and refer to it regularly as a gut check to see how my own biases and perceptions have informed my opinions on an issue and how that is reflected in my writing. While there is not necessarily anything wrong with having a point of view informed by factors like identity and education, it is crucial to recognize those forces and others are operating on our perceptions and understanding of the world rather than assuming our perceptions are neutral or universal.

To return to Adichie's talk, it's also important to be aware of how a narrative has arrived in the world and who has shaped it. The danger Adichie is referring to, in terms of the "single story," is how one culture, usually the dominant one, can shape the story of others, even with the best of intentions. She gives examples of how centuries of single stories have been detrimental to Western perceptions of certain countries and their cultures, including Mexico and her homeland of Nigeria. The consequence of the single story, Adichie says, is that "it makes our recognition of our equal humanity difficult" by focusing on our differences rather than our similarities.[7] Adichie notes that "stories matter," and as storytellers, we should be aware that they have the power to heal or to harm.[8] So, before we write, we should consider if our narrative feeds into an existing harmful stereotypical narrative, and if so, what factors contributed to this and whether we want to

---

*These authors have both engaged social issues boldly in their respective work; however, they have faced recent criticism related to other social issues.

continue to perpetuate this narrative or mitigate it by providing context and nuance or by instead supporting storytellers directly impacted by these harmful narratives. We will dive deeper into issues of cultural sensitivity and cultural appropriation in chapter 6, as we explore the question of who gets to tell whose story.

In this chapter, we examine work by George Orwell and James Baldwin, two brilliant writers who courageously and consistently probed pressing social issues of their times in their nonfiction and fiction, earning both accolades and ire. Now they are lauded as visionaries, their writing seen as prescient and relevant for grappling with thorny societal issues, many of which still plague us. In these pieces, Orwell and Baldwin turn their keen skills of observation and their writerly lenses on themselves to examine their own motivations for writing. Also included is an essay by me that speaks to what motivated me to change course to pursue writing after working in social change for close to fifteen years.

In "Why I Write," the title essay for his essay collection, Orwell self-interrogates his motivations for writing. At the start of the essay, he traces his roundabout journey to becoming a writer. He confesses that he always wanted to be a writer but faced struggles, internal and external, to realizing his ambition, noting he knew early on he had a "facility with words and a power of facing unpleasant facts." In my mind, these traits are foundational to writing about social issues—the ability to see the world for what it is, especially the unpleasant or unfair aspects, and the ability to make others see what you see by putting words to your observations.

Orwell goes on to discuss how writers of conscience are shaped by their times. "[The writer's] subject-matter will be determined by the age he lives in—at least this is true in tumultuous, revolutionary ages like our own—but before he ever begins to write he will have acquired an emotional attitude from which he will never completely escape." We can see parallels between the fraught times Orwell lived in—struggles and wars erupting against the oppressive forces of fascism and colonialism—and our own current period marked by reckonings with racial injustice, deep ideological divides, amidst the immediate devastation of a global pandemic and the looming perils of climate change. Orwell alludes to the "emotional attitude" of writers whose work is shaped by their turbulent times. In my mind, these writers, like Orwell himself, are keenly observant and use their social conscience and writerly talents to shed light on the burning social issues of their time.

Orwell identifies four motives for writing, aside from earning a living. In his estimation, these four motives act on all writers to differing degrees:

1. *"Sheer Egoism."* Orwell defines sheer egoism as the "desire to seem clever, to be talked about, to be remembered after death, to get your own back on grown-ups who snubbed you in childhood, etc., etc. . . ." As much as I admire Orwell for his commitment to holding a mirror up to the problems of society and holding those in power accountable for their abuses through his writing, I admire him just as much for his honesty in revealing that writers—even writers with a social conscience—have egos and that these egos motivate them to write and get their work out into the world. Pretending that we don't have egos or vanity when it comes to our artistic expression as writers is a fallacy, yet we don't tend to talk about the role of ego in writing. Many writers struggle for years before their work is ever published, and what helps them find the will to keep writing and submitting their work is their ego and a core belief that their work matters and that the issues they're writing about matter.

2. *"Aesthetic Enthusiasm."* As with his acknowledgment of the role of writers' egos in motivating them to write, Orwell also finds motivation in the beauty of language and the story, itself. "Perception of beauty in the external world, or, on the other hand, in words and their right arrangement. Pleasure in the impact of one sound on another, in the firmness of good prose or the rhythm of a good story." While we might want to believe that the sole purpose of writing about

a social issue is to illuminate the issue, Orwell asks us to remember to take pleasure and pride in the aesthetic choices
we make—the words we choose, the narrative elements we
use—to tell our story. We shouldn't forget that writing is an
art form as much as it is a vehicle for ideas.

3. *"Historical Impulse."* Orwell speaks to writers' desire to bear
witness to and chronicle the events of their time noting their
"desire to see things as they are, to find out true facts and
store them up for the use of posterity." Sometimes the issues
we care most about are not reflected in the media or our
literature. This has historically been true for issues of race
and sexuality and disability, making it even more imperative
for writers to chronicle these issues to ensure they are not
invisible in the present moment or become lost to history.

4. *"Political Purpose."* Here, Orwell notes that he is using "political" broadly when referring to the "desire to push the
world in a certain direction, to alter other people's idea of
the kind of society that they should strive after." Some in the
literary world frown on writing that seeks to change hearts
and minds, labeling it propaganda. Meanwhile, others in the
journalism realm extol the importance of journalists maintaining neutrality in their writing. However, there are writers in both genres for whom the desire to raise awareness
and seed change are powerful motivations. Orwell, himself,
is a testament that literature need not stand apart from politics because "no book is genuinely free from political bias."

In her remarks to fellow journalists at the International Press
Freedom Awards in November 2016, on the heels of the presidential election, award-winning journalist Christiane Amanpour
made the following observation: "It appeared much of the media
got itself into knots trying to differentiate between balance, objectivity, neutrality, and crucially, truth."[9] She goes on to articulate a key distinction that drives her approach as a journalist. "I
believe in being truthful, not neutral. And I believe we must stop

banalizing the truth."[10] This underscores that journalists do not have to see the tenets of good journalism and their own social conscience as being in conflict because both should guide them to being truthful rather than neutral, especially when bearing witness to and chronicling injustice.

Interestingly, Orwell seems to be in agreement with Amanpour when he notes that a key challenge in trying to "fuse political purpose and artistic purpose into one whole" is achieving "truthfulness." Ultimately, Orwell reminds us that his catalyst for writing is always a sense of "injustice" for which he is seeking a "hearing."

Around a decade later, in 1955, James Baldwin, who had emerged as one of the most critical Black voices in literature and a writer of conscience during the civil rights struggle, published *Notes of a Native Son*, an autobiographical set of essays. In "Autobiographical Notes," which kicks off the collection, Baldwin, like Orwell, acknowledges that he was engrossed in books as a child and harbored desires of becoming a writer from an early age. He writes about how he drew motivation from his struggle against the "indifference" of the world to his work, saying "it is only because the world looks on his talent with such a frightening indifference that the artist is compelled to make his talent important." He goes on to note how it is hard to "divorce" the impact of the things that hurt a writer from the things that help them, and states that the most difficult and rewarding factor in his life was "that I was born a Negro," noting how his Black identity and his calling as a writer were indelibly forged.

Baldwin emphasizes the influence of a writer's life experiences: "One writes out of one thing only—one's own experience . . . This is the only real concern of the artist, to recreate out of the disorder of life that order which is art." But Baldwin underscores the "dangers of [his] social situation" as a Black man and writer in a society unwilling to reckon with race. Baldwin ends "Autobiographical Notes" by acknowledging the central role of morality in his life and writing and by urging, "one must find, therefore, one's own moral center and move through the world hoping that this center will guide one aright. . . . I want to be an honest man and a good writer."

However, earlier in "Autobiographical Notes," Baldwin seems to make the contradictory point that "social affairs are not generally speaking the writer's prime concern, whether they ought to be or not." He goes on to observe that "it is absolutely necessary that he establish between himself and these affairs a distance which will allow, at least, for clarity, so that before he can look forward in any meaningful sense, he must first be allowed to take a long look back." When I take these thoughts in totality, I understand Baldwin to say that writers are not compelled to address "social affairs," but if they choose to, they must, as we've already noted, be clear in their own thoughts about those issues and in doing so, it is critical that they establish a certain distance from those issues, which allows them to reflect on these issues from not just a personal standpoint but perhaps in a historical and philosophical context as well.

Reading Baldwin's later-in-life reflections on his writing and his role as a writer seems to reveal an evolution in his appreciation for the authority rooted in his own experience as a Black man and writer. For example, in the new preface Baldwin wrote for the 1984 edition of *Notes on a Native Son*, he seems to concur with Orwell about the impact of the times in which a writer lives but then notes how he transcends these markers. "I am what time, circumstance, history, have made of me, certainly but I am, also, much more than that. So are we all."[11] Though Baldwin had long aspired to write novels, he acknowledges here that he had "never thought of [him]self as an essayist."[12] He goes on to observe that his essays came from both what he was trying to discover and avoid, within himself.[13]

In an interview with the *New York Times* following the release of his novel *Just Above My Head* in 1979, Baldwin articulated how his initial reticence to engage directly on civil rights issues as a public figure gave way to his resolve to play a part in the civil rights movement. "And I was frightened because it was not the role of a writer, or so I was told. On the other hand, I couldn't see myself sitting in some room somewhere cultivating my talent."[14] He goes on to explain how a writer has to thread the needle between upholding their craft while upholding their values. "I think what you have to do, which is the difficult thing about a writer, is avoid slogans. You have to have the [guts] to protest the slogan, no matter how noble it may sound. It always hides something else; the writer should try to expose what it hides."[15]

Baldwin discusses how in chronicling the oppressive civil rights issues of his time, he sought to act as a "witness" and to "translate" what he saw, whether or not it becomes literature.[16] At the end of the interview, Baldwin does confess to being motivated by the lofty goal of changing the world through his writing:

> The bottom line is this: You write in order to change the world, knowing perfectly well that you probably can't, but also knowing that literature is indispensable to the world. In some way, your aspirations and concern for a single man in fact do begin to change the world. The world changes according to the way people see it, and if you alter, even by a millimeter, the way a person looks or people look at reality, then you can change it.

Ultimately, the fifty-five-year-old Baldwin states, "If there is no moral question, there is no reason to write." He confesses, "I'm an old-fashioned writer and, despite the odds, I want to change the world."[17]

In interrogating my own motivations for writing about social issues, I believe I'm inspired by all the motivations discussed earlier—understanding and clarifying my own thoughts, raising awareness, changing minds, changing policies, and changing culture. Depending on the piece or the issue, one of these motivations will likely be stronger than the others. Having worked in social change for close to fifteen years, I understand how much collective work goes into manifesting social change and how slow it can be in taking root, so I tend to be motivated more by the chance to raise awareness and to provoke readers to consider an alternate perspective than aiming to change policies or culture.

When it came to writing articles and a biography about Lakshmi Shankar, the female Grammy-nominated Hindustani singer who helped bring Indian music to the West in the late 1960s, I was most motivated by the chance to bear witness to the contributions of a woman of color artist, whose music I have known and loved since childhood. But I was also motivated by the importance of pushing against the cultural forces of erasure, which obscure certain life stories and favor others. And while I knew it was unlikely that this one story about one life would change our biased culture, I also knew a biography of her would help ensure her story was not lost to history in the way that life stories and the contributions of so many people of color and other marginalized individuals are often lost. It would also serve to counter the dominant and false single story that only male artists—Western and Indian—were responsible for bringing Indian music to the West.

In my piece "Ellaji and Lakshmiji," I chart the evolution of finding my voice as a writer, catalyzed by my motivation to write Lakshmi Shankar's life story. As I labored to find my footing on how to write and publish her story and push back against my own feelings of imposter syndrome, I believed my primary motivation was that Lakshmiji, as I respectfully and affectionally referred to her, would have wanted her story told. However, as I recount in "Ellaji and Lakshmiji," I came to realize I was no less motivated by my desire to chronicle the life story of a fellow South Asian American woman, which sadly was all too rare since the realm of biography has tended to prioritize the life stories of white men and women. Around this time, I came across a quote from the great Toni Morrison from which I drew motivation: "If there's a book that you want to read, but it hasn't been written yet, then you must write it."[18]

I became consumed with the myriad steps of researching, writing, and publishing Lakshmiji's biography, motivated by the hope of seeing it out in the world and raising awareness of Lakshmiji's musical legacy. Once *Poignant Song: The Life and Music of Lakshmi Shankar* was finally released, I was astounded by all I had learned and experienced over those six years as an emerging writer. And I took account of not just my successes, but also the many obstacles I faced all along the way:

> Hitting one roadblock after another, including several agents and editors who didn't think Lakshmi Shankar's story merited a book, claiming there was no audience for it, I wondered what business I had trying to become a writer at age forty. But then, there, staring back at me from my evolving manuscript, stood the story of how Lakshmiji transformed herself from a dancer to a singer as a mother in her thirties, through commitment to her art and sheer resilience.

Without an MFA or institutional support, I was plagued by periods of self-doubt, where I would contemplate if this project was perhaps beyond my scope. Sadly, seeking guidance from the wrong sources only deepened my self-doubt—a book I read about how to write biography nearly convinced me that Lakshmiji's biography could not be written because her life lacked the type of traditional archives that typically only exist for chronicling the lives of wealthy and influential white figureheads, and an agent I met told me Lakshmiji's story was "too niche." Thankfully, even though I was unsure of myself, I pushed forward because I was certain of the merits of Lakshmiji's story and couldn't bear the thought of her story being erased from history. Positive motivation can be an instrumental engine for your writing, but in this case, negative motivation—my worry that Lakshmiji's story would be erased—was an effective spark to keep me going.

As you can see, writers have myriad motivations for writing and specifically for engaging thorny social issues in our writing, which range from seeking to clarify our own understanding to changing the way others understand and treat an injustice. While you can find inspiration in the motivations of writers you admire, ultimately, your writing will be anchored by your own. Therefore, as passionate as you might be about an issue, take some time to interrogate and articulate your motivations. Your writing will be stronger for it, and if you ever falter and have moments of self-doubt, those motivations will serve as powerful reminders of why your work matters.

■

WHY I WRITE

By George Orwell

From a very early age, perhaps the age of five or six, I knew that when I grew up I should be a writer. Between the ages of about seventeen and twenty-four I tried to abandon this idea, but I did so with the consciousness that I was outraging my true nature and that sooner or later I should have to settle down and write books.

I was the middle child of three, but there was a gap of five years on either side, and I barely saw my father before I was eight. For this and other reasons I was somewhat lonely, and I soon developed disagreeable mannerisms which made me unpopular throughout my schooldays. I had the lonely child's habit of making up stories and holding conversations with imaginary persons, and I think from the very start my literary ambitions were mixed up with the feeling of being isolated and undervalued. I knew that I had a facility with words and a power of facing unpleasant facts, and I felt that this created a sort of private world in which I could get my own back for my failure in everyday life. Nevertheless the volume of serious—i.e. seriously intended—writing which I produced all through my childhood and boyhood would not amount to half a dozen pages. I wrote my first poem at the age of four or five, my mother taking it down to dictation. I cannot remember anything about it except that it was about a tiger and the tiger had "chair-like teeth"—a good enough phrase, but I fancy the poem was a plagiarism of Blake's "Tiger, Tiger." At eleven, when the war of 1914–18 broke out, I wrote a patriotic poem which was printed in the local newspaper, as was another, two years later, on the death of Kitchener. From time to time, when I was a bit older, I wrote bad and usually unfinished "nature poems" in the Georgian style. I also, about twice, attempted a short story which was a ghastly failure. That was the total of the would-be serious work that I actually set down on paper during all those years.

However, throughout this time I did in a sense engage in literary activities. To begin with there was the made-to-order stuff which I produced quickly, easily and without much pleasure to myself. Apart from school work, I wrote *vers d'occasion*, semi-comic poems which I could turn out at what now seems to me astonishing speed—at fourteen I wrote a whole rhyming play, in imitation of Aristophanes, in about a week—and helped to edit school magazines, both printed and in manuscript. These magazines were the most pitiful burlesque stuff that you could imagine, and I took far less trouble with them than I now would with the cheapest journalism. But side by side with all this, for fifteen years or more, I was carrying out a literary exercise of a quite different kind: this was the making up of a continuous "story" about myself, a sort of diary existing only in the mind. I believe this is a common habit of children and adolescents. As a very small child I used to imagine that I was, say, Robin Hood, and picture myself as the hero of thrilling adventures, but quite soon my "story" ceased to be narcissistic in a crude way and became more and more a mere description of what I was doing and the things I saw. For minutes at a time this kind of thing would be running through my head: "He pushed the door open and entered the room. A yellow beam of sunlight, filtering through the muslin curtains, slanted on to the table, where a matchbox, half-open, lay beside the inkpot. With his right hand in his pocket he moved across to the window. Down in the street a tortoiseshell cat was chasing a dead leaf," etc., etc. This habit continued until I was about twenty-five, right through my non-literary years. Although I had to search, and did search, for the right words, I seemed to be making this descriptive effort almost against my will, under a kind of compulsion from outside. The "story" must, I suppose, have reflected the styles of the various writers I admired at different ages, but so far as I remember it always had the same meticulous descriptive quality.

When I was about sixteen I suddenly discovered the joy of mere words, i.e. the sounds and associations of words. The lines from *Paradise Lost*—

> *So hee with difficulty and labour hard*
> *Moved on: with difficulty and labour hee,*

which do not now seem to me so very wonderful, sent shivers down my backbone; and the spelling "hee" for "he" was an added pleasure. As for the need to describe things, I knew all about it already. So it is clear what kind of books I wanted to write, in so far as I could be said to want to write books at that time. I wanted to write enormous naturalistic novels with unhappy endings, full of detailed descriptions and arresting similes, and also full of purple passages in which words were used partly for the sake of their sound. And in fact my first completed novel, *Burmese Days*, which I wrote when I was thirty but projected much earlier, is rather that kind of book.

I give all this background information because I do not think one can assess a writer's motives without knowing something of his early development. His subject-matter will be determined by the age he lives in—at least this is true in tumultuous, revolutionary ages like our own—but before he ever begins to write he will have acquired an emotional attitude from which he will never completely escape. It is his job, no doubt, to discipline his temperament and avoid getting stuck at some immature stage, or in some perverse mood: but if he escapes from his early influences altogether, he will have killed his impulse to write. Putting aside the need to earn a living, I think there are four great motives for writing, at any rate for writing prose. They exist in different degrees in every writer, and in any one writer the proportions will vary from time to time, according to the atmosphere in which he is living. They are:

1. *Sheer egoism.* Desire to seem clever, to be talked about, to be remembered after death, to get your own back on grown-ups who snubbed you in childhood, etc., etc. It is humbug to pretend this is not a motive, and a strong one. Writers share this characteristic with scientists, artists, politicians, lawyers, soldiers, successful business men—in short, with the whole top crust of humanity. The great mass of human beings are not acutely selfish. After the age of about thirty they abandon individual ambition—in many cases, indeed, they almost abandon the sense of being individuals at all—and live chiefly for others, or are simply smothered under drudgery. But there is also the minority of gifted, willful people who are determined to live their own lives to the end, and writers belong in this class. Serious writers, I should say, are on the whole more vain and self-centered than journalists, though less interested in money.

2. *Aesthetic enthusiasm.* Perception of beauty in the external world, or, on the other hand, in words and their right arrangement. Pleasure in the impact of one sound on another, in the firmness of good prose or the rhythm of a good story. Desire to share an experience which one feels is valuable and ought not to be missed. The aesthetic motive is very feeble in a lot of writers, but even a pamphleteer or writer of textbooks will have pet words and phrases which appeal to him for non-utilitarian reasons; or he may feel strongly about typography, width of margins, etc. Above the level of a railway guide, no book is quite free from aesthetic considerations.

3. *Historical impulse.* Desire to see things as they are, to find out true facts and store them up for the use of posterity.

4. *Political purpose*—using the word *"political"* in the widest possible *sense*. Desire to push the world in a certain direction, to alter other people's idea of the kind of society that they should strive after. Once again, no book is genuinely free from political bias. The opinion that art should have nothing to do with politics is itself a political attitude.

It can be seen how these various impulses must war against one another, and how they must fluctuate from person to person and from time to time. By nature—taking your "nature" to be the state you have attained when you are first adult—I am a person in whom the first three motives would outweigh the fourth. In a peaceful age I might have written ornate or merely descriptive books, and might have remained almost unaware of my political loyalties. As it is I have been forced into becoming a sort of pamphleteer. First I spent five years in an unsuitable profession (the Indian Imperial Police, in Burma), and then I underwent poverty and the sense of failure. This increased my natural hatred of authority and made me for the first time fully aware of the existence of the working classes, and the job in Burma had given me some understanding of the nature of imperialism: but these experiences were not enough to give me an accurate political orientation. Then came Hitler, the Spanish Civil War, etc. By the end of 1935 I had still failed to reach a firm decision. I remember a little poem that I wrote at that date, expressing my dilemma:

A happy vicar I might have been
Two hundred years ago,
To preach upon eternal doom
And watch my walnuts grow
     But born, alas, in an evil time,
I missed that pleasant haven,
For the hair has grown on my upper lip
And the clergy are all clean-shaven.

And later still the times were good,
We were so easy to please,
We rocked our troubled thoughts to sleep
On the bosoms of the trees.

   All ignorant we dared to own
The joys we now dissemble;
The greenfinch on the apple bough
Could make my enemies tremble.

   But girls' bellies and apricots,
Roach in a shaded stream,
Horses, ducks in flight at dawn,
All these are a dream.

   It is forbidden to dream again;
We maim our joys or hide them;
Horses are made of chromium steel
And little fat men shall ride them.

   I am the worm who never turned,
The eunuch without a harem;
Between the priest and the commissar
I walk like Eugene Aram;

   And the commissar is telling my fortune
While the radio plays,
But the priest has promised an Austin Seven,
For Duggie always pays.

   I dreamt I dwelt in marble halls,
And woke to find it true;
I wasn't born for an age like this;
Was Smith? Was Jones? Were you?

The Spanish war and other events in 1936–37 turned the scale and thereafter I knew where I stood. Every line of serious work that I have written since 1936 has been written, directly or indirectly, *against* totalitarianism and *for* democratic socialism, as I understand it. It seems to me nonsense, in a period like our own, to think that one can avoid writing of such subjects. Everyone writes of them in one guise or another. It is simply a question of which side one takes and what approach one follows. And the more one is conscious of one's political bias, the more chance one has of acting politically without sacrificing one's aesthetic and intellectual integrity.

What I have most wanted to do throughout the past ten years is to make political writing into an art. My starting point is always a feeling of partisanship, a sense of injustice. When I sit down to write a book, I do not say to myself, "I am going to produce a work of art." I write it because there is some lie that I want to expose, some fact to which I want to draw attention, and my initial concern is to get a hearing. But I could not do the work of writing a book, or even a long magazine article, if it were not also an aesthetic experience. Anyone who cares to examine my work will see that even when it is downright propaganda it contains much that a full-time politician would consider irrelevant. I am not able, and do not want, completely to abandon the world view that I acquired in childhood. So long as I remain alive and well I shall continue to feel strongly about prose style, to love the surface of the earth, and to take a pleasure in solid objects and scraps of useless information. It is no use trying to suppress that side of myself. The job is to reconcile my ingrained likes and dislikes with the essentially public, non-individual activities that this age forces on all of us.

It is not easy. It raises problems of construction and of language, and it raises in a new way the problem of truthfulness. Let me give just one example of the cruder kind of difficulty that arises. My book about the Spanish civil war, *Homage to Catalonia*, is of course a frankly political book, but in the main it is written with a certain detachment and regard for form. I did try very hard in it to tell the whole truth without violating my literary instincts. But among other things it contains a long chapter, full of newspaper quotations and the like, defending the Trotskyists who were accused of plotting with Franco. Clearly such a chapter, which after a year or two would lose its interest for any ordinary reader, must ruin the book. A critic whom I respect read me a lecture about it. "Why did you put in all that stuff?" he said. "You've turned what might have been a good book into journalism." What he said was true, but I could not have done otherwise. I happened to know, what very few people in England had been allowed to know, that innocent men were being falsely accused. If I had not been angry about that I should never have written the book.

In one form or another this problem comes up again. The problem of language is subtler and would take too long to discuss. I will only say that of late years I have tried to write less picturesquely and more exactly. In any case I find that by the time you have perfected any style of writing, you have always outgrown it. *Animal Farm* was the first book in which I tried, with full consciousness of what I was doing, to fuse political purpose and artistic purpose into one whole. I have not written a novel for seven years, but I hope to write another fairly soon. It is bound to be a failure, every book is a failure, but I do know with some clarity what kind of book I want to write.

Looking back through the last page or two, I see that I have made it appear as though my motives in writing were wholly public-spirited. I don't want to leave that as the final impression. All writers are vain, selfish, and lazy, and at the very bottom of their motives there lies a mystery. Writing a book is a horrible, exhausting struggle, like a long bout of some painful illness. One would never undertake such a thing if one were not driven on by some demon whom one can neither resist or understand. For all one knows that demon is simply the same instinct that makes a baby squall for attention. And yet it is also true that one can write nothing readable unless one constantly struggles to efface one's own personality. Good prose is like a windowpane. I cannot say with certainty which of my motives are the strongest, but I know which of them deserve to be followed. And looking back through my work, I see that it is invariably where I lacked a *political* purpose that I wrote lifeless books and was betrayed into purple passages, sentences without meaning, decorative adjectives and humbug generally.

■

AUTOBIOGRAPHICAL NOTES,
FROM *NOTES OF A NATIVE SON*
By *James Baldwin*

I was born in Harlem thirty-one years ago. I began plotting novels at the time I learned to read. The story of my childhood is the usual bleak fantasy, and we can dismiss it about with the restrained observation that I certainly would not consider living it again. In those days my mother was given to the exasperating and mysterious habit of having babies. As they were born, I took them over with one hand and held a book with the other. The children probably suffered, though they have since been kind enough to deny it, and in this way I read *Uncle Tom's Cabin* and *A Tale of Two Cities* over and over and over again; in this way, in fact, I read just about everything I could get my hands on—except the Bible, probably because it was the only book I was encouraged to read. I must also confess that I wrote—a great deal—and my first professional triumph, in any case, the first effort of mine to be seen in print, occurred at the age of twelve or thereabouts, when a short story I had written about the Spanish revolution won some sort of prize in an extremely short-lived church newspaper. I remember the story was censored by the lady editor, though I don't remember why, and I was outraged.

Also wrote plays, and songs, for one of which I received a letter of congratulations from Mayor La Guardia, and poetry, about which the less said, the better. My mother was delighted by all these goings-on, but my father wasn't; he wanted me to be a preacher. When I was fourteen I became a preacher, and when I was seventeen I stopped. Very shortly thereafter I left home. For God knows how long I struggled with the world of commerce and industry—I guess they would say they struggled with *me*—and when I was about twenty-one I had enough done of a novel to get a Saxton Fellowship. When I was twenty-two the fellowship was over, the novel turned out to be unsalable, and I started waiting on tables in a Village restaurant and writing book reviews—mostly, as it turned out, about the Negro problem, concerning which the color of my skin made me automatically an expert. Did another book, in company with photographer Theodore Pelatowski, about the store-front churches in Harlem. This book met exactly the same fate as my first—fellowship, but no sale. (It was a Rosenwald Fellowship.) By the time I was twenty-four I had decided to stop reviewing books about the Negro problem—which, by this time, was only slightly less horrible in print than it was in life—and I packed my bags and went to France, where I finished, God knows how, *Go Tell It on the Mountain.*

Any writer, I suppose, feels that the world into which he was born is nothing less than a conspiracy against the cultivation of his talent—which attitude certainly has a great deal to support it. On the other hand, it is only because the world looks on his talent with such a frightening indifference that the artist is compelled to make his talent important. So that any writer, looking back over even so short a span of time as I am here forced to assess, finds that the things which hurt him and the things which helped him cannot be divorced from each other; he could be helped in a certain way only because he was hurt in a certain way; and his help is simply to be enabled to move from one conundrum to the next—one is tempted to say that he moves from one disaster to the next. When one begins looking for influences one finds them by the score. I haven't thought much about my own, not enough anyway; I hazard that the King James Bible, the rhetoric of the store-front church, something ironic and violent and perpetually understated in Negro speech—and something of Dickens' love for bravura—have something to do with me today; but I wouldn't stake my life on it. Likewise, innumerable people have helped me in many ways; but finally, I suppose, the most difficult (and most rewarding) thing in my life has been the fact that I was born a Negro and was forced, therefore, to effect some kind of truce with this reality. (Truce, by the way, is the best one can hope for.)

One of the difficulties about being a Negro writer (and this is not special pleading, since I don't mean to suggest that he has it worse than anybody else) is that the Negro problem is written about so widely. The bookshelves groan under the weight of information, and everyone therefore considers himself informed. And this information, furthermore, operates usually (generally, popularly) to reinforce traditional attitudes. Of traditional attitudes there are only two—For or Against—and I, personally, find it difficult to say which attitude has caused me the most pain. I am speaking as a writer; from a social point of view I am perfectly aware that the change from ill-will to good-will, however motivated, however imperfect, however expressed, is better than no change at all.

But it is part of the business of the writer—as I see it—to examine attitudes, to go beneath the surface, to tap the source. From this point of view the Negro problem is nearly inaccessible. It is not only written about so widely; it is written about so badly. It is quite possible to say that the price a Negro pays for becoming articulate is to find himself, at length, with nothing to be articulate about. ("You taught me language," says Caliban to Prospero, "and my profit on't is I know how to curse.") Consider: the tremendous social activity that this problem generates imposes on whites and Negroes alike the necessity of looking forward, of working to bring about a better day. This is fine, it keeps the waters troubled; it is all, indeed, that has made possible the Negro's progress. Nevertheless, social affairs are not generally speaking the writer's prime concern, whether they ought to be or not; it is absolutely necessary that he establish between himself and these affairs a distance which will allow, at least, for clarity, so that before he can look forward in any meaningful sense, he must first be allowed to take a long look back. In the context of the Negro problem neither whites nor blacks, for excellent reasons of their own, have the faintest desire to look back; but I think that the past is all that makes the present coherent, and further, that the past will remain horrible for exactly as long as we refuse to assess it honestly.

I know, in any case, that the most crucial time in my own development came when I was forced to recognize that I was a kind of bastard of the West; when I followed the line of my past I did not find myself in Europe but in Africa. And this meant that in some subtle way, in a really profound way, I brought to Shakespeare, Bach, Rembrandt, to the stones of Paris, to the cathedral at Chartres, and to the Empire State Building, a special attitude. These were not really my creations, they did not contain my history; I might search in them in vain forever for any reflection of myself. I was an interloper; this was not my heritage. At the same time I had no other heritage which I could possibly hope to use—I had certainly been unfitted for the jungle or the tribe. I would have to appropriate these white centuries, I would have to make them mine—I would have to accept my special attitude, my special place in this scheme—otherwise I would have no place in *any* scheme. What was the most difficult was the fact that I was forced to admit something I had always hidden from myself, which the American Negro has had to hide from himself as the price of his public progress; that I hated and feared white people. This did not mean that I loved black people; on the contrary, I despised them, possibly because they failed to produce Rembrandt. In effect, I hated and feared the world. And this meant, not only that I thus gave the world an altogether murderous power over me, but also that in such a self-destroying limbo I could never hope to write.

One writes out of one thing only—one's own experience. Everything depends on how relentlessly one forces from this experience the last drop, sweet or bitter, it can possibly give. This is the only real concern of the artist, to recreate out of the disorder of life that order which is art. The difficulty then, for me, of being a Negro writer was the fact that I was, in effect, prohibited from examining my own experience too closely by the tremendous demands and the very real dangers of my social situation.

I don't think the dilemma outlined above is uncommon. I do think, since writers work in the disastrously explicit medium of language, that it goes a little way towards explaining why, out of the enormous resources of Negro speech and life, and despite the example of Negro music, prose written by Negroes has been generally speaking so pallid and so harsh. I have not written about being a Negro at such length because I expect that to be my only subject, but only because it was the gate I had to unlock before I could hope to write about anything else. I don't think that the Negro problem in America can be even discussed coherently without bearing in mind its context; its context being the history, traditions, customs, the moral assumptions and preoccupations of the country; in short, the general social fabric. Appearances to the contrary, no one in America escapes its effects and everyone in America bears some responsibility for it. I believe this the more firmly because it is the overwhelming tendency to speak of this problem as though it were a thing apart. But in the work of Faulkner, in the general attitude and certain specific passages in Robert Penn Warren, and, most significantly, in the advent of Ralph Ellison, one sees the beginnings—at least—of a more genuinely penetrating search. Mr. Ellison, by the way, is the first Negro novelist I have ever read to utilize in language, and brilliantly, some of the ambiguity and irony of Negro life.

About my interests: I don't know if I have any, unless the morbid desire to own a sixteen-millimeter camera and make experimental movies can be so classified. Otherwise, I love to eat and drink—it's my melancholy conviction that I've scarcely ever had enough to eat (this is because it's *impossible* to eat enough if you're worried about the next meal)—and I love to argue with people who do not disagree with me too profoundly, and I love to laugh. I do *not* like bohemia, or bohemians, I do not like people whose principal aim is pleasure, and I do not like people who are *earnest* about anything. I don't like people who like me because I'm a Negro; neither do I like people who find in the same accident grounds for contempt. I love America more than any other country in the world, and, exactly for this reason, I insist on the right to criticize her perpetually. I think all theories are suspect, that the finest principles may have to be modified, or may even be

pulverized by the demands of life, and that one must find, therefore, one's own moral center and move through the world hoping
that this center will guide one aright. I consider that I have many
responsibilities, but none greater than this: to last, as Hemingway
says, and get my work done.

I want to be an honest man and a good writer.

■

ELLAJI AND LAKSHMIJI
By Kavita Das

When I arrived at Bryn Mawr College in the fall of 1992, the
only thing I was sure of was that I didn't want to become a
doctor like my Indian parents. Other than that guiding principle,
I had no idea what I wanted to make of my life.

Unlike many of my classmates, I hadn't brought along a
boombox. I only had a tiny selection of music—my entire tape
collection fit in a shoe box. A third of my cassettes were Western
classical music, particularly violin concertos; I had studied violin
intensively and was planning to play in the college orchestra.

Another third were bootlegs and mixtapes made by friends
who took pity on me because my parents wouldn't let me buy or
listen to pop or rock music—their misguided attempt to protect
me from the supposedly corrosive effects of American culture.
All through junior high and high school, I surreptitiously popped
these tapes into my Pepto Bismol-pink Walkman late at night,
under the covers.

The final third of my tapes were of the Hindustani singer
Lakshmi Shankar. Her soulful bhajans echoed African-American
gospel hymns, emphasizing love and belief in the Divine, especially during times of adversity and oppression. They consoled me
when I was visited by bouts of homesickness.

"Jo tum todo piya main nahi todu re," she sings, saying: "Although, Dear Lord, you might break our bond of love, I will never
break it."

I grew up in a home steeped in Indian music and culture, but we were not overly religious. I wasn't sure why Lakshmiji's bhajans brought me such comfort. Even today, when I listen to her soulful voice, I feel the same stirrings in me that I felt when I watched her perform in the vastness of Lincoln Center as a five-year-old girl.

I can't remember a time when I didn't have Lakshmiji or her music in my life. My immigrant parents helped organize arts programs in New York City, and we frequently hosted Indian artists in our home. As a child, I was fascinated by these talented strangers who rehearsed in our basement and shared meals with us. But there was one I loved above all others: Lakshmiji. I cherished her visits.

Though she was an acclaimed artist, Lakshmiji fit right into our hybrid Bengali-Tamil family; she herself was a Tamilian woman married into one of the most esteemed artistic Bengali families, that of modern Indian dance pioneer Uday Shankar and sitar maestro Ravi Shankar. She seamlessly moved from helping my mother fry up puffy pooris, to discussing Indian current events with my father in Bengali, to chatting with me and my sister about our favorite TV shows in English, to sharing tea while conversing in Tamil with my Patti, my grandmother.

When it came time for her to perform, Lakshmiji cloistered herself in our guest room, and we could faintly hear her humming. Later, she emerged, silent and serene, and remained that way until she ascended the stage. As I grew older and my musical tastes evolved, her voice continued to stir something deep within me. It had a silken texture, spanned a three-octave range, and reverberated with so much emotion.

Even when I couldn't understand most of the words in her songs, I felt I understood them on a deeper level. My parents had introduced me to Lakshmiji's music as a way of connecting me to our culture, yet her voice became an indelible part of me that mysteriously spoke to all parts of my identity: first, as a South Asian American girl; and later, as a woman making her way through college and finding her path in life. Beyond her voice, her life as a

US-based Indian musician inspired me. She was a bridge traversing South Asian and Western cultures, embodying how each one can be enriched by the other.

In college, I experienced a newfound freedom to explore and fall in love with other genres of music. I was riveted by my first ventures to rock concerts. I enjoyed trawling used tape and CD shops, up and down Philadelphia's Main Line. On one of my trips to the store Plastic Fantastic, Ella Fitzgerald came on over the sound system. After just a few strains, I stopped rummaging in the rock section, migrated to classic jazz, and, lovestruck by Ellaji's gorgeous voice, pulled out two of her tapes.

Ellaji's voice had some of the same qualities I loved most about Lakshmiji's—the tremendous range, the musicality. Her voice could be somber and soulful one minute—as on songs like "April in Paris," "Summertime," and "How Long Has This Been Going On"—then turn nimble and bright the next, as in "A-Tisket, A-Tasket," "Oh, Lady Be Good," and "Mack the Knife."

If Lakshmiji's voice was silk, then Ellaji's was satin.

Though I went from playing tapes to CDs, and my tastes shifted from pop rock to grunge, I returned, time and again, to the music of Ellaji and Lakshmiji. Just a few years later, on the cusp of the millennium, these two women sang at my wedding.

At my mehndi ceremony in Bangalore, surrounded by a sea of Indian aunties I didn't know, Lakshmiji's round visage stood out. She began to sing a bhajan as beautiful and intricate as the vines being drawn onto my hands. Despite the jitters over my impending nuptials and being thousands of miles from home, the moment I was draped in the silken strands of Lakshmiji's voice, I felt that familiar, stirring sense of comfort.

A few weeks later, at my wedding reception in New Jersey, my beloved and I danced to Ellaji and Louis Armstrong's rendition of "Cheek to Cheek," a song about finding heavenly bliss dancing cheek-to-cheek in the arms of the one you love, a song we fell in love to, singing it to each other over the phone during our long-distance relationship. I'd sing Ellaji's part, Om would croon

Louis's. As he dipped me down low and pulled me up, I watched the world turn topsy-turvy and right itself, enveloped in his arms and the satin softness of Ellaji's voice.

In April 2010, on the heels of her Grammy nomination, I traveled from New York to Los Angeles to ask eighty-three-year-old Lakshmiji for permission to write her biography. She wasn't touring much anymore, so I hadn't seen her in a few years. I worried what she would think of my plan to write about her and agonized over how she would respond.

It had been twenty years since I graduated from college. I had spent most of that time working in social change but in my most recent job addressing racial injustice it dawned on me that it can manifest in quieter, more insidious ways, like erasure. It blots out one life at a time, invalidates some histories in favor of others, and ensures marginalized lives remain in the margins.

Although I believed deeply that Lakshmiji's story must be told, I was unsure of how and where to begin. Knowing her personally seemed as much an incentive as a disincentive.

Upon seeing her, I was shocked by how gaunt Laskhmiji looked. She showed me her Grammy nomination, and the significance of it washed over me. It symbolized all Lakshmiji had done as an artist and cultural ambassador, helping to bring Indian music to the west. I had traveled across the country to ask if I could tell her life story and now was the moment to ask.

She said yes and I was overjoyed. But soon afterwards, I began worrying about not getting her story right and imperiling our relationship. I was battling a strong case of imposter syndrome in calling myself a writer and researcher. The gravity of having walked away from my career in social change to be a writer, to tell Lakshmiji's story, weighed heavily on me.

Just months after I began working on the project in earnest, Lakshmiji passed away. I was grief-stricken. Even though I had watched her grow more and more frail over the past year, I had somehow believed she, like her music, would endure. Having lost my beloved muse, I wasn't sure how to push forward.

At first, I carried on, propelled by my conviction that Lakshmiji would've wanted her story to be told. But delving deeper into her life as a person and an artist, I realized *I* needed Lakshmiji's story to be told.

As I learned of the obstacles Lakshmiji faced, I grew to appreciate her artistry in a different way. I realized Lakshmiji's struggles were probably shared by other women of color artists of her era. Being in love with Ellaji's voice and music, I wondered what obstacles she had faced on her road to renown.

I discovered startling similarities between Ellaji and Lakshmiji's artistic lives. By the time I came to her music, Ellaji was a legend, known as America's "First Lady of Song," the winner of fourteen Grammy Awards. But Ellaji, like Lakshmiji, had initially pinned her hopes on becoming a dancer. An orphan at age fifteen, she had been sent to an abusive reformatory school, where she was barred from singing in the choir because of her race.

At seventeen, Ellaji entered Harlem's Apollo Theater Amateur Night contest intending to dance. But once she saw the strong dance acts, she tried her luck singing. She won and met bandleader Chick Webb. Soon, they were performing at Harlem's famed Savoy Ballroom, and her career began to take off.

Meanwhile, young Lakshmiji was goaded into learning Bharat Natyam dance by her mother, even though dance was improper for South Indian Brahmin girls, according to cultural mores. At just thirteen, Lakshmiji journeyed from Madras to the foothills of the Himalayas to join a dance troupe led by dance innovator, Uday Shankar.

Lakshmiji's passion for dance grew stronger, but then she was struck with pleurisy. Her doctor advised her to give up dancing. Devastated, Lakshmiji turned to being a playback singer for Bollywood movies, whose heroines lip-synched to her songs. A music producer told her she had the voice and talent to be a Hindustani, or North Indian classical, singer.

Doubtful at first, Lakshmiji soon fell in love with Hindustani music and began studying it intensively. Three years later, she re-launched her artistic career as a thirty-year-old mother of two.

While Ellaji achieved fame and acclaim, she also bore the burden of being a Black female artist during the Jim Crow and Civil Rights eras. She built her reputation on legendary performances and hit records, even as she faced racism and segregated venues, travel, and accommodations. She persevered, breaking barriers, including being the first Black artist to headline New York City's famed Copacabana Club. In my mind, that Ellaji transcended poverty and racism to become America's First Lady of Song is less a testament to the American Dream, than to her own artistic brilliance and resilience.

Meanwhile, Lakshmiji was the most prominent Indian female musician in the cross-cultural movement that brought Indian music to the West in the late 1960s. Yet, despite her role as a cultural ambassador, she went largely uncelebrated in her own homeland of India. It was only decades later, in 2008, just five years before her death, that Lakshmiji received a Grammy nomination for her final album.

These women of song, whose music I love and whose lives I admire, faced inverse challenges—systemic racism and white gatekeepers hindered Ellaji, but could not hold back her success; while Lakshmiji was celebrated all over the world, but went largely unheralded in India due to patriarchy and cultural snobbery. Though their experiences as Black and brown women artists differed due to racial, cultural, and national contexts, I found solace and reassurance in Ellaji and Lakshmiji's respective spirits of resilience.

Listening to Lakshmiji and Ellaji's voices alternately navigating runs or meditating on a somber note has always been, for me, a sublime experience. Their vocal stylings provide the soundtrack to my most joyful moments and give me refuge during trying times. As I wrote Lakshmiji's biography while struggling to find my own voice as a writer, their artistic lives were a beacon of inspiration.

Hitting one roadblock after another, including several agents and editors who didn't think Lakshmi Shankar's story merited a book, claiming there was no audience for it, I wondered what business I had trying to become a writer at age forty. But then, there, staring back at me from my evolving manuscript, stood the story of how Lakshmiji transformed herself from a dancer to a singer as a mother in her thirties, through commitment to her art and sheer resilience.

Meanwhile, when I felt like an outsider in writing workshops because I was the only person of color or because I lacked an MFA, I reminded myself how privileged I was to even have the opportunity. The story of the entrenched structural racism Ellaji faced, and the success she built despite it, reminded me how fortunate I was. I focused on what mattered: improving as a writer so I could tell these crucial stories.

Eventually, I published some of my work and signed a contract for my biography of Lakshmiji. At that point, I finally felt able to call myself a writer. But instead of feeling confident, I often felt dismayed by countless rejections and missed opportunities. I turned my gaze inward and began writing and publishing deeply personal essays, even as I doubted anyone would want to hear my ruminations on my own life.

When I received messages from friends and strangers about how my personal explorations resonated with them and reflected their own experiences, I was so moved. I remembered how much Lakshmiji valued her audience more than any critic or award. They were the ones who filled the auditoriums, clapped thunderously, and stayed after for the chance to speak to her. Heartened, I keep delving into myself on the page.

The obstacles Ellaji and Lakshmiji faced during their respective lives just for the chance to pursue their artistic passions far overshadow any artistic challenges I've faced or will likely face. If I had given up trying to tell Lakshmiji's story just because of the value judgement of some agents and editors who didn't believe her story needed to be told, how would I be honoring her struggle, or the struggle of other women of color artists?

Now, when I listen to Ellaji and Lakshmiji sing, I hear a sonic reflection of their resilience in the face of adversity. Whether they're navigating vocal runs or meditating on somber notes, I discern a gritty undertone woven into their satin silk voices.

CHAPTER 2

HOW WE ARE
ALL CONNECTED

*Understanding the Relationship Between
the Writer, Reader, and Subject*

After we have delved into all our research about a social issue but before we start writing, we need to take a step back
and remind ourselves about the core responsibilities of a writer.
A writer's responsibilities are actually twofold—as a writer to our
readers and as a writer to our subject.

So, what are our responsibilities to our readers? To answer
that, we need to consider how we ourselves behave as readers.
What makes us want to read, and what keeps us reading? First
and foremost, as readers, we read what compels us. We read to
immerse ourselves in a story that captivates us while sparking our
curiosity about something we didn't know, that tugs at our hearts
while taking us along on a journey of discovery, real or imagined.

Meanwhile, when it comes to the subject of our writing—a
complex, fraught social issue and the people most impacted by
it—it is important to do it justice. We must write about the issue and the communities most affected truthfully and responsibly,
with a sense of how our words can impact the subject.

By aiming to write about social issues both compellingly and
responsibly, we seek a way to meet our dual responsibilities as a
writer—to our readers and to our subject. Focusing exclusively on

the reader might make us susceptible to sensationalizing the issue, while focusing only on the subject might make us so preoccupied with nuance and detail that we lose the interest of our readers. So, being intentional and explicit about laying out our responsibilities is integral to planning the best way to approach the issue on the page.

When we think about telling a good story for our readers, what does that entail? What are the elements of a good story that draw and keep our readers' attention? We need a compelling plot where there are risks and dangers and intrigue. As readers, we love characters who fascinate us and ignite our curiosity. Yet we are also drawn to relatable characters, who act as mirrors of ourselves. We love stories that zig and zag through time and space rather than those that follow an entirely predictable, linear, "this happened, then that happened" structure.

These elements are commonly found in our favorite novels and TV shows. In fact, it makes sense to examine a favorite novel to see what drew you to read it and kept you reading. Why does it stay with you even now? You do not necessarily need to use all of these elements in every piece, but think about what are the most compelling elements of what you are writing about—is it the plot or is it the characters?

Although we want to write a compelling story for our readers, we must be mindful to remain accurate in our depictions. Also, we should ensure that we do not cross the line into sensationalizing the issue by dramatizing or exaggerating elements. While our work needs to be anchored in facts, we can explore how to highlight the inherent drama in our story and its key elements, whether it be plot, characters, or setting.

All social issues have a moral quandary and conflict at their core. For example, do we believe guns are primarily a crucial means to defend ourselves or dangerous weapons that lead to unnecessary deaths? Do we believe protecting environmental conditions is more important than preserving people's economic livelihoods? These fraught questions are not just abstract but impact how our world functions and how people live their lives. So, all social issues have a certain dramatic element built into them because of the moral quandary at their cores.

When it comes to doing justice to our subject, it is crucial to be accurate and truthful. It is also important to provide nuance rather than depicting the issue and those impacted in broad strokes and generalizations. And one of the key ways we can ensure that we depict complex issues with nuance is by featuring the voices of those most impacted and, furthermore, to do so with integrity and with respect to their humanity.

There is a history of well-intentioned pieces about social issues that leave out the voices and perspectives of those most impacted. The result, even if unintentional, is that these individuals and communities are further marginalized, erased from and silenced in stories about issues that are central to their lives. We will be revisiting this topic in chapter 6, when we discuss cultural sensitivity and cultural appropriation.

On the next page is a graph that visually depicts the relationship between the writer, the reader, and the subject. As we see from this graph, there is a natural tension between the writer's responsibility to the reader and their responsibility to the subject. The writer's focus on the reader is captured along the x axis of this graph while their focus on the subject is captured along the y axis. The way this tension is resolved varies for each writer and for each piece, depending on their goals and key considerations. Ultimately, it means that the writer will have to make choices and trade-offs between how to address readers' needs and how to do justice to their subject. If we were to graph writing that focuses more on the reader, it would be represented by a flatter line. Writing that focuses more on the subject would be rendered as a steeper line. We'll drill more deeply into the tension between readers and subjects in the next chapter when we discuss context and narrative and the ways in which they impact this tension and help inform our choices as writers.

In order to illustrate the differences between writing that focuses on the reader and writing that focuses on the subject, I in-

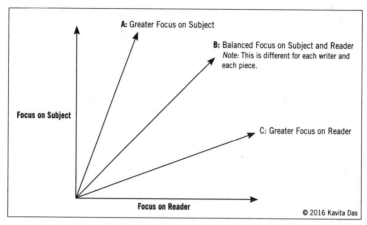

A: Greater Focus on Subject

B: Balanced Focus on Subject and Reader
Note: This is different for each writer and each piece.

Focus on Subject

C: Greater Focus on Reader

Focus on Reader

© 2016 Kavita Das

Reader Versus Subject

clude two of my own essays on the same subject, the brutal gang rape of a young woman named Jyoti Singh, in Delhi, India, in December 2012. Since many of us are often knowledgeable and passionate about a particular issue, I want to illustrate how a writer can write about the same issue in divergent ways—sometimes focusing on the reader, other times, on the subject.

As a South Asian American woman, I was stunned and horrified upon learning of Jyoti's brutal rape. I prayed for her as she clung to life and was deeply saddened when she died. I found myself enraged at her perpetrators but also at India's patriarchal forces that, in my mind, were complicit in victimizing her, by demonizing and repressing women's freedom while excusing and justifying the growing number of sexual assaults against women by men.

Going through this cycle of emotions yet feeling helpless, thousands of miles away, in a country that for all its modernism was also trying to repress and legislate women's bodies, I felt compelled to write about Jyoti and what her life and death meant to me and to the world. However, I wanted not to in any way sensationalize her already highly sensationalized rape and murder or compromise her dignity. Instead, I hoped to contextualize the incident in new and meaningful ways.

In "Tramp," I focus more on my readers by taking them through my own experience and reflections on watching an old Bollywood Hindi movie, *Awaara* ("Tramp"), on the eve of Jyoti's death. The themes of the more than sixty-year-old movie subtly, and not so subtly, echo the prevalence of patriarchy and misogyny in India and presage the rise of rape culture. I note how as I watched Leela, a pregnant woman, abandoned by her husband, a young, educated judge, because she is "tainted" for having been kidnapped by another man, I couldn't help consider the film's themes against the backdrop of the aftermath of the gang rape in India and the ways misogyny was playing out here in the United States. As I write in "Tramp":

> But I remained hung up on the plight of the judge's wife, Leela— how she was devalued and "thrown away" by her husband and society despite the fact that she was the victim. And I thought to myself, are things that different more than 60 years later? In the U.S., we have male politicians putting forth arguments about "legitimate rape." And in India we have male politicians denigrating female protesters of a brutal gang rape as "painted" and "dented" women.

In "Jyoti's Rainbow," I focus more on my subject by examining the cultural impact of this horrific rape. I look at multiple artistic works sparked by the incident and its aftermath—two movies, a play, and a digital comic—all of which seek to reckon with this senseless crime and the need for Indian society to foster an environment where girls and women can feel safe, valued, and equal:

> Both films, *Daughters of Mother India* and *India's Daughter*, are important, informative and shaped by their respective focus on how much has changed and how much has not in terms of sexual violence in India. And in a democracy, both deserve to be seen because of their opposing perspectives, rather than despite them. Meanwhile, *Nirbhaya* and *Priya's Shakti* differ greatly in

medium, yet their power and poignancy lie in how they hold up the voices, not just the stories, of sexual violence survivors.

Jyoti Singh's rape and death was horrifying, inspiring new laws, activism, and diverse works of art that follow a long tradition of art that seeks to reflect society, not only in all its beauty, but also in all its barbarity. It is arts activism, which seeks to goad society towards what it ideally could be. As unspeakable as this was, it would have been made that much more tragic, had it been followed by silence.

In "Tramp," I focus on the reader by treating myself as a character and homing in on my experience of watching *Awaara* and trying to understand how it relates to this horrific sexual assault in India and the prevalence of misogyny in both India and the US. I bring the reader with me into the living room of my parents' home during the holidays, sharing personal details that set the intimate mood and tone of the piece.

Meanwhile, in "Jyoti's Rainbow," I focus on elements of four artistic pieces that were created in response to the tragic crime, each seeking in its own way to shed light on underlying issues and the need for change. I draw parallels between the works while also showing how they differ in tone, message, and medium. I'm less a character in this piece and more a guide or narrator, keeping focus on the works of art and how they speak to the cultural and sociopolitical significance of this incident and the activism it ignited.

Also included in this chapter are two essays by writer Garnette Cadogan on the significance of inhabiting public spaces as a Black man. In "Black and Blue," Cadogan centers readers as he takes us on a journey through his intimidating experiences of walking as a Black man in US cities amidst the pervasive perils of racism perpetuated by not just fellow citizens but also members of law enforcement, the very individuals tasked with protecting us. In "Black and Blue," Cadogan introduces us to how his love of walking began in his hometown of Kingston, Jamaica. Here, the dangers he faced on late-night walks through the city are as familiar to him as the terrain he traversed. When Cadogan travels to New Orleans for college, however, he becomes aware that his love of walking endangers him, not because of criminal elements about which he's warned, but because *he* is now perceived as the criminal element.

Cadogan arrives in New York City, a liberal, multiracial city that is home to the most diverse county in the country, and falls in love with discovering its myriad neighborhoods and cultural enclaves by foot. However, he soon realizes despite the city's cosmopolitanism, he, as a Black man, is not afforded the freedom of walking its streets without suspicion. He must, as he notes, return to his old rules for walking while Black:

> I realized that what I least liked about walking in New York City wasn't merely having to learn new rules of navigation and socialization—every city has its own. It was the arbitrariness of the circumstances that required them, an arbitrariness that made me feel like a child again, that infantilized me. When we first learn to walk, the world around us threatens to crash into us. Every step is risky. We train ourselves to walk without crashing by being attentive to our movements, and extra-attentive to the world around us. As adults we walk without thinking, really. But as a black adult I am often returned to that moment in childhood when I'm just learning to walk. I am once again on high alert, vigilant. Some days, when I am fed up with being considered a troublemaker upon sight, I joke that the last time a cop was happy to see a black male walking was when that male was a baby taking his first steps.

Cadogan depicts the violent and troubling incidents he's experienced walking while Black in New York City through vivid, immersive scenes. Some readers, who have had similar experiences, will relate and understand while many others will be shocked and left with a deeper understanding and empathy for how the insidious patterns of structural racism circumscribe the movements of Black citizens, endangering them while simultaneously casting suspicion on them. Cadogan's "Black and Blue" underscores the power of story and narrative elements like character, scene, and dialogue. Sometimes a personal account that brings the reader into a particular issue in an immersive way can be more powerful and convincing than reams of data and evidence.

Meanwhile, in "Football, Free on the Streets," Cadogan keeps the focus on how soccer's ubiquitous popularity is evidenced by West African youth bringing their love of the game to public spaces, temporarily transforming them into informal stadiums. Alongside evocative images from Nigerian photographer Andrew Esiebo, the essay chronicles the ways in which devotees of this sport adapt public spaces into makeshift altars for communion with fellow true believers:

> The sight of people playing football daily in public spaces around the world is visual testimony of how the presence of bodies can turn the commonplace into the marvelous; proof, too, that football is a world game not because of the millions drawn to watch the World Cup, but because of the millions for whom the game is alive every day on the street, tournament or none. Andrew Esiebo's "Goal Diggers"—an exhibition of photographs on the irrepressible love West Africans have for football—reminds us that the simple desire to chase a ball is one of our commonalities. From Nigeria to Ghana to Sierra Leone to Senegal, groups of resourceful young people play the game on sidewalks, under bridges, in hallways, on narrow streets filled with more obstacles than players, on dusty grounds adorned with ad hoc goalposts, on beaches with no barriers but the horizon.

And of the tableau captured through Esiebo's evocative images, Cadogan observes:

> Sometimes the bodies have the force of symbols, as if poised to become fantasy; the game is both recreation and reverie. You rarely see any player's face in detail. What you cannot miss,

though, are the rich assembly of black bodies—in motion, sublime and alluring in their dips and leans and twists and lunges and runs and pauses, caught in a poetic choreography, at once jubilant and self-possessed.

Although Cadogan is focused on the meanings of soccer to West African youth and how it is embodied spatially and through Esiebo's photographs, he still engages the reader by immersing us in the scenes of resourceful youth playing in repurposed public spaces, in the bend and speed of their bodies as they chase the ball and each other. Cadogan is playing the role of witness and guide, but he lets us know he's also been a participant in his homeland of Jamaica. So, while "Football, Free on the Streets," is centered around exploring the visual spectacle of soccer in West Africa, Cadogan never forgets to provide immersive details and imagery.

Cadogan seems keenly aware of the reader's need for story, which is evident in how he crafts his narrative arc. Yet, as a thinker, he is committed to fleshing out ideas and issues in ways that respect their importance and complexity.

As we delve into writing, we must not forget that the purpose of writing is to be read, and the reason we write about social issues is because we want to highlight their importance. Keeping our readers and our subject at the forefront of our minds ensures that, as writers, we ultimately meet our dual responsibilities—being compelling yet truthful.

■

TRAMP

By Kavita Das

On what would turn out to be the eve of the death of the recent gang rape victim in Delhi, my family and I gathered together to watch a Hindi film that my parents had ordered on Netflix. The 1951 movie, *Awaara*, which translates to "tramp" in English, was produced, directed, and starred in by the early champion of Bollywood films Raj Kapoor and featured Nargis, the most famous leading lady of that time. I was feeling feverish so I was huddled under the brand new Slanket I had presented to my father for Christmas. We're all Hindus but our Christmas tree stood twinkling in the corner of the room.

The black and white film opens with a courthouse scene where the accused, Raj (Raj Kapoor) is a young man who tried to kill a highly respected judge, Raghunath. When the judge presiding over the case asks who is defending the accused, a female attorney, Rita (Nargis) makes a dramatic entrance just in the nick of time and declares that she is here to mount a defense, while looking over at Raj with loving eyes. She begins to cross-examine Raghunath by asking him if he had any children to which he replies he doesn't. She presses him and asks if he denies abandoning his wife and child many years ago. And then we are treated to a flashback in which all is revealed and explained.

The theme of the movie, which is taken up by the villains and heroes alike, is this: If you're the child of a bandit, are you destined to a life of criminality? Or put more broadly, does where you are born determine your destiny? But I was less interested in this question of nature versus nurture. Instead, I found myself more preoccupied by another theme contained in the film's plot, which in my mind was reminiscent of both the *Ramayana*, one of the most revered ancient Hindu texts, as well as the recent gang rape in Delhi.

The flashback showed how Raghunath, a young judge, bucked tradition by marrying a widow, Leela. This was almost unheard of given that even in the early part of this century, there were still those who called for Hindu widows to be burned alive on the funeral pyres of their husbands because what life is there for them once their husbands are dead?

But then one night, Leela is kidnapped by Jagga, an infamous bandit. It turns out that Jagga specifically planned to kidnap Leela as a vendetta because he claimed Raghunath had wrongly thrown him in jail for an alleged rape based on a determination that as the son and grandson of career criminals, he must be guilty. Jagga plans to rape Leela, as retribution but doesn't when he learns that she is in the early stages of pregnancy. He returns Leela to Raghunath knowing that by kidnapping her he has "tainted" her and that will bring ruin to not only her but also to Raghunath and his unborn child.

Raghunath, at first is thrilled to see Leela, however, their happy reunion is soon marred because his elder sister tells him that "everyone" is talking about how Leela has brought shame to their house by being with another man. She insists that Leela and her unborn child should be thrown out before they bring further shame to the family name. Raghunath, an educated and powerful man, succumbs to this barbaric thinking and just as Rama casts away Sita for the sake of propriety, in the epic *Ramayana*, Raghunath abandons Leela and his unborn child. The movie follows Raj, their child as he grows up in a Bombay slum, depicting how he gets pulled into a life of crime by Jagga, the bandit, himself. Kapoor lifted the persona and antics of his tramp from the master tramp, Charlie Chaplin, and set it to Hindi music.

I eventually gave up on the movie because I was feeling increasingly lousy—it turned out I had a 24-hour stomach bug. Anyways, I was pretty sure by this point that through a dramatic twist worthy of a telenovela, the accused, Raj, would be revealed to be none other than the judge's own abandoned son. But I remained hung up on the plight of the judge's wife, Leela—how she was devalued and "thrown away" by her husband and society despite the fact that she was the victim. And I thought to myself, are things that different more than 60 years later? In the U.S., we have male politicians putting forth arguments about "legitimate rape." And in India we have male politicians denigrating female protesters of a brutal gang rape as "painted" and "dented" women.

India is the world's most populous democracy but it's also by some measures the worst country for women, despite the fact that it was led by a female Prime Minister for many years. Bollywood, India's Hindi film industry is known the world over because it makes more movies than Hollywood, but very few of these movies actually move the genre forward. Through its mastery of science and technology, India is on a path to economic and political power but that path will prove illusory if it doesn't take concrete steps to address the very real systemic issues it faces in terms of women's rights, poverty, and corruption. Meanwhile, here in the U.S., as we recover from our own wounds from gun violence, hopefully the painful echoes of the protests in India over this horrific crime will rouse us and keep us ever-vigilant of those who seek to condone sexual violence against women or curtail women's rights.

I am encouraged because over the last few weeks in India, women and men have turned out by the thousands for vigils to honor the victim and for protests to demand better law enforcement and justice for rape cases. Here in the U.S., voters "kicked out" congressional members who had backwards views on women's reproductive rights. This makes me hopeful that despite the fact that democracies are messy and don't in and of themselves guarantee equal rights to all their citizens, it gives its citizens the chance, even if it is a narrow one, at times, to call for justice and be heard.

Awaara, which was nominated for the Grand Prize at the Cannes Film Festival, avoided the conventional formula for Bollywood films that persists to this day, which requires a shining hero to rescue a beautiful damsel in distress from an ominous villain. Instead, in *Awaara*, some heroes emerge as villains, such as Raghunath, the illustrious judge, who let social pressure and backwards thinking cloud over his rationality. Meanwhile, some villains are revealed to have heroic traits, such as the judge's son, Raj, who came up as a tramp but is redeemed by the power of love. Similarly, women are portrayed as both the oppressor and the savior, with the judge's sister seeking to leave her pregnant sister-in-law destitute while Rita, the female attorney comes to the rescue of Raj, the lovable tramp. In my mind, the more than sixty-year-old film serves as a cross-cultural time capsule showing how women's lives played out on the black and white screens of yesteryears. Now we need to figure out how they will play out on the high-definition, three-dimensional, screens of tomorrow.

■

JYOTI'S RAINBOW

By Kavita Das

The gang rape and death of Jyoti Singh in New Delhi, India in December 2012 triggered a wave of activism and seeded societal changes. It also, like tragedies before, inspired art. This spring, I watched two films, attended a play, and viewed a digital comic over a three-month span. Each was catalyzed by the same event, but their perspective and approach to the somber subject varied.

First was Leslee Udwin's BBC film, *India's Daughter*, which I saw amidst the maelstrom of controversy that surrounded it and its director in early March. I was struck by how many people were decrying the film without having seen it, primarily because it portrays India negatively and because Udwin is not an Indian. Debates raged within the Indian government and amongst the public, and on March 4th, just four days before its planned worldwide release set to coincide with International Women's Day on March 8th, the Indian government banned the film from theaters in India, citing concerns that it might incite violence and because it featured damning interviews with one of the rapists, who had a pending appeal before the court. The government of India, the most populous democracy in the world, went even farther, banning the film online in India through YouTube and on the BBC web site.

I managed to stream the film online during the narrow window of time while it was still available on an Indian culture site—and I wasn't alone. In some ways, the ban had the opposite effect, with many Indians both in India and in the diaspora seeking out and watching the film online. Ultimately, a film with India as its focus was screened and broadcast in cities outside India, including London, New York, and Chicago.

India's Daughter reveals many ugly truths about gender and sexual violence in India, but, importantly, these truths do not come from foreigners. Rather, they are spoken by those central to the atrocity. Udwin talks to Mukesh Singh, one of Jyoti's rapists, who not only shows no remorse for his heinous actions, but expounds on how women who are raped are just as culpable as their male rapists. "You can't clap with one hand—it takes two hands . . . a decent girl won't roam around at 9 o'clock at night; a girl is far more responsible for rape than a boy." Here, Udwin complicates the narrative by showing the destitution in which the rapists were raised and now live. Puneeta Devi, wife of rapist Akshay Thakur, wonders why, in all of this, no one seems to care about her welfare. "Am I not a daughter of this country? Don't I have a right to live?"

While it's hard to stomach Mukesh Singh's lack of remorse and views on rape and women's role in Indian society, it's even more shocking to hear similar views from the rapists' attorneys. The film shows a TV broadcast where a lawyer threatens: "If my daughter or sister engaged in pre-marital activities and disgraced herself and allowed herself to lose face and character by doing such things, I would most certainly take this sort of sister or daughter to my farmhouse, and in front of my entire family, I would put petrol on her and set her alight." Comments by these attorneys cross far beyond creating a convincing argument into victim-blaming, underscoring that education is not necessarily a cure for such deeply entrenched societal views.

Jyoti Singh became a symbol to girls and women all over India standing up to sexual violence, but first, she was the daughter of Asha and Badri Singh, who tell Udwin of the joy Jyoti brought them. "We were given a gift of light and happiness when she was born," Asha says. Badri speaks of the pride they felt at their daughter's promising future as a medical student: "Happiness was a few steps ahead." They discuss the devastation of her death, but also what her life has come to mean to them and to others. In the film's closing, her father describes how Jyoti challenged Indian society's views on gender by posing the question, "What is the meaning of 'a woman?' How is she looked on by society today?" Udwin is unflinching in also depicting their outrage at not only the brutal death of their daughter but at the delay in getting justice. While the four adult rapists were convicted and sentenced to death in September 2013, the case has been languishing in a final appeal to the Indian Supreme Court. Meanwhile, the juvenile rapist was sentenced to only three years in prison and is due to be released in December 2015.

India's Daughter emphasizes not only how threatening sexual violence is against girls and women in India, but also how it's connected to deeply entrenched and pervasive views on women's role in society. Meanwhile, the banning of the film set off debates about the curtailing of freedom of speech, from the floor of the Indian Parliament to the pages and broadcasts of Indian and international outlets, including *OpIndia*, *Firstpost*, *NDTV*, *The Hindu*, *Al Jazeera America*, and *Poynter*. Ultimately, those who vehemently opposed the ban—some of whom expressed concerns about the film and how it was made—wondered how India could meaningfully address sexual violence while silencing the very voices speaking about it.

On May 5th, two months later, I watched Vibha Bhakshi's *Daughters of Mother India* at the 2015 New York Indian Film Festival. Like *India's Daughter*, this film uses the brutal rape of Jyoti Singh as the starting point. However, it has a decidedly different perspective: it focuses on the positive changes wrought in the wake of this tragedy. It opens with a narration about Jyoti Singh's case, however Bakshi doesn't talk to anyone involved directly in that case. Instead, the film quickly turns to highlight the weeks of protests by hundreds of thousands of people in Delhi, especially youth, which were sparked by this case. The film goes on to focus on the changes that were created in the legal and law enforcement systems due to this case and the resulting social movement. Changes have been made to the legal definition of rape and sexual assault and new rape laws were drafted and passed. Then Bakshi takes us into the Delhi Police Department, which is assigning more women officers to the domestic and sexual violence hotline, and conducting sensitivity trainings for the city's largely male police force. *Daughters of Mother India* also depicts how art activists are using street theater to create awareness and change minds about sexual violence against women and how educators are making children aware of sexual abuse.

In Bakshi's film, it's as if everyone wants and is engaged in change, from the youth, to the government, to the police. And yet, we know that cultural change comes slowly and not without resistance, and given India's deep and diverse cultural history, it might come even more slowly.

Daughters of Mother India's focus on the positive changes that have transpired since Jyoti's death is neither subtle nor tempered, and not surprisingly, it has garnered a positive response in India and within the Indian government. At the 2015 National Film Awards, which is overseen by the Indian Government's Directorate of Film Festivals, *Daughters of Mother India* nabbed the National Film Award for Best Film on Social Issues. Beyond accolades, following the film's premiere in Mumbai, the director of the National Police Academy issued an internal memo urging that the film be seen by the entire force as part of their sensitivity training on gender violence, demonstrating that the film both focuses on positive change, and seeks to be a tool for that change.

The very next day, on May 6th, I attended Yael Farber's riveting play, *Nirbhaya*. The play has shown in Mumbai, Edinburgh, and Dublin, and its title, which means, "one who is not afraid," refers to the name Jyoti came to be called by the media and public when her identity was still unknown. The cast features six female actors and one male actor, who not only powerfully portray Jyoti's brutal rape and its aftermath but also deftly weave in their own traumatic stories of gender violence. It is part theater, and part confessional, but it is entirely engrossing, and deeply affecting.

I was stunned by the courage of the five actresses who share their own experiences of sexual trauma and gender violence. Sneha Jawale was severely beaten and burned by her husband, who then absconded with their young son. Weeping on stage, she says to the son lost to her, "I search for you in the stars and in the face of every stranger." Meanwhile, Priyanka Bhose, who endured repeated sexual molestation during her childhood, says with disgust, "like half the children in our country, we spent our childhoods cleaning other people's scents from ourselves," speaking both of her own trauma as well as the sad pervasiveness of childhood sexual abuse. I marveled at how these women relive their traumas night after night on stage, turning their pain into art. And while *Nirbhaya* does not take a position or inform you of what has changed and what has not, you leave understanding that Jyoti's story is at once singularly horrific and tragically universal.

The next day, on May 7th, *Priya's Shakti*, an exhibit featuring an augmented comic book experience opened at City Lore Gallery in New York City as part of the 2015 PEN World Voices Festival. *Priya's Shakti* is the brainchild of filmmaker Ram Devineni, and uniquely combines Hindu mythology, comic book storytelling, and digital technology to address sexual violence in India. Drawn by comic book artist Dan Goldman, it portrays Priya, a young Dalit woman who is raped and finds no support within her family and community. In desperation, she invokes Hindu Goddess Parvati for solace and strength. Priya's mythical story is powerful, but so are the real stories of Indian women who have survived sexual violence, which Devineni and his creative partners have woven into the exhibit. Each woman and their story have been rendered in comic book form to protect their identity and to integrate their story into Priya's narrative, as well as the broader narrative of sexual violence.

As a child, I devoured *Amar Chitra Kathas*, Indian comic books; however, their portrayal of women was often problematic, ideologically as well as visually. Given that *Amar Chitra Kathas* did not address rape, let alone sex, I was encouraged to see *Priya's Shakti's* take on sexual violence. The use of cutting-edge mobile and digital technologies in the comic book and related exhibit, along with the bold yet nuanced treatment of sexual violence, makes *Priya's Shakti* a model for the future of Indian comic books.

Both films, *Daughters of Mother India* and *India's Daughter*, are important, informative and shaped by their respective focus on how much has changed and how much has not in terms of sexual violence in India. And in a democracy, both deserve to be seen because of their opposing perspectives, rather than despite them. Meanwhile, *Nirbhaya* and *Priya's Shakti* differ greatly in medium, yet their power and poignancy lie in how they hold up the voices, not just the stories, of sexual violence survivors.

Jyoti Singh's rape and death was horrifying, inspiring new laws, activism, and diverse works of art that follow a long tradition of art that seeks to reflect society, not only in all its beauty, but also in all its barbarity. It is arts activism, which seeks to goad society towards what it ideally could be. As unspeakable as this was, it would have been made that much more tragic, had it been followed by silence.

■

BLACK AND BLUE

By Garnette Cadogan

My only sin is my skin.
What did I do, to be so black and blue?

—"(What Did I Do to Be So)
Black and Blue?" (Fats Waller, composer;
lyrics by Harry Brooks and Andy Razaf)

Manhattan's streets I saunter'd, pondering.

—WALT WHITMAN,
"Manhattan's Streets I Saunter'd, Pondering"

My love for walking started in childhood, out of necessity. No thanks to a stepfather with heavy hands, I found every reason to stay away from home and was usually out—at some friend's house or at a street party where no minor should be—until it was too late to get public transportation. So I walked.

The streets of Kingston, Jamaica, in the 1980s were often terrifying—you could, for instance, get killed if a political henchman thought you came from the wrong neighborhood, or even if you wore the wrong color. Wearing orange showed affiliation with one political party and green with the other, and if you were neutral or traveling far from home you chose your colors well. The wrong color in the wrong neighborhood could mean your last day. No wonder, then, that my friends and the rare nocturnal passerby declared me crazy for my long late-night treks that traversed warring political zones. (And sometimes I did pretend to be crazy, shouting non sequiturs when I passed through especially dangerous spots, such as the place where thieves hid on the banks of a storm drain. Predators would ignore or laugh at the kid in his school uniform speaking nonsense.)

I made friends with strangers and went from being a very shy and awkward kid to being an extroverted, awkward one. The beggar, the vendor, the poor laborer—those were experienced wanderers, and they became my nighttime instructors; they knew the streets and delivered lessons on how to navigate and enjoy them. I imagined myself as a Jamaican Tom Sawyer, one moment sauntering down the streets to pick low-hanging mangoes that I could reach from the sidewalk, another moment hanging outside a street party with battling sound systems, each armed with speakers piled to create skyscrapers of heavy bass. These streets weren't frightening. They were full of adventure when they weren't serene. There I'd join forces with a band of merry walkers, who'd miss the last bus by mere minutes, our feet still moving as we put out our thumbs to hitchhike to spots nearer home, making jokes as vehicle after vehicle raced past us. Or I'd get lost in Mittyesque moments, my young mind imagining alternate futures. The streets had their own safety: Unlike at home, there I could be myself without fear of bodily harm. Walking became so regular and familiar that the way home became home. The streets had their rules, and I loved the challenge of trying to master them. I learned how to be alert to surrounding dangers and nearby delights, and prided myself on recognizing telling details that my peers missed. Kingston was a map of complex, and often bizarre,

cultural and political and social activity, and I appointed myself
its nighttime cartographer. I'd know how to navigate away from
a predatory pace, and to speed up to chat when the cadence of a
gait announced friendliness. It was almost always men I saw. A
lone woman walking in the middle of the night was as common a
sight as Sasquatch; moonlight pedestrianism was too dangerous
for her. Sometimes at night as I made my way down from hills
above Kingston, I'd have the impression that the city was set on
"pause" or in extreme slow motion, as that as I descended I was
cutting across Jamaica's deep social divisions. I'd make my way
briskly past the mansions in the hills overlooking the city, now
transformed into a carpet of dotted lights under a curtain of stars,
saunter by middle-class subdivisions hidden behind high walls
crowned with barbed wire, and zigzagged through neighborhoods of zinc and wooden shacks crammed together and leaning
like a tight-knit group of limbo dancers. With my descent came
an increase in the vibrancy of street life—except when it didn't;
some poor neighborhoods had both the violent gunfights and the
eerily deserted streets of the cinematic Wild West. I knew well
enough to avoid those even at high noon.

I'd begun hoofing it after dark when I was ten years old. By
thirteen I was rarely home before midnight, and some nights
found me racing against dawn. My mother would often complain,
"Mek yuh love street suh? Yuh born a hospital; yuh neva born a
street." ("Why do you love the streets so much? You were born in
a hospital, not in the streets.")

I left Jamaica in 1996 to attend college in New Orleans, a city
I'd heard called "the northernmost Caribbean city." I wanted to
discover—on foot, of course—what was Caribbean and what was
American about it. Stately mansions on oak-lined streets with
streetcars clanging by, and brightly colored houses that made
entire blocks look festive; people in resplendent costumes dancing to funky brass bands in the middle of the street; cuisine—and

aromas—that mashed up culinary traditions from Africa, Europe, Asia, and the American South; and a juxtaposition of worlds old and new, odd and familiar: Who wouldn't want to explore this?

On my first day in the city, I went walking for a few hours to get a feel for the place and to buy supplies to transform my dormitory room from a prison bunker into a welcoming space. When some university staff members found out what I'd been up to, they warned me to restrict my walking to the places recommended as safe to tourists and the parents of freshmen. They trotted out statistics about New Orleans' crime rate. But Kingston's crime rate dwarfed those numbers, and I decided to ignore these well-meant cautions. A city was waiting to be discovered, and I wouldn't let inconvenient facts get in the way. These American criminals are nothing on Kingston's, I thought. They're no real threat to me.

What no one had told me was that I was the one who would be considered a threat. Within days I noticed that many people on the street seemed apprehensive of me: Some gave me a circumspect glance as they approached, and then crossed the street; others, ahead, would glance behind, register my presence, and then speed up; older white women clutched their bags; young white men nervously greeted me, as if exchanging a salutation for their safety: "What's up, bro?" On one occasion, less than a month after my arrival, I tried to help a man whose wheelchair was stuck in the middle of a crosswalk; he threatened to shoot me in the face, then asked a white pedestrian for help.

I wasn't prepared for any of this. I had come from a majority-black country in which no one was wary of me because of my skin color. Now I wasn't sure who was afraid of me. I was especially unprepared for the cops. They regularly stopped and bullied me, asking questions that took my guilt for granted. I'd never received what many of my African-American friends call "The Talk": No parents had told me how to behave when I was stopped by the police, how to be as polite and cooperative as possible, no matter what they said or did to me. So I had to cobble together my own rules of engagement. Thicken my Jamaican accent. Quickly mention my college. "Accidentally" pull out my college identification card when asked for my driver's license.

My survival tactics began well before I left my dorm. I got out of the shower with the police in my head, assembling a cop-proof wardrobe. Light-colored oxford shirt. V-neck sweater. Khaki pants. Chukkas. Sweatshirt or T-shirt with my university insignia. When I walked I regularly had my identity challenged, but I also found ways to assert it. (So I'd dress Ivy League style, but would, later on, add my Jamaican pedigree by wearing Clarks Desert Boots, the footwear of choice of Jamaican street culture.) Yet the all-American sartorial choice of white Tshirt and jeans, which many police officers see as the uniform of black troublemakers, was offlimits to me—at least, if I wanted to have the freedom of movement I desired. In this city of exuberant streets, walking became a complex and often oppressive negotiation. I would see a white woman walking towards me at night and cross the street to reassure her that she was safe. I would forget something at home but not immediately turn around if someone was behind me, because I discovered that a sudden backtrack could cause alarm. (I had a cardinal rule: Keep a wide perimeter from people who might consider me a danger. If not, danger might visit me.) New Orleans suddenly felt more dangerous than Jamaica. The sidewalk was a minefield, and every hesitation and self-censored compensation reduced my dignity. Despite my best efforts, the streets never felt comfortably safe. Even a simple salutation was suspect.

One night, returning to the house that, eight years after my arrival, I thought I'd earned the right to call my home, I waved to a cop driving by. Moments later, I was against his car in handcuffs. When I later asked him—sheepishly, of course; any other way would have asked for bruises—why he had detained me, he said my greeting had aroused his suspicion. "No one waves to the police," he explained. When I told friends of his response, it was my behavior, not his, that they saw as absurd. "Now why would you do a dumb thing like that?" said one. "You know better than to make nice with police."

■ ■ ■

A few days after I left on a visit to Kingston, Hurricane Katrina slashed and pummeled New Orleans. I'd gone not because of the storm but because my adoptive grandmother, Pearl, was dying of cancer. I hadn't wandered those streets in eight years, since my last visit, and I returned to them now mostly at night, the time I found best for thinking, praying, crying. I walked to feel less alienated— from myself, struggling with the pain of seeing my grandmother terminally ill; from my home in New Orleans, underwater and seemingly abandoned; from my home country, which now, pre- cisely because of its childhood familiarity, felt foreign to me. I was surprised by how familiar those streets felt. Here was the corner where the fragrance of jerk chicken greeted me, along with the warm tenor and peace-and-love message of Half Pint's "Greet- ings," broadcast from a small but powerful speaker to at least a half-mile radius. It was as if I had walked into 1986, down to the soundtrack. And there was the wall of the neighborhood shop, adorned with the Rastafarian colors red, gold, and green along with images of local and international heroes Bob Marley, Marcus Garvey, and Haile Selassie. The crew of boys leaning against it and joshing each other were recognizable; different faces, similar sto- ries. I was astonished at how safe the streets felt to me, once again one black body among many, no longer having to anticipate the many ways my presence might instill fear and how to offer some reassuring body language. Passing police cars were once again merely passing police cars. Jamaican police could be pretty brutal, but they didn't notice me the way American police did. I could be invisible in Jamaica in a way I can't be invisible in the United States. Walking had returned to me a greater set of possibilities. And why walk, if not to create a new set of possibilities? Following serendipity, I added new routes to the mental maps I had made from constant walking in that city from childhood to young adult- hood, traced variations on the old pathways. Serendipity, a mentor once told me, is a secular way of speaking of grace; it's unearned favor. Seen theologically, then, walking is an act of faith. Walking is, after all, interrupted falling. We see, we listen, we speak, and we trust that each step we take won't be our last, but will lead us into a richer understanding of the self and the world.

In Jamaica, I felt once again as if the only identity that mattered was my own, not the constricted one that others had constructed for me. I strolled into my better self. I said, along with Kierkegaard, "I have walked myself into my best thoughts."

When I tried to return to New Orleans from Jamaica a month later, there were no flights. I thought about flying to Texas so I could make my way back to my neighborhood as soon as it opened for reoccupancy, but my adoptive aunt, Maxine, who hated the idea of me returning to a hurricane zone before the end of hurricane season, persuaded me to come to stay in New York City instead. (To strengthen her case she sent me an article about Texans who were buying up guns because they were afraid of the influx of black people from New Orleans.)

This wasn't a hard sell: I wanted to be in a place where I could travel by foot and, more crucially, continue to reap the solace of walking at night. And I was eager to follow in the steps of the essayists, poets, and novelists who'd wandered that great city before me—Walt Whitman, Herman Melville, Alfred Kazin, Elizabeth Hardwick. I had visited the city before, but each trip had felt like a tour in a sports car. I welcomed the chance to stroll. I wanted to walk alongside Whitman's ghost and "descend to the pavements, merge with the crowd, and gaze with them." So I left Kingston, the popular Jamaican farewell echoing in my mind: "Walk good!" Be safe on your journey, in other words, and all the best in your endeavors.

I arrived in New York City, ready to lose myself in Whitman's "Manhattan crowds, with their turbulent musical chorus!" I marveled at what Jane Jacobs praised as "the ballet of the good city sidewalk" in her old neighborhood, the West Village. I walked up past midtown skyscrapers, releasing their energy as lively people onto the streets, and on into the Upper West Side, with its regal Beaux Arts apartment buildings, stylish residents, and buzzing streets. Onward into Washington Heights, the sidewalks spilled over with an ebullient mix of young and old Jewish and Dominican-American residents, past leafy Inwood, with parks whose grades rose to reveal beautiful views of the Hudson River, up to my home in Kingsbridge in the Bronx, with its rows of brick bungalows and apartment buildings nearby Broadway's bustling sidewalks and the peaceful expanse of Van Cortlandt Park. I went to Jackson Heights in Queens to take in people socializing around garden courtyards in Urdu, Korean, Spanish, Russian, and Hindi. And when I wanted a taste of home, I headed to Brooklyn, in Crown Heights, for Jamaican food and music and humor mixed in with the flavor of New York City. The city was my playground.

I explored the city with friends, and then with a woman I'd begun dating. She walked around endlessly with me, taking in New York City's many pleasures. Coffee shops open until pre-dawn; verdant parks with nooks aplenty; food and music from across the globe; quirky neighborhoods with quirkier residents. My impressions of the city took shape during my walks with her.

As with the relationship, those first few months of urban exploration were all romance. The city was beguiling, exhilarating, vibrant. But it wasn't long before reality reminded me I wasn't invulnerable, especially when I walked alone.

One night in the East Village, I was running to dinner when a white man in front of me turned and punched me in the chest with such force that I thought my ribs had braided around my spine. I assumed he was drunk or had mistaken me for an old enemy, but found out soon enough that he'd merely assumed I was a criminal because of my race. When he discovered I wasn't what he imagined, he went on to tell me that his assault was my own fault for running up behind him. I blew off this incident as an aberration, but the mutual distrust between me and the police was impossible to ignore. It felt elemental. They'd enter a subway platform; I'd notice them. (And I'd notice all the other black men registering their presence as well, while just about everyone else remained oblivious to them). They'd glare. I'd get nervous and glance. They'd observe me steadily. I'd get uneasy. I'd observe them back, worrying that I looked suspicious. Their suspicions would increase. We'd continue the silent, uneasy dialogue until the subway arrived and separated us at last.

I returned to the old rules I'd set for myself in New Orleans, with elaboration. No running, especially at night; no sudden movements; no hoodies; no objects—especially shiny ones—in hand; no waiting for friends on street corners, lest I be mistaken for a drug dealer; no standing near a corner on the cell phone (same reason). As comfort set in, inevitably I began to break some of those rules, until a night encounter sent me zealously back to them, me having learned that anything less than vigilance was carelessness.

After a sumptuous Italian dinner and drinks with friends, I was jogging to the subway at Columbus Circle—I was running late to meet another set of friends at a concert downtown. I heard someone shouting and I looked up to see a police officer approaching with his gun trained on me. "Against the car!" In no time, half a dozen cops were upon me, chucking me against the car and tightly handcuffing me. "Why were you running?" "Where are you going?" "Where are you coming from?" "I said, why were you running?!" Since I couldn't answer everyone at once, I decided to respond first to the one who looked most likely to hit me. I was surrounded by a swarm and tried to focus on just one without inadvertently aggravating the others.

It didn't work. As I answered that one, the others got frustrated that I wasn't answering them fast enough and barked at me. One of them, digging through my already-emptied pockets, asked if I had any weapons, the question more an accusation. Another badgered me about where I was coming from, as if on the fifteenth round I'd decide to tell him the truth he imagined. Though I kept saying—calmly, of course, which meant trying to manage a tone that ignored my racing heart and their spittle-filled shouts in my face—that I had just left friends two blocks down the road, who were all still there and could vouch for me, to meet other friends whose text messages on my phone that could verify that, yes, sir, yes, officer, of course, officer, it made no difference.

For a black man, to assert your dignity before the police was to risk assault. In fact, the dignity of black people meant less to them, which was why I always felt safer being stopped in front of white witnesses than black witnesses. The cops had less regard for the witness and entreaties of black onlookers, whereas the concern of white witnesses usually registered on them.

A black witness asking a question or politely raising an objection could quickly become a fellow detainee. Deference to the police, then, was sine qua non for a safe encounter. The cops ignored my explanations and my suggestions and continued to snarl at me. All except one of them, a captain. He put his hand on my back, and said to no one in particular, "If he was running for a long time he would have been sweating." He then instructed that the cuffs be removed. He told me that a black man had stabbed someone earlier two or three blocks away and they were searching for him. I noted that I had no blood on me and had told his fellow officers where I'd been and how to check my alibi—unaware that it was even an alibi, as no one had told me why I was being held, and of course, I hadn't dared ask. From what I'd seen, anything beyond passivity would be interpreted as aggression.

The police captain said I could go. None of the cops who detained me thought an apology was necessary. Like the thug who punched me in the East Village, they seemed to think it was my own fault for running.

Humiliated, I tried not to make eye contact with the onlookers on the sidewalk, and I was reluctant to pass them to be on my way. The captain, maybe noticing my shame, offered to give me a ride to the subway station. When he dropped me off and I thanked him for his help, he said, "It's because you were polite that we let you go. If you were acting up it would have been different." I nodded and said nothing.

I realized that what I least liked about walking in New York City wasn't merely having to learn new rules of navigation and socialization—every city has its own. It was the arbitrariness of the circumstances that required them, an arbitrariness that made me feel like a child again, that infantilized me. When we first learn to walk, the world around us threatens to crash into us.

Every step is risky. We train ourselves to walk without crashing by being attentive to our movements, and extra-attentive to the world around us. As adults we walk without thinking, really. But as a black adult I am often returned to that moment in childhood when I'm just learning to walk. I am once again on high alert, vigilant.

Some days, when I am fed up with being considered a troublemaker upon sight, I joke that the last time a cop was happy to see a black male walking was when that male was a baby taking his first steps. On many walks, I ask white friends to accompany me, just to avoid being treated like a threat. Walks in New York City, that is; in New Orleans, a white woman in my company sometimes attracted more hostility. (And it is not lost on me that my woman friends are those who best understand my plight; they have developed their own vigilance in an environment where they are constantly treated as targets of sexual attention.) Much of my walking is as my friend Rebecca once described it: A pantomime undertaken to avoid the choreography of criminality.

Walking while black restricts the experience of walking, renders inaccessible the classic Romantic experience of walking alone. It forces me to be in constant relationship with others, unable to join the New York flaneurs I had read about and hoped to join. Instead of meandering aimlessly in the footsteps of Whitman, Melville, Kazin, and Vivian Gornick, more often, I felt that I was tiptoeing in Baldwin's—the Baldwin who wrote, way back in 1960, "Rare, indeed, is the Harlem citizen, from the most circumspect church member to the most shiftless adolescent, who does not have a long tale to tell of police incompetence, injustice, or brutality. I myself have witnessed and endured it more than once." Walking as a black man has made me feel simultaneously more removed from the city, in my awareness that I am perceived as suspect, and more closely connected to it, in the full attentiveness demanded by my vigilance. It has made me walk more purposefully in the city, becoming part of its flow, rather than observing, standing apart.

But it also means that I'm still trying to arrive in a city that isn't quite mine. One definition of home is that it's somewhere we can most be ourselves. And when are we more ourselves but when walking, that natural state in which we repeat one of the first actions we learned? Walking—the simple, monotonous act of placing one foot before the other to prevent falling—turns out not to be so simple if you're black. Walking alone has been anything but monotonous for me; monotony is a luxury.

A foot leaves, a foot lands, and our longing gives it momentum from rest to rest. We long to look, to think, to talk, to get away. But more than anything else, we long to be free. We want the freedom and pleasure of walking without fear—without others' fear—wherever we choose. I've lived in New York City for almost a decade and have not stopped walking its fascinating streets. And I have not stopped longing to find the solace that I found as a kid on the streets of Kingston. Much as coming to know New York City's streets has made it closer to home to me, the city also withholds itself from me via those very streets. I walk them, alternately invisible and too prominent. So I walk caught between memory and forgetting, between memory and forgiveness.

Jamestown 2018. Andrew Esiebo Photo.

■

FOOTBALL, FREE ON THE STREETS
By Garnette Cadogan

The sight of people playing football daily in public spaces around the world is visual testimony of how the presence of bodies can turn the commonplace into the marvelous; proof, too, that football is a world game not because of the millions drawn to watch the World Cup, but because of the millions for whom the game is alive every day on the street, tournament or none. Andrew Esiebo's "Goal Diggers"—an exhibition of photographs on the irrepressible love West Africans have for football—reminds us that the simple desire to chase a ball is one of our commonalities. From Nigeria to Ghana to Sierra Leone to Senegal, groups of resourceful young people play the game on sidewalks, under bridges, in hallways, on narrow streets filled with more obstacles than players, on dusty grounds adorned with ad hoc goalposts, on beaches with no barriers but the horizon.

"In Africa, the beautiful game isn't confined to the stadium," Esiebo writes. "From farmland to city roads, from beaches to markets, football belongs everywhere." His images testify that kinship is found in play, and declare that this game doubles as a diasporic handshake.

Football invites you to lose yourself in other people's stories; their play becomes yours as you follow the ball and intertwine your enthusiasm with theirs. The ritual of watching bodies at play draws us to them and allows us—our bodies—to join a shared rhythm. Football is therefore not just competition, but is generous, collective participation.

Esiebo is preoccupied with rituals of the everyday—the myriad ways they show creativity, empowerment, and survival. As if in gentle rebuke, he turns his lens to activities that highlight how simple daily experiences carry the shine of magnificence, revealing the significance of the overlooked and the dignity of the excluded.

He focuses on urban environments where there aren't enough spaces for formalized recreation, where poor urban infrastructure and planning stifle cultural and social life. Players move out of defiance as much as pleasure. In Lagos, young men under a bridge play between makeshift goalposts composed of piles of tires joined at their peaks by a rope made from plastic strings. In Jamestown, Accra, children scamper on a tiny sidewalk around adults selling tomatoes to gain control of a ball; in the same district, another group of children imaginatively turn a narrow corridor into a football field. And whoever said that a small walkway between houses, with people cooking and going about their business, was off-bounds for a game of football? Present, but not in the way, these little ones in Lagos stand before the viewer as evidence that scoring is beside the point—the drama is in the dance: bodies making their way through the world with grace and exuberant glow.

As a kid myself, I never knew my country to be as international as when the World Cup came around. The quadrennial tournament made emigrés of us Jamaicans, and we became competing West Germans and Argentinians and Brazilians. We wore the national colors of our new countries proudly, hoisting flags and raising voices with such fervor that if a consular official saw us they'd grant us visas on sight. This was the great appeal of the recent World Cup for me: one nation becomes many, if even superficially. We jump the fence of sovereignty to cheer alongside fans of other countries, share in their joy. Or anguish. That crowd—away from the stadiums, gathered in living rooms and restaurants and bars, hushed and screaming before television screens—was what pulled me to the World Cup.

And no crowd I know of celebrates like a Jamaican crowd— banging pot covers they've converted to madcap cymbals, slamming palms on every flat surface in sight, turning the built environment into a drum kit. I was habituated, then, to believe a game isn't worth seeing if there's no pulsating energy around it; there's no real action at a game if I can't watch the watchers. The show is in the areas far beyond the stadium.

When I visited Lagos a few months ago, I instinctively looked, as I often do when I'm abroad, for signs of the one Jamaican everyone knows. Sure enough, I spotted more than a few people in Bob Marley T-shirts, and made a new friend, the Afrobeat musician Edaoto Olaolu Agbeniyi, in part because of our shared love for my countryman's music and his support for pan-African struggle and unity. But as I explored the city's teeming sidewalks and streets with Edaoto as my guide, I noticed just about everyone rushing by at warp speed. Lagos in a hurry is nothing unusual—the city is so fast-paced that one is reluctant to make any claims about it lest the place revise itself before you finish writing down your observations. But I felt an enthusiastic gale pushing everyone along to the same end.

Edaoto explained that people were quickening their paces to see a football game. With the World Cup approaching, and Nigeria's beloved national team readying for Russia, I thought the Super Eagles must have had a warm-up match, so I asked whom Nigeria was playing. Edaoto turned to me, with a grin: "It's not Nigeria. It's Liverpool and Real Madrid."

One wonders if his being born and raised in Lagos, and based not far from there, has drawn Esiebo's eye to the ways people reshape their environment. Lagos is, after all, not merely a city on the move but also one preoccupied with change—self-improvement literature is hawked in the middle of streets overflowing with people intent on reinventing themselves and remaking their environs. It's a city of constant improvisation. A city that seems made for people who find inventive ways to carve out space for leisure in the face of—really, under the actual shadow of—urban renewal and too-often merciless change.

How do people strengthen their identities by sharing space with strangers? How do they lose themselves with abandon in community, and gain a richer sense of self or personal freedom? How is being black, and part of a community of blacks, a bridge to unity and pathway to variegated expression? Esiebo pursues those questions across West Africa, and ends up in barbershops and hair salons, documenting—in the project *Pride* (2012)—stories of how strangers who co-exist share intimacies and thereby transform their spaces into places of trust and joy. Traveling around West Africa, he recognizes that football, like barbershops, reveals people's inclination to reinvent themselves and transform their surroundings.

As attentive to the game as he is to setting, Esiebo fills his frame with the beauty of movement. Bodies are arranged like musical notes on a staff—whether they are playing alongside their reflections in a puddle of rain water in Olodi-Apapa, Lagos, or set in silhouette on a beach in Freetown, Sierra Leone—and bold color imbues them with an otherworldly feel. Sometimes the bodies have the force of symbols, as if poised to become fantasy; the game is both recreation and reverie. You rarely see any player's face in detail. What you cannot miss, though, are the rich assembly of black bodies—in motion, sublime and alluring in their dips and leans and twists and lunges and runs and pauses, caught in a poetic choreography, at once jubilant and self-possessed.

His perspective rarely betrays the distance of a spectator—he brings us onto the field, inserts us in the game, releases us in its vibrancy, ready to receive or steal the ball from the player headed our way. I found myself running alongside the players, cheering them on from up close. (All the more so when I stood in Rele Gallery, in Lagos, surrounded by the large-scale photographs printed on Hahnemühle Museum Etching paper, which has a natural, non-glossy, texture and sometimes resembles a watercolor print. Alongside these prints is a video installation of a montage of football games where we see players chasing a ball that has been digitally removed, leaving us to focus on the game as a movement of bodies; one is reminded of the touching, heartbreaking, funny scene from Abderrahmane Sissako's *Timbuktu* (2014), where a group of young men play a match with an invisible football, an act of spirited resistance after the game is banned by jihadists.) In the photographs, I experienced football as a communal activity, and was happy to abandon my role as a bystander. These images insist that we not be a spectator of spectators. They demand, too, that we see football as a diasporic language: the vocabulary might change from place to place, but the grammar remains the same.

With this last World Cup over, and the accompanying global fever evaporating, the bars and cafés and restaurants and living rooms have emptied out. But the energy of football, abundant and unfading, has returned to its true locus, away from the stadiums. After the spectacle has gone, there are still the many who are often overlooked—some displaced from their homes by stadiums built for previous World Cup tournaments—playing the game that Andrew Esiebo lovingly portrays. They'll come for what many have come for since the game began eons ago: the beauty of community; the inventive spirit of strangers and neighbors who readily turn whatever is under their feet into a playground; the joy of seeing bodies in motion, in relation to each other; the pleasure of being alive. Football is a shared beauty, a reminder that we find our better selves in company. And perhaps our best selves are our playful selves.

CHAPTER 3

DIVING IN DEEP OR CASTING WIDE

*Considering Context Versus Narrative
to Shape Our Stories*

Once we have determined whether we are going to focus on the subject or on the reader, this drives our decisions about how we shape our writing. If we're focusing on subject, we have the latitude to delve into the background, or the context of the issue, providing more details and nuance. If we aim to convey an in-depth and comprehensive understanding of the issue, that may require us to include historical, scientific, or technical details in order to do the subject justice. However, if we are focusing on the reader, then we are driven more by the story and its narrative elements, like plot, character, and dialogue. We use these dramatic elements to illustrate the issue and its impact on people's lives in a compelling way.

When we are seeking to find the right balance between context and narrative for our writing, we should ask ourselves the following questions:

- What does the reader need to know in order to meaningfully understand the story and the issue that is central to it?
- How much contextual information is necessary?
- How much contextual information is too much?

Sometimes when we are passionate about an issue or if we are an expert on a topic, it is tempting to tell our readers everything we know about it—every detail, every piece of research. We assume they want to know as much as we do. But does that make sense for our piece? In order to determine how much emphasis should be placed on contextual information and, therefore, how much context to provide, we should keep in mind the audience we are trying to reach and the type of outlets in which we are hoping to publish. For example, if we are issue experts writing for other experts, in an academic journal or a topical journal perhaps, then we should focus on addressing the subject in a rigorous way with as much context and technical details as is required for an in-depth understanding.

If our piece is a deep exploration of an issue that requires a great deal of context, but we are writing for an audience broader than other topical experts, we should do our best to avoid jargon. Every field is rife with jargon, some of which is academic, technical, or shorthand understood by other insiders, and it is easy to become used to only being able to discuss an issue using these terms. But jargon is exclusionary to lay readers, who may be interested in the topic but feel intimidated or put off by terminology they do not understand or see in a daily context.

Instead, if you feel there is a technical term that is crucial to understanding the issue, use your own expertise to define the term in a way that is understandable by a lay audience and lends itself to the narrative. This is a more inclusive approach to writing about an issue while maintaining nuance and depth. It brings more people "into the tent," engaging them in learning about the issue rather than excluding them because they are not topical experts.

Often our goal is not to make our readers experts on an issue but to spark their interest and prick their conscience enough for them to be aware of the issue and why it matters. So, we must figure out how much contextual information is truly necessary and then determine when and how to introduce this information within the piece, while keeping our focus on a narrative that

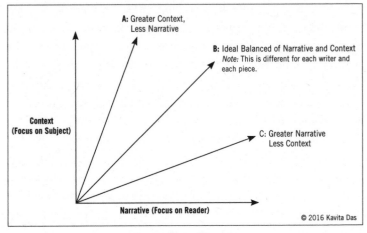

Context Versus Narrative

illustrates the significance of the issue rather than its background and details.

The tension between how much to focus on the context versus how much to focus on the narrative stems from and is parallel to the tension between focusing on our subject versus focusing on our reader. We see this parallel in the graph above, which is similar to the graph in the previous chapter depicting the tension for the writer between focusing on their reader or subject. This graph builds on that by depicting the tension for the writer between discussing an issue through its context versus depicting it through narrative.

If you determine, based on your target reader and intended goals for the piece, it is best served by having a balance of context and narrative, here are some ways you can achieve greater balance:

- *Stagger the contextual information along the narrative.* Consider which background information and details the reader needs at what point along the story arc rather than placing all of the contextual information at the beginning. This will keep the reader engaged in the narrative while ensuring that they understand the issue through important background details.

- *Use narrative elements including scene setting, character development, and revealing dialogue.* Break up the contextual information, like historical background or scientific explanations, with a story that has the issue at its center, keeping the reader engaged even as they learn more about the issue.
- *Use a mix of macro and micro perspectives.* We can tell a story from a broad angle, such as the issue's impact on a whole society or geographic area, or we can focus on a narrow perspective, like that of an individual or a small group of people. For example, we might tell a story about the impact of climate change on an Indigenous people or we might tell the story of its impact on a specific member of that community. It can be particularly powerful to combine macro and micro perspectives; we might use one person's story as a lens on a broader issue and toggle back and forth between micro and macro perspectives.
- *Start and end with a scene.* Dramatic elements like scenes—where we meet the main characters who are taking action and who are in dialogue with each other—pull readers in because they want to know what happens next. These elements also personalize the issue in a way that is hard to do when we rely solely on context, such as historical background or scientific information.

In this chapter, I've included two of my essays, "Red Ink of Revisionist History" and "Selective Perception of Disinformation," which both explore the impact of historical erasure—the erasure of certain groups of people from our history books and from our collective understanding of our American culture. Although they are focused around the same topic, they approach it in different ways. "Red Ink of Revisionist History" provides a contextual examination of how historical erasure ope ices in American classrooms, delving into the problematic pr ctices in the history textbook industry and local education governance. Meanwhile, "Selective Perception of Disinformation" takes a more creative approach, mixing context and narrative, depicting how historical erasure happens, and underscoring its impact on our culture.

"Red Ink of Revisionist History" focuses on the revisionist history about race being taught in America's classrooms. I turn to James Baldwin's prescient words, spoken almost sixty years ago, to a group of this country's teachers, to highlight the lessons of the turbulent civil rights era and how they have or have not made it into our history books, and most importantly, into our collective conscience. "The political level in this country now, on the part of people who should know better, is abysmal," observed Baldwin in his speech. My essay goes on to provide a contextual exploration of how history textbooks get developed by publishers, who seek approval from education regulatory bodies at the local level, some of whom are more invested in teaching a whitewashed version of America's history than an objective, accurate version.

This context helps us understand how problematic and inaccurate textbooks, including ones that depict slavery as "economic migration" rather than cruel and forced labor while erasing the contributions of Black, Indigenous, and people of color (BIPOC) Americans, have been making their way into American classrooms. It also serves to reinforce the essay's narrative and core theme: we didn't arrive at our current impasse on race by chance but rather by perpetuating a flawed understanding of history, and unless we confront and correct this, we are doomed to repeat it. Therefore, this essay is more contextual than narrative because it focuses on a deep dive of how history is taught and codified in textbooks and who is involved in that process. It does not use narrative elements like scene, plot, and character, and in lieu of animating the piece through dialogue, I use quotes from Baldwin that illustrate his incisiveness about our society's lack of accountability for our troubling history around race. Its narrative flow is built on exploring moments of time from the civil rights era to the present day that build to show how history and history education have been politicized by conservative forces. Ultimately, the context and narrative of the piece revolve around its central question: Can we build our future if we can't reconcile our past?

"Selective Perception of Disinformation" blends context and narrative as I explore the cultural impact of historical erasure. I wanted to underscore the central question: How can something or someone be culturally relevant if they and their contributions are unacknowledged? So, I methodically built the first section of the piece by investigating and naming some of the myriad BIPOC individuals and their contributions left out of cultural historian E. D. Hirsch's seminal work, *Cultural Literacy: What Every American Needs to Know* (1987), which catalogued the five thousand things of cultural significance to Americans. I decided to open the piece without any context or explanation, using a lyrical form to articulate missing individuals and their contributions so the reader would know who and what was excluded and feel the weight and consequence of their erasure:

There is neither *Langston Hughes* nor *Zora Neale Hurston*,
but then again, there is no *Harlem Renaissance*.

There is neither *Inuit* nor *Hopi*,
but then again, there is no *tribe*.

There is no *Aretha Franklin*,
but then again, there is no *gospel (music)*.

How can there be *corruption*, when there is no *economic violence*?

The piece is in the form of a serial essay—an essay with clearly delineated sections—but it is not until the second section that I delve into the context of how these individuals and items were left out of Hirsch's *Cultural Literacy: What Every American Needs to Know*. Each subsequent section of the essay reveals more of the narrative about the consequences of historical erasure, culminating in the final section, focusing on the 2016 election of President

Trump. Thereby, underscoring how historical erasure does not just harm the individuals and communities who are excluded but erodes the fabric of our own collective culture, conscience, and democracy. The narrative revolves around this central question: What are the cultural consequences—personal and societal—of historical erasure? Meanwhile, each section provides additional context, moving the narrative along, illustrating how context and narrative work together to provide a more complete depiction of the issue.

To provide further examples about how we use context and narrative to shape our work, I have included three pieces: 1) the introduction to *An Indigenous Peoples' History of the United States*, by Roxanne Dunbar-Ortiz; 2) an excerpt from Imani Perry's *Breathe: A Letter to My Sons*; and 3) "How Could I Write About Women Whose Existence Is Barely Acknowledged?," an essay by Gaiutra Bahadur. Dunbar-Ortiz's work is focused on providing the context for a new historical narrative, while Perry's is driven by a narrative she is writing as a Black mother to her Black sons. Bahadur's essay reflects on the experience of writing the book *Coolie Woman: The Odyssey of Indenture*.

In the introduction to *An Indigenous Peoples' History of the United States*, Dunbar-Ortiz begins to lay the groundwork for a new and revised narrative to the one we have been taught about the history of the Indigenous peoples of the United States by providing crucial context that has been overlooked. Even though the history of these factual events is documented, it tends to be either erased or whitewashed since it does not support the dominant narrative promoted through our schools and history books, which seeks to alternately justify or minimize the displacement, genocide, and ongoing mistreatment of Indigenous peoples by not only the American government but by our broader society. This dominant "narrative of progress" tends to leave out or minimize the horrors of the US's role in killing and displacing countless Indigenous people and the depravity of hundreds of years of slavery of Black Americans as well as the exploitation of waves of immigrants, whose journeys were sometimes the consequence of America's conflicts in the world.

Dunbar-Ortiz rightly notes that there is a collective cost to the broad denial of the US's settler colonialism:

> US history, as well as inherited Indigenous trauma, cannot be understood without dealing with the genocide that the United States committed against Indigenous peoples. From the colonial period through the founding of the United States and continuing in the twentieth century, this has entailed torture, terror, sexual abuse, massacres, systematic military occupations, removals of Indigenous peoples from their ancestral territories, and removals of Indigenous children to military-like boarding schools. The absence of even the slightest note of regret or tragedy in the annual celebration of the US independence betrays a deep disconnect in the consciousness of US Americans.

Dunbar-Ortiz makes clear that US history requires a deeper examination that takes into account the context that has long been ignored, revealing a different narrative, one not just relevant to America's Indigenous peoples but to our collective conscience and welfare as a society. "Strengthening Indigenous sovereignty and self-determination to prevent that result will take general public outrage and demand, which in turn will require that the general population, those descended from settlers and immigrants, know their history and assume responsibility. Resistance to these powerful corporate forces continues to have profound implications for US socioeconomic and political development and the future." By recontextualizing US history from Indigenous peoples' perspective, Dunbar-Ortiz is not only creating a new, more honest, and just narrative but also inviting all Americans—of Indigenous, settler, or immigrant backgrounds—to be aware of this narrative and its implications for the future of our diverse democratic society.

In *Breathe: A Letter to My Sons*, Imani Perry uses an epistolary, or a letter form, to shape the narrative she wishes to impart as a Black mother to her Black sons amidst a time when despite having had our first Black president, the lives of Black boys and men remain in peril. Through *Breathe*, Perry seeks to provide her sons with a new, corrective narrative that contradicts the dominant and flawed narrative of America and American history, which lacks accountability for the impact of hundreds of years of slavery and racial injustice while also devaluing the lives and contributions of Black individuals in the present moment. Her sons are her primary intended readers; we are witnesses overhearing this intimate conversation from mother to sons. That Perry's sons are her primary intended readers is underscored by her opening line: "You were both little bits when President Obama was elected."

Although *Breathe* focuses on the dual narrative Perry is seeking to convey to her sons—about their own histories amidst America's own history—she deftly weaves in historical context to ground these narratives. The context provided is always in service of the narrative and the narrative is always in service to the readers, her sons. Perry introduces us to some of the implications around racial injustice in America and then reveals their personal impact. For example, against the backdrop of the epidemic of Black men and boys being targeted and killed by law enforcement, she recounts how, after her home security system was activated and police arrived, she was more fearful for her sons' lives at the hands of the police than she was of a possible intruder. In this section, she examines the collective and personal trauma reaped from unrelenting cycles of injustice and violence faced by Black Americans:

> The ethics of living with a roulette wheel of Black death are complicated. "Sufficient unto the day is the evil thereof." We do the fight today for the living. Grief must not be distorted into the constant imagination of death. We ward and guard and try to protect but know that there is no warding or guarding lest your whole life become their impunity . . . Sons, I will not allow that to be your life. Your testimony is living with the passionate intensity of one whose presence matters despite the violence of this world towards your beautiful flesh.

The central question *Breathe*'s narrative explores is how does a Black mother impart truth and hope, reality and possibility, strength and vulnerability to her Black sons whose birthplace has yet to reckon with and rectify its history of racism?

This nation that is yours by inheritance and birth is in a state of panic and disaster. Its imperial grandeur is ending. Upward mobility is waning; precariousness is multiplying. And yet the rich keep getting richer. Whiteness is ebbing. And those who are afraid are turning to a game of cowboys and gangsters, going out with a viral blaze of glory. Children keep dying. The world keeps turning them bitter and demonic indeed . . . And I know that, despite my fear, I cannot clip your wings, as though cowering is a respectful tribute to the beauty we have lost. No, I want your wingspan wide. To honor the departed, ancestral, and immediate—BE. Living defined by terror is itself destructive of the spirit. And it is submission. The truth is that life is unsafe. And genius, more often than not, remains unvalidated or, even worse, dormant. But joy, even in slivers, shows up everywhere. Take it. And keep taking it.

With her epistolary narrative, Perry holds tight to her dreams for her sons even as she holds her country accountable for the nightmares it perpetrates on Black lives. Meanwhile, we the reader become invested in the narrative Perry is weaving and what it reveals about the worldview she seeks to convey to her sons. With each instance of racial injustice she relates, past and present, we feel called to consider the personal impact on Perry and her sons but also the collective impact on Black families throughout America.

In 2013, Gaiutra Bahadur published *Coolie Woman: The Odyssey of Indenture*, which explores the journeys and lives of female migrant indentured workers from India to the West Indies, including the journey of her own great-grandmother, Sujaria. Bahadur reflected on the archival constraints she faced and the narrative decisions she made in telling the stories of these marginalized individuals in her essay for the *Guardian*, "How Could I Write About Women Whose Existence Is Barely Acknowledged?" Archival records were sparse and most often written from the perspective of a stranger, at best, or that of an oppressor, at worst. In this piece, Bahadur alternates between narrating her personal observations and reflections and offering context about the system of migrant indentured servitude:

> Missing from the written record, however, was her own testimony, the story in her own words of how she came to leave and who she truly was. A waylaid pilgrim, A widow? A fugitive from an abusive marriage? A woman deserted by her husband? These were experiences shared by other recruits. So which was her story? Did my great-grandmother choose to go and work on a Caribbean sugar plantation, or was she forced? On these and other crucial questions, the record is silent, stranding me at the very edges of the archives, at the limits of what can be known.
>
> *Coolie Woman* is not only a family history, but a broader social and narrative history of indenture; the system that, for roughly 80 years after the abolition of slavery in the British empire, provided exploitable labour to plantation owners across the globe. More than a million Indians were transported to colonies from the Indian Ocean to the West Indies, in a traffic one-third the size of the British slave trade . . . History had left these women voiceless. The existing archives that document indenture contain biases and elisions.

So, we see how Bahadur weaves together her own ponderings about her great-grandmother's motivations for making the fateful journey from India to the Caribbean and enduring life as an indentured worker with crucial background on the history and scope of the system of indenture.

As noted in the essay's title, given these glaring omissions in archival records, Bahadur is left wondering, "How could I write about women whose very existence the official sources barely acknowledged?" And this central question is answered both through the narrative of Bahadur's reflections on her journey writing *Coolie Woman* and by the context she provides about the journey of her great-grandmother and countless other migrant indentured workers whose stories are obscured. As readers, we wonder alongside Bahadur how she as a writer and great-granddaughter will deal with the significant holes and mysteries in her great-grandmother's story. When she reveals her decision to write herself into the narrative and use her questions as the basis for a "speculative history," the reader feels the importance of this epiphany:

> Where the voices of indentured women were absent, I used my own, as their descendant, to question the records as aggressively as I could . . . Whole sections of *Coolie Woman* unfold entirely in questions: mine, my great-grandmother's, the reader's, one relentlessly following the next. These questions allow me to imagine interiorities withheld by the written record. They paint landscapes, advance plot, convey a tone. They communicate my own attitude to the archive and its elisions and biases: I could never be neutral because I am, after all, a product of the history I've written.

Bahadur's piece focuses on the story behind the story of her great-grandmother's life and by bringing us along on her own journey as both a researcher and writer, but also as a great-granddaughter, Bahadur pulls back the curtain on her family's story revealing how it fits into a larger, global narrative.

Through the range of pieces in this chapter, it is clear whatever issue we are trying to unpack on the page, we must make decisions about how much context and how much narrative we need in order to illuminate it. Knowing our goals and who we are trying to reach helps guide our decisions on the right balance of context and narrative. If we are topical experts trying to reach a broader audience, we want to write in a way that conveys our knowledge and authority while also making the issue accessible and relevant to those who might find it intimidating or view themselves as outside its sphere. In casting this wider net, we have the opportunity to raise awareness in a critical mass of people, increasing our chances of moving the needle on issues we care about.

■

RED INK OF REVISIONIST HISTORY
By Kavita Das

On October 16, 1963, James Baldwin delivered a speech to a group of teachers entitled "The Negro Child—His Self-Image," which was later that year published in the *Saturday Review* as "A Talk to Teachers." This was a year of great turbulence and strife as the fight for Civil Rights was being waged and a toll was being exacted on Black lives, young and old. On August 28, 1963, Martin Luther King, Jr., gave his now iconic "I Have a Dream" speech, in front of more than a quarter of a million people gathered at the March on Washington. A few months before that, on June 12, 1963, Medgar Evers, pioneering civil rights leader and field secretary for the Mississippi chapter of the National Association for the Advancement of Colored People (NAACP), was murdered outside his home. And just a month before Baldwin's talk, on September 15, 1963, four young Black girls were brutally murdered when the Sixteenth Street Baptist Church in Birmingham, Alabama, a frequent gathering site for civil rights meetings, was bombed. Baldwin, outraged by the cruel theft of these young girls' lives, was also deeply concerned by what he viewed as a lack of broad "public uproar," outside the Black community. And though he was not a teacher himself, he seemed to harbor a desperate hope that sounding a warning to those who shape young minds in classrooms across the country might be a way forward.

Baldwin opens his remarks, leaving no ambiguity about the crisis. "Let's begin by saying that we are living through a very dangerous time . . . We are in a revolutionary situation, no matter how unpopular that word has become in this country. The society in which we live is desperately menaced, not by Krushchev, but from within." He goes on to explain that, "What is upsetting the country is a sense of its own identity."

Fifty-four years later, as we continue to reel from the impact of the election of Donald J. Trump as the 45th president and contemplate the "menacing" forces at work that made his election and his regressive campaign and policies possible, Baldwin's words ring just as true. We are a deeply divided nation. Each week, the President and his administration find new ways to roll back civil rights protections for marginalized populations. And correspondingly, there continues to be an alarming uptick in hate crimes and instances of xenophobic harassment. Disproving that all progress made on civil rights is irreversible, our current socio-political climate reflects some of the essence of Baldwin's observations of that turbulent era. "The political level in this country now, on the part of people who should know better, is abysmal."

All manner of theories has been put forth by political pundits as to how the country descended into its current socio-political state—some of the same pundits who inaccurately predicted the outcome of the election. Ultimately, to truly move forward as a nation, we must embrace shared ideals shaped by the crucible of a true and shared understanding of our nation's history, an understanding that acknowledges not just our triumphant moments, but moments when we fell gravely short of upholding these ideals. And to arrive at this shared understanding of our nation's true history, we must revisit our classrooms, where many of us first learned about American history, albeit a version which often was incomplete and incongruent. We must follow the trail of the red ink of revisionist history that fills many of our textbooks, classrooms, and consequently, our own understanding of our national identity.

Baldwin's talk is so prescient of our current situation because of his unerringly perceptive understanding of how some of our country's most entrenched ills are rooted in our inability to grapple with our true history, as well as our lack of meaningful progress on this front over the last several decades. Baldwin asks the gathering of teachers to imagine the impact of a paradigm shift in teaching American history. "If, for example, one managed to change the curriculum in all the schools so that Negroes learned more about themselves and their real contributions to this culture, you would be liberating not only Negroes, you'd be liberating white people who know nothing about their own history. And the reason is that if you are compelled to lie about one aspect of anybody's history, you must lie about it all. If you have to lie about my role here, if you have to pretend that I hoed all that cotton just because I love you, then you have done something to yourself."

However, despite Baldwin's plea, many obstacles continue to prevent us from teaching and learning history in a meaningful way. "History Class and the Fictions About Race in America," published in *The Atlantic* in 2015, details these myriad issues. The article explains that when it comes to history teachers, according to a 2012 report by the American Academy of Arts and Sciences focused on high school educators, 34 percent of history teachers had not majored in history or received certification to teach it, and points to lax and varied licensing policies and requirements from state to state. It goes on to cite another report by the National History Education Clearinghouse which showed that only a small percentage of states require college course hours in history for certification, and no states require a major or minor in history for teachers. The article points to a 2013 Gallup Poll that reveals that few Americans "valued" their history classes, and quotes a Carnegie Corporation report on the consequences of this: "students who receive effective education in social studies are more likely to vote, four times more likely to volunteer and work on community issues, and are generally more confident in their ability to communicate ideas with their elected representatives."

James W. Loewen, the author of the 1995 book, *Lies My Teacher Told Me: Everything Your American History Textbook Got Wrong*, observes that many history teachers use textbooks as a "crutch." There have been several examples of inadequate and problematic content in textbooks and educational materials, but one of the most egregious examples recently involved textbook giant McGraw-Hill. In October 2015, a controversy unfolded when it was revealed that a McGraw-Hill world geography textbook explained immigration patterns for the Southeast corridor of the United States with a caption that stated: "The Atlantic Slave Trade between the 1500s and 1800s brought millions of workers from Africa to the southern United States to work on agricultural plantations." McGraw-Hill was blasted, and rightly so, for so blatantly mischaracterizing slaves as willing "workers," and forced capture and migration as immigration. But while this was a particularly glaring error, it's not certain that errors like this one are all that rare. *The Atlantic* article noted a National Clearinghouse on History Education brief reviewing four elementary and middle-school textbooks which found that they "left out or misordered the cause and consequence of historical events and frequently failed to highlight main ideas." If one is not taught the causes and consequences of a historical event or social issue, what historical lesson has been gleaned, what truth has been conveyed? These factual errors are not only betrayals of our youth by our education system, but impediments to achieving a true and shared understanding of our history and national identity. And can we build our future if we can't reconcile our past?

How do substantive factual and contextual "errors" like the one in the McGraw-Hill textbook happen and how do they find their way into textbooks throughout a state and throughout the country? First, there is the often-noted fact that the publishing industry, including its editorial staff, is woefully undiverse (79% to 89% white, varies by source of survey data). However, while this might elucidate how history books reflect an incomplete or biased version of history, this doesn't fully explain egregious factual errors or mischaracterizations. Sometimes, these "errors" reflect successful attempts to infuse curriculums with regressive ideologies or agendas. For example, in 2010, the Texas school board passed a ban on books with "anti-Christian, pro-Islamic slant(s)." Similarly, in January 2013, Arizona instituted a ban on the use of the Mexican-American studies curriculum used in Tucson high schools. And most recently, in March of this year, a state representative of Arkansas introduced legislation to prohibit the inclusion of books and materials by *A People's History of the United States* author Howard Zinn within Arkansas public school curriculum. Meanwhile, textbook publishers like McGraw-Hill are eager to win contracts for large state public schools systems, of which Texas is amongst the largest and most influential, and are at the very least indirectly influenced to draft content for their textbooks in a way that is perceived as inoffensive and uncontroversial to these states' textbook adoption bodies. Ultimately, all these issues and influences jockey with actual facts and the true context of history in classrooms across the nation, but especially in classrooms in "red" states.

However, it's not just conservative white Americans who are looking to make American classrooms the sites for their revisionist history. In January of 2016, California's State Board of Education requested input for its History-Social Science Framework curriculum and was besieged by controversial and contradictory public input for the South Asia component of the Framework. Pro-Hindu and India-centric organizations, including the Hindu American Foundation and the Uberoi Foundation were pushing for revisions to the Framework including replacing certain references to "South Asia" with "India," and revising descriptions and characterizations of India's caste system to be more tied to social and economic class rather than Hindu doctrine and practices. These groups went so far as to say that the Framework's depiction of caste was anti-Hindu and could be stigmatic to California's Hindu students. Meanwhile, a loose coalition of organizations representing broader South Asian interests, including Sikhs, Muslims, and Dalits, as well as an inter-institution South Asia Faculty Group, sought to push back against what they viewed as pro-Hindu and India-centric revisions, characterizing them as both revisionist and reductive history, even creating a Twitter campaign: #DontEraseOurHistory. The California State Board of Education body ultimately rejected most of the Pro-Hindu, and India-centric proposed revisions, however the controversy illustrates once again that the American classroom has become a battlefield for those who seek to revise history. But it also makes evident this battle is not just between white and minority Americans over their respective roles in American history, but also within marginalized populations, grappling with their own divided and contested histories.

Beyond expressing his deep concerns about the long-term sociopolitical impact of being a nation unwilling to grapple with its true and whole history in the classroom, in his speech, James Baldwin also expresses his thoughts on the core purpose of education in society. "The purpose of education finally, is to create in a person the ability to look at the world for himself, to make his own decisions, to say to himself this is black or this is white . . ." Baldwin acknowledges that, "what societies, really, ideally want is a citizenry which will simply obey the rules of society," yet he warns that, "if a society succeeds in this, that society is about to perish." And he notes that this is the paradox of education within a fraught social framework. Baldwin concludes, "The obligation of anyone who thinks of himself as responsible is to examine society and try to change it and to fight it—at no matter what risk. This is the only hope society has. This is the only way societies change."

A true and meaningful education, Baldwin suggests, empowers students to not only examine fraught aspects of their society but also their role within the system. Students of color are subjected to inequitable accounts of history in the classroom, minimizing the contributions of their respective communities, but also face inequities in their lives outside the classroom. Baldwin expresses his hopes for the student of color:

> "I would try to make him know that just as American history
> is longer, larger, more various, more beautiful, and more terri-
> ble than anything anyone has ever said about it, so is the world

larger, more daring, more beautiful and more terrible, but prin-
cipally larger—and that it belongs to him. I would teach him
that he doesn't have to be bound by the expediencies of any
given administration, any given policy, any given morality; that
he has the right and the necessity to examine everything."

Meanwhile, when it comes to white students, he fears the
harm also caused to them by internalizing inequitable historical
accounts in and out of the classroom, thwarting their understanding of themselves. "And a price is demanded to liberate all those
white children—some of them near forty—who have never grown
up, and who never will grow up, because they have no sense of
their identity."

With the election of President Trump, we are left to contemplate not just how we got here, but whether this marks the beginning of a stark new reality or the inevitable continuation of our
nation's history. But if we seek to alter our course, we must know
from whence we came. Baldwin concluded his speech delivered to
teachers during the midst of the Civil Rights movement by saying
the following, and 54 years later, his words echo, not as a history
lesson, but as a vision for our future. "America is not the world and
if America is going to become a nation, she must find a way—and
this child must help her to find a way to use the tremendous potential and tremendous energy which this child represents. If this
country does not find a way to use that energy, it will be destroyed
by that energy."

■

SELECTIVE PERCEPTION
OF DISINFORMATION
By Kavita Das

1.

There is neither *Langston Hughes* nor *Zora Neale Hurston*,
but then again, there is no *Harlem Renaissance.*

There is neither *Inuit* nor *Hopi*,
but then again, there is no *tribe.*

There is no *Aretha Franklin*,
but then again, there is no *gospel (music).*

How can there be *corruption*, when there is no *economic violence?*

There is neither *Betty Freidan* nor *Jane Fonda*,
but then again, there is neither *misogyny* nor *gynecology.*

There is neither *Davis, Miles* nor *Billie Holiday*,
but then again, there is no *cool (personality attribute).*

There is neither *James Baldwin* nor *Lorraine Hansberry*
(Raisin in the Sun),
but then again, there is no *Afro-American.*

There is no *rap music*,
but then again, there is no *boom box.*

Is there a *Krishna*, if there is no *Bhagavad Gita?*

There is neither *Nelson Mandela* nor *Desmond Tutu*,
neither *Rosa Parks* nor *Medgar Evers*,
but then again, there is no *White Supremacy.*

There is no *Marvin Gaye*,
but then again, there is no *funk*.

How are there neither *internment camps* nor *Asian Exclusion Act?*

There is no *Margaret Mead*,
but then again, there are no *pesticides*.

There is no *Bob Marley*,
but then again, there is no *reggae*.

There is no *Joseph McCarthy*, but then again,
there is no *Christian radicalism*.

There is neither *Toni Morrison* nor *Alice Walker*,
but then again, there is no *Truth, Sojourner.*

How can there be *endangered species* when there is no *extinction?*

There is neither *Muddy Waters* nor *Wolf, Howlin'*,
but then again, there is no *rhythm and blues (music)*.

There is neither *aborigine* nor *migrant worker*,
but then again, there is no *indigenous*.

There is neither *Kahlo, Frida* nor *Isamu Noguchi*,
but then again, there is neither *Pablo Neruda* nor
Gabriel García Márquez.

How can there be a *Rumi*, if there is no *Sufi?*

There is no *Charlie (Bird) Parker*,
but then again, there is no *jam session*.

There is neither *soul music* nor *soul food*,
but then again, there are no *Souls of Black Folk, The (Title)*.

How is there neither *homophobia*, nor *racial slur?*

2.

In 1987, E.D. Hirsch, Jr., a respected professor of English at the University of Virginia in Charlottesville, publishes a book entitled *Cultural Literacy: What Every American Needs to Know*. Hirsch, a committed education reformer, decries that American children are lacking basic knowledge about matters of key cultural significance which would hinder their success as individuals, and our society collectively. Included in *Cultural Literacy* is a list of 5,000 things, names, proverbs, quotes, and concepts compiled by Hirsch and two of his colleagues, aptly entitled *"What Literate Americans Know."* Hirsch's book and list spark a key battle in the ensuing "culture war" over what qualifies as culturally significant and who gets to decide.

The following year, independent publisher Graywolf releases *Multi-Cultural Literacy*, an anthology in response to the culture war and the works which perpetuated it, in particular Hirsch's *Cultural Literacy*. In their introduction, Rick Simonson and Scott Walker, the editors of *Multi-Cultural Literacy*, note that while they agree with Hirsch's assertion that education needs to be a national priority, they are alarmed by his "overridingly static, and so shallow, definition of culture," and conclude that it derives, in part, "from a particular white, male, academic, eastern U.S., Eurocentric bias."

Multi-Cultural Literacy is filled with writings on culture from across the decades, with a diversity of writers including James Baldwin, Wendell Berry, Michelle Cliff, Carlos Fuentes, and David Mura, and is dedicated to James Baldwin and Joseph Campbell, two writers who unflinchingly held a mirror up to American society. Simonson and Walker concur that "culture is largely contained and carried in the word," and given the inherent problems with Hirsch's list, they create their own supplementary list of close to six hundred words "not included in the Hirsch book, the sorts of things too commonly excluded from U.S. educational texts, political thinking, or social planning."

3.

When I review Simonson and Walker's list *of exclusions*, I am struck by the vast and varied cultural creations and creators not included in Hirsh's own. I form Section 1 by selecting and pairing excluded cultural concepts or creations with their proponents or creators, of particular significance to me. I can't imagine my life untouched or my perspective unenriched by them. Yet it lays bare for me the nebulous mechanisms of erasure, which work gradually on an everyday basis as memories fade and work goes unheralded and undocumented, but also in one fell swoop, through lists of significance, like the one compiled by Hirsch and his colleagues, of "what every American should know." Ultimately, why would the creator be acknowledged as culturally significant when their creation is not?

In truth, although the mechanisms of erasure might be nebulous, they are not foreign to me. For the past four years, I've been working on a biography of Lakshmi Shankar, a Grammy-nominated Indian American singer who helped to bring Indian music to the West in the late 1960s, yet whose story is all but unknown by the broader public. So as I uncover the contours of her remarkable yet unknown story, I've often pondered the reasons it requires uncovering, and the forces that have kept it unknown.

In 2014, a year after I began working on this biography, I attend the *American Cool* exhibit at Smithsonian's National Portrait Gallery in Washington, D.C., exploring the quintessentially American concept of "cool"—a concept created by Black American jazz artists of the 1940s, but espoused and embodied by so many American iconic figures over the past seventy-five years of American cultural history. According to the exhibit notes, "Cool is an earned form of individuality. Each generation has certain individuals who bring innovation and style to a field of endeavor while projecting a certain charismatic self-possession. They are the figures selected for this exhibition: the successful rebels of American culture."

Although Black American artists coined the term "cool" in part as a transgressive response to the racism they faced, they only account for thirty of the one hundred figures whose portraits and bios make up the *American Cool* exhibit. And of the remaining seventy, sixty-five are white, while only three are Hispanic, and just two are Asian American. I walk through the exhibit three times in disbelief to come up with these rough tallies. As an Asian American, I'm in search of those from recent decades who inspire me as much with their accomplishments as with their personas—from master musician Ravi Shankar (Lakshmi Shankar's brother-in-law and frequent collaborator), actor George Takei of *Star Trek* fame, and civil rights activist Yuri Kochiyama, to comedian Margaret Cho, jazz musician Vijay Iyer, and Pulitzer Prize-winning writer Jhumpa Lahiri. Yet they are missing from the walls. Worse yet, when I come to the end of the exhibit, there is a note about how these one hundred figures were chosen after much discussion and debate and since not everyone could be included, they created a "runner-up" list of another one hundred—and this list includes no Asian Americans at all.

The list of *What Literate Americans Know* contained in *Cultural Literacy* was created thirty years ago by three individuals. Meanwhile, *American Cool*, a national exhibit by the Smithsonian, was conceptualized and shaped just three years ago by many individuals through, as noted, discussion and debate. So what do you do when your opponent in a resurgent battle of the culture war is the museum of national record, whose bare walls serve as a stark reminder of your erasure not just from cultural history but present-day culture? You wield your only weapon, the almighty pen, to bear witness to this latest instance of *selective perception* of *disinformation*, which too are terms excluded from Hirsch's list of cultural literacy.

4.

In *What Every American Should Know*, a July 3, 2015 article in *The Atlantic*, Eric Liu revisits Hirsch's *Cultural Literacy*, and its purpose and pitfalls, through the lens of our "increasingly diverse nation," one that has had our first Black president. Liu, executive director of the Aspen Institute Program on Citizenship and American Identity who served as a speechwriter and deputy domestic policy adviser for President Bill Clinton, begins by asking the question, "Is the culture war over?" He answers his own question by pointing to the racial and cultural turmoil we've been experiencing which he attributes to the increasing "delinking" of Americanness and whiteness, and then proceeds to pose and answer his next question: "What is the story of 'us' when 'us' is no longer by default 'white'? The answer, of course, will depend on how aware Americans are of what they are, of what their culture already (and always) has been. And that awareness demands a new kind of mirror."

In fact, Liu is not overly critical of either Hirsch's definition of cultural literacy or the intent behind his list, asserting, "Literacy in the culture confers power, or at least access to power. Illiteracy, whether willful or unwitting, creates isolation from power." So he views Hirsch's effort, while inherently flawed, as "progressive," for its attempt to "close the opportunity gap," and points out that Hirsch, whose work on cultural literacy was often heralded by conservatives and lambasted by liberals, was a Democrat and considered himself progressive. Instead he takes greater issue with the insular and static method in which Hirsch and colleagues compiled their list, totally unsuited for our increasingly diverse nation and rapidly shifting times. He intones, "Americans need a list made new with new blood. Americans are such a list," a reflection of every American's "right to be recognized. The right to be counted. The right to make the means of recognition and accounting."

5.

On November 8, 2016, nearly thirty years after the publication of Hirsch's *Cultural Literacy* and twenty-nine years following that of Graywolf's *Multi-Cultural Literacy*, America elects Donald Trump, a morally bankrupt but cash-flush businessman with no government experience, who ran a campaign rife with hate speech, playing into the fears and hopes of white nationalists and disaffected white Americans alike. With his trademark red baseball cap bearing his slogan "Make America Great Again," Trump, on the campaign trail, reignites the culture war, making clear through his vow to build a wall along the U.S. southern border and his calls to keep Syrian refugees out, his view on who and what makes America great. Unlike Hirsch's inadvertent erasure from his list of the contributions made by marginalized people to American culture, President Trump, with the support of social conservatives, is working concertedly to erase the very lives and rights of vulnerable populations. And he has proposed his own lists—a weekly list of the crimes committed by undocumented immigrants, the list of seven countries he sought to ban travel from through his Executive Order, among the first he signed in office, the list of health service organizations providing abortion who will no longer be eligible for federal funding, and finally, his list of agencies whose budgets he proposes drastically cutting or eliminating, which includes the National Endowment for the Arts (NEA), a crucial lifeline for writers and artists.

More recently, Trump announced a proposed overhaul to immigration policy favoring highly skilled workers and those who speak English, a sinister echo of the xenophobic "English only" language debates of previous years that raged in certain cities and towns in reaction to demographic shifts caused by immigration. And despite a considerable spike in hate crimes against marginalized populations which accompanied Trump's election, the Department of Justice chose to direct its resources to investigate and sue universities whose affirmative action policies are deemed to discriminate against white applicants.

But even as these latest battles rage on, spawning an amorphous resistance movement, what is the broader culture war? Was it sparked thirty years ago in the halls of the ivory towers of academia, or did it start with the founding of this country? Or does it pre-date even that? Calling it a war when most of the cultural power and weaponry has been historically held by one side is akin to Trump flagrantly assigning "blame on both sides" for deadly violence perpetrated by white supremacists and neo-Nazis against counter-protesters in Charlottesville, Virginia. Perhaps it is more accurately an enduring and insidious tradition of cultural domination through cultural erasure, replacement, and appropriation. Ironically, it was the potential removal of a statue of Confederate general Robert E. Lee—mischaracterized as cultural erasure by those who have grown so used to being culturally dominant—that transformed Charlottesville into a literal and figurative battleground in the culture war.

Whatever the framing or nomenclature, there is no doubt this country is embroiled in an imperative and visceral moral struggle for the very human rights its founding documents hold "unalienable." Given this real struggle, can we justify our continued engagement in an ideological culture war? Yes, because the culture war and its resulting battles being waged involve and impact those most imperiled by autocratic policies, who not coincidentally are also those most marginalized in American culture. It might seem futile, perhaps even indulgent, to hold space, to hold a candle up to our threads in the mottled fabric of American cultural history, while just as importantly, continuing to create new threads of culture through our work as writers. However, fighting the culture war, or alternately, resisting cultural oppression, in the present may be our only chance at securing our legacy, a future where we might seamlessly be seen, heard, and understood as part of "what every American should know."

■

INTRODUCTION: THIS LAND, FROM *AN INDIGENOUS PEOPLES' HISTORY OF THE UNITED STATES*

By Roxanne Dunbar-Ortiz

We are here to educate, not forgive.
We are here to enlighten, not accuse.[1]

—WILLIE JOHNS,
Brighton Seminole
Reservation, Florida

Under the crust of that portion of Earth called the United States of America—"from California . . . to the Gulf Stream waters"—are interred the bones, villages, fields, and sacred objects of American Indians.[2] They cry out for their stories to be heard through their descendants who carry the memories of how the country was founded and how it came to be as it is today.

It should not have happened that the great civilizations of the Western Hemisphere, the very *evidence* of the Western Hemisphere, were wantonly destroyed, the gradual progress of humanity interrupted and set upon a path of greed and destruction.[3] Choices were made that forged that path toward destruction of life itself—the moment in which we now live and die as our planet shrivels, overheated. To learn and know this history is both a necessity and a responsibility to the ancestors and descendants of all parties.

What historian David Chang has written about the land that became Oklahoma applies to the whole United States: "Nation, race, and class converged in land."[4] Everything in US history is about the land—who oversaw and cultivated it, fished its waters, maintained its wildlife; who invaded and stole it; how it became a commodity ("real estate") broken into pieces to be bought and sold on the market.

98 | KAVITA DAS

US policies and actions related to Indigenous peoples, though often termed "racist" or "discriminatory," are rarely depicted as what they are: classic cases of imperialism and a particular form of colonialism—settler colonialism. As anthropologist Patrick Wolfe writes, "The question of genocide is never far from discussions of settler colonialism. Land is life—or, at least, land is necessary for life."[5]

The history of the United States is a history of settler colonialism—the founding of a state based on the ideology of white supremacy, the widespread practice of African slavery, and a policy of genocide and land theft. Those who seek history with an upbeat ending, a history of redemption and reconciliation, may look around and observe that such a conclusion is not visible, not even in utopian dreams of a better society.

Writing US history from an Indigenous peoples' perspective requires rethinking the consensual national narrative. That narrative is wrong or deficient, not in its facts, dates, or details but rather in its essence. Inherent in the myth we've been taught is an embrace of settler colonialism and genocide. The myth persists, not for a lack of free speech or poverty of information but rather for an absence of motivation to ask questions that challenge the core of the scripted narrative of the origin story. How might acknowledging the reality of US history work to transform society? That is the central question this book pursues.

Teaching Native American studies, I always begin with a simple exercise. I ask students to quickly draw a rough outline of the United States at the time it gained independence from Britain. Invariably most draw the approximate present shape of the United States from the Atlantic to the Pacific—the continental territory not fully appropriated until a century after independence. What became independent in 1783 were the thirteen British colonies hugging the Atlantic shore. When called on this, students are embarrassed because they know better. I assure them that they are not alone. I call this a Rorschach test of unconscious "manifest destiny," embedded in the minds of nearly everyone in the United

States and around the world. This test reflects the seeming inevitability of US extent and power, its destiny, with an implication that the continent had previously been *terra nullius*, a land without people.

Woody Guthrie's "This Land Is Your Land" celebrates that the land belongs to everyone, reflecting the unconscious manifest destiny we live with. But the extension of the United States from sea to shining sea was the intention and design of the country's founders. "Free" land was the magnet that attracted European settlers. Many were slave owners who desired limitless land for lucrative cash crops. After the war for independence but preceding the writing of the US Constitution, the Continental Congress produced the Northwest Ordinance. This was the first law of the incipient republic, revealing the motive for those desiring independence. It was the blueprint for gobbling up the British-protected Indian Territory ("Ohio Country") on the other side of the Appalachians and Alleghenies. Britain had made settlement there illegal with the Proclamation of 1763.

In 1801, President Jefferson aptly described the new settler-state's intentions for horizontal and vertical continental expansion, stating: "However our present interests may restrain us within our own limits, it is impossible not to look forward to distant times, when our rapid multiplication will expand itself beyond those limits and cover the whole northern, if not the southern continent, with a people speaking the same language, governed in similar form by similar laws." This vision of manifest destiny found form a few years later in the Monroe Doctrine, signaling the intention of annexing or dominating former Spanish colonial territories in the Americas and the Pacific, which would be put into practice during the rest of the century.

Origin narratives form the vital core of a people's unifying identity and of the values that guide them. In the United States, the founding and development of the Anglo-American settler-state involves a narrative about Puritan settlers who had a covenant with God to take the land. That part of the origin story is supported and reinforced by the Columbus myth and the "Doctrine of Discovery." According to a series of late-fifteenth-century papal bulls, European nations acquired title to the lands they "discovered" and the Indigenous inhabitants lost their natural right to that land after Europeans arrived and claimed it.[6] As law professor Robert A. Williams observes about the Doctrine of Discovery:

> Responding to the requirements of a paradoxical age of Renaissance and Inquisition, the West's first modern discourses of conquest articulated a vision of all humankind united under a rule of law discoverable solely by human reason. Unfortunately for the American Indian, the West's first tentative steps towards this noble vision of a Law of Nations contained a mandate for Europe's subjugation of all peoples whose radical divergence from European-derived norms of right conduct signified their need for conquest and remediation.[7]

The Columbus myth suggests that from US independence onward, colonial settlers saw themselves as part of a world system of colonization. "Columbia," the poetic, Latinate name used in reference to the United States from its founding throughout the nineteenth century, was based on the name of Christopher Columbus. The "Land of Columbus" was—and still is—represented by the image of a woman in sculptures and paintings, by institutions such as Columbia University, and by countless place names, including that of the national capital, the District of Columbia.[8] The 1798 hymn "Hail, Columbia" was the early national anthem and is now used whenever the vice president of the United States makes a public appearance, and Columbus Day is still a federal holiday despite Columbus never having set foot on the continent claimed by the United States.

Traditionally, historians of the United States hoping to have successful careers in academia and to author lucrative school textbooks became protectors of this origin myth. With the cultural upheavals in the academic world during the 1960s, engendered by the civil rights movement and student activism, historians came to call for objectivity and fairness in revising interpretations of US history. They warned against moralizing, urging instead a dispassionate and culturally relative approach. Historian Bernard Sheehan, in an influential essay, called for a "cultural conflict" understanding of Native–Euro-American relations in the early United States, writing that this approach "diffuses the locus of guilt."[9] In striving for "balance," however, historians spouted platitudes: "There were good and bad people on both sides." "American culture is an amalgamation of all its ethnic groups." "A frontier is a zone of interaction between cultures, not merely advancing European settlements."

Later, trendy postmodernist studies insisted on Indigenous "agency" under the guise of individual and collective empowerment, making the casualties of colonialism responsible for their own demise. Perhaps worst of all, some claimed (and still claim) that the colonizer and colonized experienced an "encounter" and engaged in "dialogue," thereby masking reality with justifications and rationalizations—in short, apologies for one-sided robbery and murder. In focusing on "cultural change" and "conflict between cultures," these studies avoid fundamental questions about the formation of the United States and its implications for the present and future. This approach to history allows one to safely put aside present responsibility for continued harm done by that past and the questions of reparations, restitution, and reordering society.[10]

Multiculturalism became the cutting edge of post-civil-rights-movement US history revisionism. For this scheme to work—and affirm US historical progress—Indigenous nations and communities had to be left out of the picture. As territorially and treaty-based peoples in North America, they did not fit the grid of multiculturalism but were included by transforming them into an inchoate oppressed racial group, while colonized Mexican Americans and Puerto Ricans were dissolved into another such group, variously called "Hispanic" or "Latino." The multicultural approach emphasized the "contributions" of individuals from oppressed groups to the country's assumed greatness. Indigenous peoples were thus credited with corn, beans, buckskin, log cabins, parkas, maple syrup, canoes, hundreds of place names, Thanksgiving, and even the concepts of democracy and federalism. But this idea of the gift-giving Indian helping to establish and enrich the development of the United States is an insidious smoke screen meant to obscure the fact that the very existence of the country is a result of the looting of an entire continent and its resources. The fundamental unresolved issues of Indigenous lands, treaties, and sovereignty could not but scuttle the premises of multiculturalism.

With multiculturalism, manifest destiny won the day. As an example, in 1994, Prentice Hall (part of Pearson Education) published a new college-level US history textbook, authored by four members of a new generation of revisionist historians. These radical social historians are all brilliant scholars with posts in prestigious universities. The book's title reflects the intent of its authors and publisher: *Out of Many: A History of the American People*. The origin story of a supposedly unitary nation, albeit now multicultural, remained intact. The original cover design featured a multicolored woven fabric—this image meant to stand in place of the discredited "melting pot." Inside, facing the title page, was a photograph of a Navajo woman, dressed formally in velvet and adorned with heavy sterling silver and turquoise jewelry. With a traditional Navajo dwelling, a hogan, in the background, the woman was shown kneeling in front of a traditional loom, weaving a nearly finished rug. The design? The Stars and Stripes! The authors, upon hearing my objection and explanation that Navajo weavers make their livings off commissioned work that includes the desired design, responded: "But it's a real photograph." To the authors' credit, in the second edition they replaced the cover photograph and removed the Navajo picture inside, although the narrative text remains unchanged.

Awareness of the settler-colonialist context of US history writing is essential if one is to avoid the laziness of the default position and the trap of a mythological unconscious belief in manifest destiny. The form of colonialism that the Indigenous peoples of North America have experienced was modern from the beginning: the expansion of European corporations, backed by government armies, into foreign areas, with subsequent expropriation of lands and resources. Settler colonialism is a genocidal policy. Native nations and communities, while struggling to maintain fundamental values and collectivity, have from the beginning resisted modern colonialism using both defensive and offensive techniques, including the modern forms of armed resistance of national liberation movements and what now is called terrorism. In every instance they have fought for survival as peoples. The objective of US colonialist authorities was to terminate their existence as peoples—not as random individuals. This is the very definition of modern genocide as contrasted with premodern instances of extreme violence that did not have the goal of extinction. The United States as a socioeconomic and political entity is a result of this centuries-long and ongoing colonial process. Today's Indigenous nations and communities are societies formed by their resistance to colonialism, through which they have carried their practices and histories. It is breathtaking, but no miracle, that they have survived as peoples.

To say that the United States is a colonialist settler-state is not to make an accusation but rather to face historical reality, without which consideration not much in US history makes sense, unless Indigenous peoples are erased. But Indigenous nations, through resistance, have survived and bear witness to this history. In the era of worldwide decolonization in the second half of the twentieth century, the former colonial powers and their intellectual apologists mounted a counterforce, often called neocolonialism, from which multiculturalism and postmodernism emerged. Although much revisionist US history reflects neocolonialist strategy—an attempt to accommodate new realities in order to retain the dominance—neocolonialist methods signal victory for the colonized. Such approaches pry off a lid long kept tightly fastened.

One result has been the presence of significant numbers of Indigenous scholars in US universities who are changing the terms of analysis. The main challenge for scholars in revising US history in the context of colonialism is not lack of information, nor is it one of methodology. Certainly difficulties with documentation are no more problematic than they are in any other area of research. Rather, the source of the problems has been the refusal or inability of US historians to comprehend the nature of their own history, US history. The fundamental problem is the absence of the colonial framework.

Through economic penetration of Indigenous societies, the European and Euro-American colonial powers created economic dependency and imbalance of trade, then incorporated the Indigenous nations into spheres of influence and controlled them indirectly or as protectorates, with indispensable use of Christian missionaries and alcohol. In the case of US settler colonialism, land was the primary commodity. With such obvious indicators of colonialism at work, why should so many interpretations of US political-economic development be convoluted and obscure, avoiding the obvious? To some extent, the twentieth-century emergence of the field of "US West" or "Borderlands" history has been forced into an incomplete and flawed settler-colonialist framework. The father of that field of history, Frederick Jackson Turner, confessed as much in 1901: "Our colonial system did not start with the Spanish War [1898]; the U.S. had had a colonial history and policy from the beginning of the Republic; but they have been hidden under the phraseology of 'interstate migration' and 'territorial organization.'"[11]

Settler colonialism, as an institution or system, requires violence or the threat of violence to attain its goals. People do not hand over their land, resources, children, and futures without a fight, and that fight is met with violence. In employing the force necessary to accomplish its expansionist goals, a colonizing regime institutionalizes violence. The notion that settler-indigenous conflict is an inevitable product of cultural differences and misunderstandings, or that violence was committed equally by the colonized and the colonizer, blurs the nature of the historical processes. Euro-American colonialism, an aspect of the capitalist economic globalization, had from its beginnings a genocidal tendency.

The term "genocide" was coined following the Shoah, or Holocaust, and its prohibition was enshrined in the United Nations convention adopted in 1948: the UN Convention on the Prevention and Punishment of the Crime of Genocide. The convention is not retroactive but is applicable to US-Indigenous relations since 1988, when the US Senate ratified it. The terms of the genocide convention are also useful tools for historical analysis of the effects of colonialism in any era. In the convention, any one of five acts is considered genocide if "committed with intent to destroy, in whole or in part, a national, ethnical, racial or religious group":

killing members of the group;
causing serious bodily or mental harm to members of the group;
deliberately inflicting on the group conditions of life calculated
to bring about its physical destruction in whole or in part;
imposing measures intended to prevent births within the group;
forcibly transferring children of the group to another group.[12]

In the 1990s, the term "ethnic cleansing" became a useful descriptive term for genocide.

US history, as well as inherited Indigenous trauma, cannot be understood without dealing with the genocide that the United States committed against Indigenous peoples. From the colonial period through the founding of the United States and continuing in the twentieth century, this has entailed torture, terror, sexual abuse, massacres, systematic military occupations, removals of Indigenous peoples from their ancestral territories, and removals of Indigenous children to military-like boarding schools. The absence of even the slightest note of regret or tragedy in the annual celebration of the US independence betrays a deep disconnect in the consciousness of US Americans.

Settler colonialism is inherently genocidal in terms of the genocide convention. In the case of the British North American colonies and the United States, not only extermination and removal
were practiced but also the disappearing of the prior existence of
Indigenous peoples—and this continues to be perpetuated in local
histories. Anishinaabe (Ojibwe) historian Jean O'Brien names this
practice of writing Indians out of existence "firsting and lasting." All
over the continent, local histories, monuments, and signage narrate
the story of first settlement: the founder(s), the first school, first
dwelling, first everything, as if there had never been occupants who
thrived in those places before Euro-Americans. On the other hand,
the national narrative tells of "last" Indians or last tribes, such as
"the last of the Mohicans," "Ishi, the last Indian," and *End of the
Trail*, as a famous sculpture by James Earle Fraser is titled.[13]

Documented policies of genocide on the part of US adminis-
trations can be identified in at least four distinct periods: the Jack-
sonian era of forced removal; the California gold rush in Northern
California; the post–Civil War era of the so-called Indian wars in
the Great Plains; and the 1950s termination period, all of which
are discussed in the following chapters. Cases of genocide carried
out as policy may be found in historical documents as well as in the
oral histories of Indigenous communities. An example from 1873
is typical, with General William T. Sherman writing, "We must
act with vindictive earnestness against the Sioux, even to their extermination, men, women and children . . . during an assault, the
soldiers can not pause to distinguish between male and female,
or even discriminate as to age."[14] As Patrick Wolfe has noted, the
peculiarity of settler colonialism is that the goal is elimination of
Indigenous populations in order to make land available to settlers. That project is not limited to government policy, but rather
involves all kinds of agencies, voluntary militias, and the settlers
themselves acting on their own.[15]

In the wake of the US 1950s termination and relocation policies, a pan-Indigenous movement arose in tandem with the powerful African American civil rights movement and the broad-based

social justice and antiwar movements of the 1960s. The Indigenous rights movement succeeded in reversing the US termination policy. However, repression, armed attacks, and legislative attempts to undo treaty rights began again in the late 1970s, giving rise to the international Indigenous movement, which greatly broadened the support for Indigenous sovereignty and territorial rights in the United States.

The early twenty-first century has seen increased exploitation of energy resources begetting new pressures on Indigenous lands. Exploitation by the largest corporations, often in collusion with politicians at local, state, and federal levels, and even within some Indigenous governments, could spell a final demise for Indigenous land bases and resources. Strengthening Indigenous sovereignty and self-determination to prevent that result will take general public outrage and demand, which in turn will require that the general population, those descended from settlers and immigrants, know their history and assume responsibility. Resistance to these powerful corporate forces continues to have profound implications for US socioeconomic and political development and the future.

There are more than five hundred federally recognized Indigenous communities and nations, comprising nearly three million people in the United States. These are the descendants of the fifteen million original inhabitants of the land, the majority of whom were farmers who lived in towns. The US establishment of a system of Indian reservations stemmed from a long British colonial practice in the Americas. In the era of US treaty-making from independence to 1871, the concept of the reservation was one of the Indigenous nation reserving a narrowed land base from a much larger one in exchange for US government protection from settlers and the provision of social services. In the late nineteenth century, as Indigenous resistance was weakened, the concept of the reservation changed to one of land being carved out of the public domain of the United States as a benevolent gesture, a "gift" to the Indigenous peoples. Rhetoric changed so that reservations were said to have been "given" or "created" for Indians. With this shift, Indian reservations came to be seen as enclaves within state boundaries. Despite the political and economic reality, the impression to many was that Indigenous people were taking a free ride on public domain.

Beyond the land bases within the limits of the 310 federally recognized reservations—among 554 Indigenous groups—Indigenous land, water, and resource rights extend to all federally acknowledged Indigenous communities within the borders of the United States. This is the case whether "within the original or subsequently acquired territory thereof, and whether within or without the limits of a state," and includes all allotments as well as rights-of-way running to and from them.[16] Not all the federally recognized Indigenous nations have land bases beyond government buildings, and the lands of some Native nations, including those of the Sioux in the Dakotas and Minnesota and the Ojibwes in Minnesota, have been parceled into multiple reservations, while some fifty Indigenous nations that had been removed to Oklahoma were entirely allotted—divided by the federal government into individual Native-owned parcels. Attorney Walter R. Echo-Hawk writes:

> In 1881, Indian landholdings in the United States had plummeted to 156 million acres. By 1934, only about 50 million acres remained (an area the size of Idaho and Washington) as a result of the General Allotment Act of 1887. During World War II, the government took 500,000 more acres for military use. Over one hundred tribes, bands, and Rancherias relinquished their lands under various acts of Congress during the termination era of the 1950s. By 1955, the indigenous land base had shrunk to just 2.3 percent of its original size.[17]

As a result of federal land sales, seizures, and allotments, most reservations are severely fragmented. Each parcel of tribal, trust, and privately held land is a separate enclave under multiple laws and jurisdictions. The Diné (Navajo) Nation has the largest contemporary contiguous land base among Native nations: nearly sixteen million acres, or nearly twenty-five thousand square miles, the size of West Virginia. Each of twelve other reservations is larger than Rhode Island, which comprises nearly eight hundred thousand acres, or twelve hundred square miles, and each of nine other reservations is larger than Delaware, which covers nearly a million and a half acres, or two thousand square miles. Other reservations have land bases of fewer than thirty-two thousand acres, or fifty square miles.[18] A number of independent nation-states with seats in the United Nations have less territory and smaller populations than some Indigenous nations of North America.

Following World War II, the United States was at war with much of the world, just as it was at war with the Indigenous peoples of North America in the nineteenth century. This was total war, demanding that the enemy surrender unconditionally or face annihilation. Perhaps it was inevitable that the earlier wars against Indigenous peoples, if not acknowledged and repudiated, ultimately would include the world. According to the origin narrative, the United States was born of rebellion against oppression—against empire—and thus is the product of the first anticolonial revolution for national liberation. The narrative flows from that fallacy: the broadening and deepening of democracy; the Civil War and the ensuing "second revolution," which ended slavery; the twentieth-century mission to save Europe from itself—twice; and the ultimately triumphant fight against the scourge of communism, with the United States inheriting the difficult and burdensome task of keeping order in the world. It's a narrative of progress. The 1960s social revolutions, ignited by the African American liberation movement, complicated the origin narrative, but its structure and periodization have been left intact. After the 1960s, historians incorporated women, African Americans, and immigrants as contributors to the commonweal. Indeed, the revised narrative produced the "nation of immigrants" framework, which obscures the US practice of colonization, merging settler colonialism with immigration to metropolitan centers during and after the industrial revolution. Native peoples, to the extent that they were included at all, were renamed "First Americans" and thus themselves cast as distant immigrants.

The provincialism and national chauvinism of US history production make it difficult for effective revisions to gain authority. Scholars, both Indigenous and a few non-Indigenous, who attempt to rectify the distortions, are labeled advocates, and their findings are rejected for publication on that basis. Indigenous scholars look to research and thinking that has emerged in the rest of the European-colonized world. To understand the historical and current experiences of Indigenous peoples in the United States, these thinkers and writers draw upon and creatively apply the historical materialism of Marxism, the liberation theology of Latin America, Frantz Fanon's psychosocial analyses of the effects of colonialism on the colonizer and the colonized, and other approaches, including development theory and postmodern theory. While not abandoning insights gained from those sources, due to the "exceptional" nature of US colonialism among nineteenth-century colonial powers, Indigenous scholars and activists are engaged in exploring new approaches.

This book claims to be a history of the United States from an Indigenous peoples' perspective but there is no such thing as a collective Indigenous peoples' perspective, just as there is no monolithic Asian or European or African peoples' perspective. This is not a history of the vast civilizations and communities that thrived and survived between the Gulf of Mexico and Canada and between the Atlantic Ocean and the Pacific. Such histories have been written, and are being written by historians of Diné, Lakota, Mohawk, Tlingit, Muskogee, Anishinaabe, Lumbee, Inuit, Kiowa, Cherokee, Hopi, and other Indigenous communities and nations that have survived colonial genocide. This book attempts to tell the story of the United States as a colonialist settler-state, one that, like colonialist European states, crushed and subjugated the original civilizations in the territories it now rules. Indigenous peoples, now in a colonial relationship with the United States, inhabited and thrived for millennia before they were displaced to fragmented reservations and economically decimated.

This is a history of the United States.

■

FROM "FEAR" IN BREATHE: A LETTER TO MY SONS
By Imani Perry

You were both little bits when President Obama was elected. That night was jubilant. We celebrated with friends, then, on the ride home, Black people cheered and danced in the streets. It reminded me of the night when Harold Washington won as mayor of Chicago, and strangers hugged me and my father. Such joy. It was a palate cleanse for a fragment of a moment. A season in which pundits speculated we might be postracial, in which scholars speculated that Black children would be less wounded; they called it a turning point, a point of no return. When Obama won, for a time Black tongues were scraped of bitterness and bile. Then the aftertaste came back like an earthquake.

Troy Davis. He was the first whose name you knew. Before either of you were born he witnessed a fight. A cop tried to break it up and was shot. And died. Troy Davis saw everything, but he insisted he wasn't the shooter. Someone else said he was.

The police were looking for Davis and so he turned himself in. Someone still said he did it, and there was a trial, and Davis was convicted. This was Georgia, a death penalty state. And Troy Davis was sentenced to death. His appeal for habeas relief—the potential grace note for unjust and unlawful detention—was denied.

Troy Davis became a household name because there were so many holes in the case. Seven witnesses recanted their (apparently coerced) testimonies. Eyewitnesses said it was his accuser and not Davis who did the shooting. The evidence of fabrication grew, and so did attention to Davis's plight. Archbishop Desmond Tutu and Pope Benedict both insisted on a halt to the killing machine. Former presidents and parliaments, even Republicans, implored. This man was innocent, and that fact was clear irrespective of what the court's procedures would recognize.

We went to demonstrations. We talked about the case. We joined the chorus pleading for Troy Davis's life. In the same way I was taught, I was teaching you how to think about injustice from an early age. No one understands fairness as much as young children. If you explain the way the world works, its pernicious efficacy, you will create justice warriors for a lifetime. They know what is right and wrong.

We sat together, me and you, Freeman, on that pretty pale-yellow denim couch. It wasn't stained yet from juice boxes and pizza. The night was September 20. You were up way past your bedtime. The news cameras covered the crowd outside the prison. The journalists told us what was happening inside, in that echoing lonely quiet. Troy Davis died at 11:08 p.m.

You looked at me, wide-eyed. "They killed him?"

They killed him. *They*. America. It. And whenever we forget and say the word *we*, it slices deep into our flesh. "Remember, nigger. Remember your place," is the national coda. I cried. You nestled in my arms. My poor child. You know intuitively that there are far more Troy Davises than Obamas. You are too smart for the surface jubilee to ever last. Sweet gets too sweet and turns bitter. It sticks and goes thick. Like cotton candy.

More protest. That was my first answer. That was what I knew to do. When I was a child and was prohibited from celebrating the Fourth of July (because, as Frederick Douglass asked, "What to the Slave is the Fourth of July?" and what is Independence Day to the oppressed?), I asked for a demonstration instead. The first time I was in the newspaper it was under a sign that read "Stop the War against Black America." I was much younger than five.

Something distinct has happened in your time. It is the product of camera phones, the diminishing whiteness of America, the backlash against a Black presidency, the persistence of American racism, the money-making weapons industry, the value added for murder in police dossiers, law-and-order policing. The epistrophe of our era: Hands up, don't shoot, can't breathe, can't run, can't play, can't drive, can't sleep, can't lose your mind unless you are ready to lose your life, dead dead dead. We wail and cry, how many pietàs? We protest their deaths; we protest for our lives.

Once our house alarm was tripped twice in one night. I tried to remain calm. But there was a loud banging sound at the back door the second time. The alarm company called again. I had said the police officers should not come the first time. I agreed the second time. You both were frightened. I was too. I called you, Freeman. Thank goodness you had a cell phone. I told you, softly, to lock your bedroom door and to not come out until I told you to. The first degree of fear, and I wonder at this, was not about the intruder who I thought was trying to get in. It was about the police, who I knew could get in, had a responsibility to get in, because they had been called.

I said lock your door because the possibility flashed before my face. You might be tipping out of your room, looking to come upstairs to me, or, in your breathtaking and youthful courage, looking to protect the home. And what if the police officers saw you, Mahogany in the shadows, tall and lean and dreadlocked, and decided you were the intruder, the one who didn't belong in this big house with lilac bushes and manicured Japanese trees in front? And what if they took you out?

There are fingers itching to have a reason to cage or even slaughter you. My God, what hate for beauty this world breeds. They say they are afraid. I do not believe it is fear. It is bloodlust.

People will say I'm being melodramatic. They have. But police kill middle-class Black children and adults too. Not with the same frequency, but class is no prevention. It is a reduction of the odds at best. As a Black mother, when I read about one of those children whose life has been snatched, at first blush I think, "That could have been my child." But I have demanded of myself that

I turn away from such egotism. The truth is that is not my child. My children are here, and they stand with me, to honor their dead.

When Mamie Till shared the bloated distended face of her beautiful son Emmett, who was murdered, she did not offer other Black parents possession. Mamie Till's pietà was one in which she could not hold his wounded but still beautiful body across her lap. Hers was a pietà, instead, of distended, inflamed, and bloated remains from a distance; a pieta of a mother made empty-handed by virtue of the cruelty of the execution remains with us. That funeral service, a martyrdom, sending off a patron saint for those who survive after deaths, is an ever present haunting. I have not raised you in the church. Maybe that is a mistake. Faith helps us hold on. What do you do other than pray, an intercession not to bring the baby back, after all he is with God, but one to make stepping out of bed possible?

Mamie Till did it. She shared her testimony. Personal tragedy became the public's grief, one of so many during the freedom movement. Emmett's horrifyingly abused face resonated. Yet and still he was her baby and not the onlookers'. The same is true of the myriad who have followed. We witness private grief and feel it turn into our collective grief. But we must not snatch it up out of their loved ones' hearts and colonize it with our fears. Instead we stand in the chorus of mourners. I am sorry, Mrs. Till, Mrs. Fulton, Mr. Martin, Mrs. Davis, I am sorry we did not protect your child with every fiber of our beings. I am sorry we go on doing the same as yesterday while you collect the shards. It is not enough, but we will try to prevent the next. And we will fail. And our elegies grow reedy and more mournful. And our ache more confused and desperate. Ashen.

The ethics of living with a roulette wheel of Black death are complicated. "Sufficient unto the day is the evil thereof."[19] We do the fight today for the living. Grief must not be distorted into the constant imagination of death. We ward and guard and try to protect but know that there is no warding or guarding lest your whole life become their impunity.

When I stopped watching the killings, and declared it, people argued with me. They insisted that public executions would turn the tide. They were wrong. They just ratified the truth: summary execution is a feature of American life. Awareness is not a virtue in and of itself, not without a moral imperative. I knew the imperative wasn't there. I wanted to be wrong. But I wasn't. And I won't beat my chest, beat our minds to a bloody pulp in order to keep trying to have faith in a place that doesn't deserve it, in an American consciousness that hates more than it recognizes.

We cannot make of our lives a nightmarish *Fortnite* game with the guns cocked and ready for you as a target and our hands inexplicably empty of self-protection. Sons, I will not allow that to be your life. Your testimony is living with the passionate intensity of one whose presence matters despite the violence of this world towards your beautiful flesh.

Sufficient unto the day is the evil thereof. That is to say, we cannot even think about tomorrow; there is enough evil in this moment. Sufficient for each day is God's grace thereof, meaning I have the grace of your presence today. I have to hold on to that. "Finish each day and be done with it. You have done what you could. Some blunders and absurdities no doubt crept in; forget them as soon as you can. Tomorrow is a new day. You shall begin it serenely and with too high a spirit to be encumbered with your old nonsense," is what Emerson said.[20] But the truth is such haunting and trauma that I cannot help but ask the forward-looking questions.

How many pietàs? Holding the husk, praying for the spirit to have never departed. The life force escaped into a place that cannot be touched. Heart plummeted, this is what we do. Make me wanna holler, the way they do our lives. As Toni Cade Bambara said, "Those bones are not my child."[21] They are simply the remnants of a cruel world. The child has spread so vast that they become air and light, a thunderous rain, a sun shower, a rainbow.

Fairly soon, Issa, the protests became too much for you. You and your brother watched as we failed. We marched, we spoke out. We testified, we cried. And then there was another one, and another one. We lost, repeatedly. We watched conflagrations that burned into ashes and nothing was changed. The next day, or week, someone else was choked or shot in the back or stomped to death. Someone else encased in brown flesh like us. It was too much. No more marches; it made life too terrifying.

I had hoped that standing shoulder to shoulder with people of conscience, people who knew like us that the tocsin peal of Black death is wrong, would help you feel powerful, a part of something. I may have been right, but it was never enough.

When I took you down to the fiftieth anniversary of Freedom Summer, it was with a different sense of purpose. We flew to Jackson, Mississippi. I am always stunned that there is a state that feels so much like Alabama, like Mississippi does. Sound, taste, smell. Though most northerners treat the South as an undifferentiated mass, it is so specific, so local, so varied. But Alabama and Mississippi? They are twins, identical yet fed different diets, raised in different homes.

I would like to take you to Africa one day. I am one of those Black people who believes in the value of return. However, you have already been to your ancestral home many times. It is the Deep South. Of course, the further back you go, the bulk of ancestors were from a motley of West African peoples, a vast genetic variety, and some, as a consequence of rape, were from Europe. But the WE to which you belong was born in the South of the United States, though there were stops in the Caribbean and Maryland. Even New York was in there. The fact of becoming a people, to which you were born, happened on plantations. In slavery. I bristle when folks tell me that Black children should know their history didn't begin with slavery, as though slavery is shameful. Yes, of course, precolonial African history is important. Every child should have the fictions of imperialism aggressively bleached from their minds. Teach Songhay and Mali and Akan and Nubia. Stop narrowly constraining the idea of the classical and calling violent and vile conquest exploration. True. Yes. That's important. But I do not believe the acts of oppressors are my people's shame. For me, that my people became, created, and imagined from a position of unfreedom is a source of deep pride, not shame. I hope you learn that too. What better evidence of human beauty and resilience could there be?

And, if those genealogy tests are right, and that is a big if, when you trace your mother's mother's mother . . . far back as the sample can ride, it takes us back to an indigenous woman of the Americas. You are literally children of this place, from before it was a slave-holding settler-colonialist imperial country. You are survival. You have survived. We have.

I took you to Mississippi to catch a hold of who you are. I rented a car, an inexpensive one. The seats were plastic and the smell was just like my dad's old VW bug in which we rode through Alabama and sometimes down to Pensacola. We drove to the campus of Tougaloo, a historically Black college founded in 1869 to serve the educational aspirations of the freedpeople, fresh from slavery. It was where Anne Moody and Joyce Ladner, among other members of the Student Nonviolent Coordinating Committee, attended college. It was where the organizers rested at the end of the March Against Fear, the one that brought the call for Black Power to the center of the movement. And then, in 2014, it was where they chose to remember fifty years later, how Black youth changed the South and the nation.

Though you were seven and ten, you had already watched documentaries of the freedom movement. Issa, you said, wide-eyed, that you liked Professor Cleveland Sellers's overalls. He, a college president, wore a shirt and tie. He, a SNCC veteran, wore their workers' uniform. Poised, dignified, tall, lean. Past and present in one body. Everyman and exceptional man. I was hoping you saw some of that in yourself, a genealogy from whence you came, and where you might be going. How to remain.

In the gymnasium, Freeman, you sat transfixed as Mukasa Ricks preached from his memory, the story of his call and response with Stokely Carmichael, for Black Power. An elder, he bounded, his voice ricocheted, the spirit of a revolutionary had kept every bit of his energy youthful even as his body evidenced the years of struggle.

You both sat quietly, in the back of a classroom, to listen to the soft-spoken architect of Freedom Summer, Bob Moses. Glistening mahogany skin, a slow smile, and that riveting quiet intellect took over the room. He is your grandmother's friend, who you usually see on Martha's Vineyard with his wife, Miss Janet, playing with their grands. There you realized he was someone historic and both steely and soft.

On the campus there were organizers young and old. A pastor from Jamaica Plain, Massachusetts, by way of Arkansas, with a fedora on his head and dreadlocks hanging to his waist, sang the old-time blues, and a young eye-glassed short-locked dream defender from Florida and the second generation of hip-hop responded to his call with joy. There was love and legacy everywhere. And out of the fray, there were young men in orange jumpsuits. They trimmed hedges, cleaned walkways, labored steadily amongst the freedom fighters. They didn't catch our eyes. I noticed one with locks that hung to his wide shoulders. I saw his hands, broad and, at one moment, upturned as though pitifully empty. A prisoner among the freedom fighters, a human bellwether, a sacrificial lamb. There we all were, almost to a one, the descendants of slaves and croppers, and rapist slavers . . . and the Jim Crow rapists. Some literally held captive, some remembering a different form of captivity, some naming it all. And I think all of us knew that we hadn't yet realized the dreams of freedpeople who'd first settled down at Tougaloo.

I got lost on the way out of Mississippi. At one point we hit a dead-end road and my heart raced. An old man, leather-faced, overalled, with a cap on his head and gaunt sharp cheeks of a sort I've only seen in three places—the Dominican Republic, Louisiana, and Mississippi—led us out to the freeway. And we made our way home.

Driving from Jackson to Birmingham was easy. We ate donuts and listened to the scratchy radio, and 2014 felt like 1974 to me, except you were there, people I only dreamed of when I was little and playing with so many baby dolls. And that was the best feeling in the world.

I was born nine years after four little girls were killed in Birmingham, Alabama, and two other boys later the same day. On that trip, Auntie Thelma took us to Kelly Ingram Park. We circumambulated around the path, where the marchers had gathered, where the hoses and dogs lashed out at children, right in front of the Sixteenth Street Baptist Church, where the girls had died, across from the Civil Rights Institute, where the memories are held. The beating heart of Birmingham's freedom fighting.

The park is named after Osmond Kelly Ingram, a Navy man who was killed by Germans in World War I. He was the son of a Confederate veteran. Ingram senior devoted his life to keeping your ancestors bound to the evil of enslavement. That is not irony. That's the texture of our history. Every place is a battleground.

Kelly Ingram Park is quiet. The sculpture garden has the children behind bars, the clergy preaching freedom, the attacks on the people. It is so quiet and so vivid, cool dark metal statues surrounded by living green under a blazing hot Alabama sun. Not like a cemetery, better than most memorials because the haunting is visceral. You feel it when you stand close.

We walked around the sculptures, to the path converging in the center. There were children your sizes, I thought, who fought for you. For me. They fought for the ones in orange jumpsuits too.

An old man sitting on a park bench commented on your thick black curls, Freeman: "I used to have long pretty hair like that. But my daddy said he didn't want me to look like a sissy." My auntie thankfully shut him up. He wanted us to know he had been beautiful, and it made my chest hurt, because it was a belief that his beauty had something to do with looking a little bit less African, a little more Indian. He couldn't help but share a childhood hurt over an insecure masculinity, a cruel charge that beauty is gay and therefore somehow inferior. These things are things we have to grapple with, too, the ongoing work of trying to get free. There are parts to kill and parts to reincarnate, again and again.

You are gifted with something and it is important. You have seen Black men of every stripe, of every sort, for the entirety of your life. Famous and homeless. Athlete, intellectual, musician, teacher. Businessman, public servant, fast-food worker. Seen, and I do not mean simply knowing who they are, I mean hearing their stories. The range of dispositions and tones of laughter. Accents and nationalities and drawls and swagger and awkwardness. Hypermasculine and elegantly feminine and every variation in between. A common thread, a dramatic assortment. And you are members of this collaged confederacy, which, as a through line through all manner of circumstance, can share the Marvin Gaye refrain "Makes me wanna holler, the way they do my life . . . Makes me wanna holler, throw up both my hands."

In your own distinctive ways, you fit into the collective, even as there are moments when you may, by virtue of your rarefied circumstance, feel on its margins. I suppose that is why I have always insisted that you travel with me into the hood. Literally, the hood, as in the abbreviation for the neighborhood, as in the Blackest of spaces, also known as being all up in the cut. I'm talking about the ghetto. The word "hood" reverberates, pointed white, tall Klan hoods, and the businessmen and politicians underneath who carved out pyramids of exclusion and containment. The hoodies, a relatively cheap way to keep warm, to encase the body, to protect it, become narrative symbols for an undesired Blackness. "No hoodies allowed" the signs say, or they are simply justifications for trigger-happy police. The hood, the hoods. There is something about that word that speaks to our beating hearts. I want you to know it is with you even when you don't know it that well. You carry it like an invisible backpack. Of course they discern it, in the echo of your brown faces, but they do not see its riches, its resilience, in the carriage of your square shoulders. You must.

This is not some pat romanticism. Trust me. We do not want the trials of poverty. We do not want the wrecking ball instead of the hammer. That can only be a colonizer's fantasy. The province of those who want to eat up everything, even the suffering they create. But we know the story of Brer Rabbit. How he outwitted being punished for theft by begging, "Whatever you do, please don't throw me into the briar patch." And then, tossed there, he gleefully sang, "Born and bred in the briar patch." Don't be afraid of being cast with the briar patch. Know the bounty that is there. The lush forestation, the deep roots. The roping connections under the surface, that persist beyond life.

We cried for Trayvon. You heard every bit of how a child was made a demon. And hunted. A child like you. You wore hoodies as resistance, like a million more, innocent and beautiful, a target but more importantly an unapologetic human being. It was moving. And then it was heartbreaking.

I told you not to raise your hands up in the don't-shoot position that was common then. I told you to raise your right fists, how I was taught. Power.

The massacre happens in police violence. In hoods flooded with guns. In survivalists and antisocialists for whom murder gives purpose. This nation that is yours by inheritance and birth is in a state of panic and disaster. It's imperial grandeur is ending. Upward mobility is waning; precariousness is multiplying. And yet the rich keep getting richer. Whiteness is ebbing. And those who are afraid are turning to a game of cowboys and gangsters, going out with a viral blaze of glory. Children keep dying. The world keeps turning them bitter and demonic in deed.

My children. You have seen us, the adults in your world, impotent to bring our lost ones back, to protect the children or the mothers or the fathers, or to even avenge their deaths as useless as retribution would be when it comes to broken hearts. We have completely failed at making those who act with violent impunity stop what they're doing. In fact, a call to the police is an audaciously wielded weapon of white discontent these days. With each sin the violent hateful ones grow bolder. They know they can take our lives without consequence. And if not that, stage theaters of our humiliation. And yet, your power sustains.

My father had the poem "Who Killed McDuffie?" above his desk while I was growing up. It is a harrowing account of the unsolved murder of a Black man in Miami in 1979. I learned, practically from birth, that judicial procedure was a cruel choreography and not a fact finding when it came to violence against Black people. That is the terror that makes me want to say, "That could have been my child," and also, "That could have been me," even though thoughts of the self cannot, should not, take over our collective outrage and grief. And I know that, despite my fear, I cannot clip your wings, as though cowering is a respectful tribute to the beauty we have lost. No, I want your wingspan wide. To honor the departed, ancestral, and immediate—BE. Living defined by terror is itself destructive of the spirit. And it is submission. The truth is that life is unsafe. And genius, more often than not, remains unvalidated or, even worse, dormant. But joy, even in slivers, shows up everywhere. Take it. And keep taking it.

HOW COULD I WRITE ABOUT WOMEN WHOSE EXISTENCE IS BARELY ACKNOWLEDGED?

By Gaiutra Bahadur

My great-grandmother Sujaria didn't leave behind letters or diaries describing the circumstances that led her to climb aboard a ship bound for the other side of the world on a summer's day in 1903, in the middle of the monsoon, while four months pregnant and alone.

A decaying emigration pass in a ship's manifest in Guyana told me that, when she departed Calcutta to work as an indentured labourer—or "coolie"—in British Guiana, she was 27 years old and high-caste. It provided the name of her father and her native village and, with remarkable intimacy, hinting at possible trauma, even recorded a burn mark on her left leg. Missing from the written record, however, was her own testimony, the story in her own words of how she came to leave and who she truly was. A waylaid religious pilgrim? A widow? A fugitive from an abusive marriage? A woman deserted by her husband?

These were experiences shared by other recruits. So which was her story? Did my great-grandmother choose to go and work on a Caribbean sugar plantation, or was she forced? On these and other crucial questions, the record is silent, stranding me at the very edges of the archives, at the limits of what can be known.

Coolie Woman is not only a family history, but a broader social and narrative history of indenture; the system that, for roughly 80 years after the abolition of slavery in the British empire, provided exploitable bonded labour to plantation owners across the globe. More than a million Indians were transported to colonies from the Indian Ocean to the West Indies, in a traffic one-third the size of the British slave trade. My book focuses on the women in this group, two-thirds of whom had quit India without men by their sides. Uprooted from families and villages, they were the subcontinent's most dispossessed: widows, sex workers or outcasts, running from or thrown out by husbands.

History had left these women voiceless. The existing archives that document indenture contain biases and elisions. I found a rich paper trail in India Office and Colonial Office records in London: statistical reports and diaries by captains and surgeons aboard the ships that transported the indentured; transcripts of inquiries into uprisings on the plantations; confidential dossiers on overseers who slept with Indian women. These documents allowed me, partially, to reconstruct the texture of the women's lives.

But what the archive didn't do, and could not do, was reveal their thoughts or their feelings: indentured women appear in the records only when something goes awry, in moments of tragedy or scandal. They are only described by others, by the various white men who held power over them; the ships' surgeons and captains, planters and overseers, immigration agents and magistrates. I could read the women only through the often sexist, racist eyes of government and plantation officials who had vested interests—economic, careerist, sexual—in telling the story from their own perspectives. Since indentured women were, for the most part, illiterate, they didn't leave behind written traces of themselves. Just as there isn't a single existing narrative from a woman or girl who survived the Middle Passage, the rare first-person accounts of indenture—there are three—are all by men. The stealing of the voices of indentured women, born into the wrong class, race and gender to write themselves into history, was structural.

How could I write about women whose very existence the official sources barely acknowledged? To enter their unknown and to some extent unknowable history, I had to turn to alternative, unofficial sources. I looked for clues in visual traces and the oral tradition: folk songs, oral histories, photographs and colonial-era postcards, even a traditional tattoo on the forearms of elderly Indo-Caribbean women. Perhaps most daringly, I turned to the self and wrote about my own journeys: to India, to visit my great-grandmother's native village in order to uncover why she left; and back to Guyana, where I was born, to explore how gender-based violence there—currently a problem of disturbing proportions—could be a legacy of indenture. In weaving myself into the narrative, I was tracing not only roots but also the inheritance of harm. I was calling on my own experience in two ways, both as a former newspaper reporter and as a child immigrant: my professional and personal background converged to suggest a strategy, a gambit for restoring the stolen voices.

A child immigrant's way of seeing the world has much in common with a journalist's way of seeing the world. Both ask questions: in the reporter's case, this is about scepticism; in the immigrant's case, it's about identity. Those who cross cultures at a young age often ask not only "Who am I?" and "Where do I belong?" but also "Who might have I been, had my family never emigrated?" We are primed to speculate, to imagine multiple possible endings.

Coolie Woman is, as such, a speculative history. Where the voices of indentured women were absent, I used my own, as their descendant, to question the records as aggressively as I could.

This solution presented itself by accident. About the time when I sat down to write my first chapter, I heard Salman Rushdie read Donald Barthelme's "Concerning the Bodyguard" on a *New Yorker* podcast. The short story, told through the eyes of a bodyguard assigned to a politician in an unnamed Latin American country, is written almost entirely in question form. The device is meant to mirror the bodyguard's uncertainty and anxiety when he views the world; he never knows who or what precisely is coming at him, or what threats they might pose. It occurred to me to try a similar experiment to deal with gaps and silences in indenture's archive. Whole sections of *Coolie Woman* unfold entirely in questions: mine, my great-grandmother's, the reader's, one relentlessly following the next. These questions allow me to imagine interiorities withheld by the written record. They paint landscapes, advance the plot, convey a tone. They communicate my own attitude to the archive and its elisions and biases: I could never be neutral because I am, after all, a product of the history I've written.

CHAPTER 4

WRITING FROM OUTSIDE
IN OR INSIDE OUT

Reporting, Personal Narrative,
or a Hybrid Approach

There is no one right way to approach social issues on the page. Social issues can be written about engagingly by examining and investigating them from a reported perspective. They can also be explored through a compelling personal perspective when the writer has firsthand experience with the issue and its personal impact.

A reported perspective takes a journalistic approach, building a narrative around facts, providing necessary contextual details, and featuring multiple perspectives, including from those most impacted—witnesses, and topical experts. Typically, the writer is outside of the frame of events. In this approach, the writer is a trusted guide illuminating an issue for a reader who shares their curiosity about this new frontier and all its fascinating terrain. Reported perspectives are ideal for broad-scope, expansive pieces and for deep dives and investigations. A reported perspective does the following:

- Provides facts and data about the featured issue
- Provides context, whether historical, scientific, or technical, or industry background, etc.

- Addresses the complexity of the issue through multiple perspectives
- Establishes the author as an objective authority on the topic

Meanwhile, a personal narrative centers the personal impact of an issue. It is grounded in the subjective and experiential aspects of the story, immersing the reader in observations, feelings, and sensations. Where a reported perspective gives broader context, a personal narrative tends to focus more narrowly on personal history and circumstances. The writer is either central to or part of the story. Personal narratives are ideal for covering the topic on a human scale, thereby humanizing a complex or fraught issue, allowing for the following:

- In-depth explorations of character(s) from a subjective and familiar standpoint
- Establishing the writer as an inside expert with a personal stake in the issue

Personal narratives offer readers the unique opportunity to view an issue from the inside, a chance to understand the human dimensions of an issue that may seem too complex or remote.

Both approaches can raise awareness amongst those who are new to the issue as well as galvanize readers who already care about it. Whichever approach you select will determine the scope of research and the shape of your narrative. The more a writer's identity and experience distance them from the issue and the community most impacted by it, the more they need to make sure their research involves the perspectives of those most affected. Your level of expertise but also your level of distance and the type of piece you are trying to write determine the kinds of research you do. I will talk more about this in chapter 6, where I discuss cultural sensitivity and avoiding cultural appropriation.

It is often assumed that since reported perspectives are centered around facts and context and personal narratives emphasize personal perspective and experience, then reported perspectives are inherently more objective. Perhaps. However, as noted in chapter 1, the aspiration for objectivity and neutrality in journalism is being challenged. The question is increasingly being asked: Is neutrality the ideal perspective when chronicling social justice issues? Relatedly, how does the lack of diversity in newsrooms impact their ability to equitably report on issues of racial injustice?

I observed the value and importance of an intentional racial justice lens when covering issues of race while serving as marketing and communications director for Race Forward, the publisher of *Colorlines*, "a daily news site where race matters." From police brutality to immigration and detention to LGBTQ+ rights to arts and culture, *Colorlines* covers issues with a race-explicit lens—articulating and analyzing their impact on race and vice versa. Embedded in Race Forward, a multicultural racial justice organization, *Colorlines* stands out not just for its coverage of race but its truly diverse and inclusive newsroom.

In my estimation, it's better to view the reported perspective and the personal perspective in a non-oppositional way, as two different approaches to getting at the truth of an issue and why it matters; one approach does so from the outside while the other does so from the inside.

We have also seen the emergence of a third approach—a hybrid approach—which blends aspects of reported perspective with aspects of personal narrative to tell the story in a creative way, defying simple categorization. Often, the author is a topical expert with a personal stake in the issue and both perspectives are reflected in one piece, showing the issue simultaneously from the outside in and the inside out.

A hybrid approach is a balancing act to figure out how much context the reader requires versus how much personal narrative serves the piece and how to weave together the two perspectives to enhance one another in telling the story rather than creating confusion by muddling the narrative flow. When done masterfully, it can result in powerful writing, which appeals equally to the heart and mind, especially to readers open to more experimental writing.

Hybrid essays play with narrative form by bringing together multiple genres and approaches in one piece, including memoir, poetry, fiction, mythology, and visual arts. A hybrid essay might alternate between personal narrative and journalistic perspective. Given their genre-defying form, hybrid pieces tend to be published on platforms that are open to creative nonfiction and experimental work rather than traditional journalistic pieces.

The good news about hybrid essays, in my mind, is that there are no hard and fast rules on how to blend perspectives. The bad news, however, is also that there are no clear rules on how best to blend perspectives. When a hybrid piece works well, it reads seamlessly, as if the different perspectives fit together to form a cohesive whole, united by the voice of the writer. There are some established types of hybrid essays. Probably the best-known form is the braided essay, where the author weaves back and forth between at least two narrative strains to reveal a broader narrative. Another, looser type is the collage or mosaic essay, which arranges narrative fragments to form an overall narrative, such as multiple perspectives on the same event.

Ultimately, the two best ways to learn about hybrid essays and determine if they are the right form for the story you're seeking to tell is to (1) read masters of the hybrid essay, including Eula Biss, Imani Perry, Hanif Abdurraqib, and Kiese Laymon, and (2) experiment with writing your own hybrid essays. Bear in mind that they work particularly well when you are both a topical expert or enthusiast and are personally impacted by the issue. Hybrid essays might be a good form to explore when you feel that no singular perspective is sufficient for conveying all that you want to express about an issue.

Let us examine some examples of reported pieces, personal narratives, and hybrid essays. I have included in this chapter two pieces I wrote about the importance of vaccines and the perils of the anti-vaccine movement and vaccine hesitancy, each of which approaches this topic in a different way. During the COVID-19 pandemic, I observed that while access to vaccines and vaccine hesitancy were being covered in the media, they were not being covered with a nuanced lens on race. I did not see any pieces addressing the differences in vaccine hesitancy in Black communities versus in rural white Evangelical communities. While vaccine hesitancy in the Black community was often driven by historical and present-day racism faced by Black patients in their encounters with the medical sector and the resulting health implications on Black lives, vaccine hesitancy in rural white Evangelical communities tended to be driven more by their desire for unfettered personal and religious freedom. And while targeted outreach by Black providers to Black community members was showing promising outcomes in vaccination rates, this was not the case in rural white Evangelical communities, where vaccination rates were lagging despite the availability of vaccines. I wrote this piece to draw attention to the contrast between these experiences and to how the pandemic further underscored the impact of rampant equity issues in public health:

> The stark contrast we see in the reasons for hesitancy in these two communities as well as their respective reactions to vaccination outreach efforts reflects the historical and present-day story of racism in America. When it comes to Black Americans, despite this group's justified fears and mistrust of the health care system due to historical and ongoing systemic racism, they are taking the advice of experts in their communities by getting vaccinated, protecting themselves and others. Meanwhile, white conservatives, who have not had to endure struggles against a racist health care system, behave as if their beliefs are more important than the nation's public health and collective safety. In truth, their vaccine hesitancy is willful vaccine resistance, risking lives and prolonging the pandemic. Theirs is a virulent privilege, rooted in delusions of white supremacy masquerading as faith and ideals.

To inform this reported piece, I talked to a leader of a philanthropic organization that was spearheading a nationwide COVID-19 outreach initiative to Black communities as well as to the Black head of a network of community health centers whose patient population was largely Black and part of this outreach initiative. Given that I don't belong to this community and was reporting for a racial justice news site, it was particularly critical that the perspectives of those in this community inform the piece.

Meanwhile, in "A Virulent Privilege," using a hybrid narrative approach, which blends personal narrative and narrative nonfiction in a serial essay, I explore the role that white privilege played in the emergence of the anti-vaccine movement. Prior to the pandemic, the anti-vaccine movement was largely overlooked by the media or portrayed as a disparate group of misinformed individuals rather than as a virulent movement, eroding collective vaccine protections and jeopardizing public health:

> By contrast, the anti-vaccine movement has remained relatively uncovered by the mainstream media for years, hiding in plain sight. Their members have been viewed as more bohemian and eccentric than threatening or harmful. Anti-vaccine moms are cast as misguided but well-meaning rather than neglectful or selfish. . . .
>
> It underscores dual narratives: one of choice, one of circumstance. It also begs the question: would this movement have been allowed to grow, endangering the lives of all children, if it was largely populated by poor families of color rather than driven by middle-class white families? Would its members have been generously perceived as misguided but well-intentioned rather than misinformed and dangerous? Ultimately, these individuals working to undermine the protection offered by vaccinations to our nation's children have been protected by their own race and class privilege—benefiting from another type of herd immunity.

This more experimental piece was published in the literary magazine *Nat. Brut* several years before the rise of the COVID-19 pandemic, when I struggled to get journalistic and literary outlets to be interested in an examination of the dangerous anti-vaccine movement, an issue that would soon come to consume our lives as we contemplate how our fellow citizens, who are vaccine skeptics, are jeopardizing our chances of seeing an end to the pandemic. Although both pieces were sparked by my deep belief in the importance of vaccines and health equity, this second piece reveals my personal motivations stemming from my identity and experiences.

Also included are two essays by Puerto Rican writer Jaquira Díaz that demonstrate two compelling approaches to exploring the lives of at-risk Latinx teens. "La Otra," adapted from Díaz's moving memoir *Ordinary Girls*, offers an immersive and deeply personal portrait of fierce internal and external struggles endured by Díaz and her family during her childhood in Puerto Rico and Miami, and the ways these struggles haunt her as a troubled teenager:

> Everything seemed to slow down, Pito and Levy and Eggy, all of them, disappearing until it was just me and my mother and my mother's knife, the three of us echoing through the years, propelled forward in time, and because I am my mother's daughter more than I have ever been my father's, it will be this moment I think of when I'm a 14-year-old hoodlum tucking razor blades into the sides of my Jordans, brass knuckles and Master combination locks and pocket knives in my backpack; when I am 15 and getting jumped by five girls at the bus stop; when I am 16 and trying to decide how to deal with a friend who has betrayed me; when I am 17 and fighting with my brother. How I would always come back to this, my mother and her knife and all that rage, la vecina leaping back out of her way.

Meanwhile, in "The School-to-Prison Pipeline Is Getting Worse for Black and Brown Girls," Díaz takes a hybrid approach, fusing her own personal experiences as a traumatized teenager struggling to come to terms with her sexual identity, with a reported perspective on how systems—educational and correctional—are set up not to support but to further victimize Black and brown teens.

> The police eventually dropped the breaking and entering charges, but I was, from that day onward, deemed a delinquent. I lived under a kind of surveillance, with cop cars constantly pulling me over for random searches, and I eventually became exactly what they expected. I wound up dropping out of school, moving through the pipeline to the juvenile justice system. But I was lucky: I'm a light-skinned Latina in addition to being black, and in school was rarely read as the latter. If I had been visibly black, all the statistics suggest, things would have been much worse for me. Of this I am sure. Ask any black woman.

Finally, in "99 Years After the Tulsa Race Massacre, an Artist Reflects," visual artist and writer Crystal Z Campbell brings together personal narrative, narrative nonfiction, poetry, and visual art in this epistolary piece addressed to their hometown of Tulsa, Oklahoma, seeking a reckoning for the horrific and deadly Tulsa Race Massacre of 1921 whose legacy continues to shape lives, including their own. Campbell's investigation of the event and its legacy is reflected throughout the piece—from their artistic renditions of archival photos of the thriving Black neighborhood of Greenwood, attacked and destroyed as residents were massacred by white mobs, to their research into Greenwood's history, to their exploration of their family ancestry, to their personal interrogation of their own conflicted feelings as a Black resident of a hometown unwilling to truly reckon with its own history:

> Oklahoma's history is riddled with pioneers on Indigenous land, land grabs, oil extraction, boomtowns, unchecked privilege, and waves of settler colonialism. I never imagined as a child that some parcels of Oklahoma would be someone's version of

utopia. However, I find comfort in picturing the over fifty Black townships that Oklahoma boasted after the Civil War.

I have always found this state beautiful—and ugly too. I ask, in 2020: How can we be truthful? How can we revisit history in a reparative way? How can we move closer to the impossibility of this utopian vision?

Hopefully, it is now evident that reported, personal, and hybrid perspectives each have their merits and purposes. Writers should consider which approach best serves their story, the requirements of their target publication, and most importantly, their intent and skills as a writer. While each piece we write requires us to make a choice, remember, we can write about the same issue using different approaches, giving us the opportunity to reach and raise awareness in new audiences. Just as importantly, exploring different approaches gives us the chance to discover different aspects of the craft of writing. I close this chapter with this stirring, lyrical evocation of narrative's power to reckon with historical injustice from Campbell's work:

Narratives are skins.
Narratives are tools.
Narratives are weapons.
Narratives are scars.

■

COVID-19 VACCINE: WHAT WHITE CONSERVATIVES CAN LEARN FROM BLACK AMERICANS

By Kavita Das

In November 2020, news broke about the successful development of the first vaccines against COVID-19 and people began to debate whether or not they would be inoculated. As Dr. Anthony S. Fauci, the director of the National Institute of Allergy and Infectious Diseases (NIAID), and the leaders of the Centers for Disease Control (CDC) sought to distribute information to diminish fears about the vaccine's safety and efficacy, and most importantly, its crucial necessity in halting the pandemic; virulent misinformation about the virus and the safety of the injection was spreading rapidly across social media. In the United States alone, COVID-19 has killed nearly 600,000 and sickened more than 33,340,000.

One group that was understandably hesitant about receiving the vaccine was Black Americans. According to the Kaiser Family Foundation, in December 2020, 52% of Black Americans said they would take a wait-and-see approach to the vaccine with only 20% saying that they wanted to be vaccinated as soon as possible. In comparison, skepticism about the COVID-19 vaccine was lower in white (36%) and Latino populations (43%). This was particularly concerning since according to the CDC, Black Americans were 2.9 times more likely to require hospitalization for COVID-19 and 1.9 times more likely to die from the disease than white Americans.

Much of the hesitancy from Black Americans around trusting medical guidance about a new vaccine for an emergent disease is justifiably rooted in the long history of unconscionable racism embedded in the American medical establishment. This is evidenced by Dr. James Marion Sims, who is considered to be the "father" of modern gynecology, conducting experimental surgical procedures on enslaved people without anesthetics or their consent. As well as the infamous Tuskegee Syphilis study, where Black men were denied treatment for syphilis in order to study the disease's long-term impacts. Meanwhile, white Americans reaped the benefits of these medical breakthroughs which came at the expense of Black Americans' health and wellbeing.

However, hesitancy amongst Black Americans is not just rooted in the history of medicine, but is also tied to rampant present-day inequities in American health care. Black Americans contend with myriad health disparities and adverse outcomes. Black mothers are three times more likely to die in childbirth compared to white mothers while Black adults and children are less likely to receive adequate pain medication during an emergency room visit. These inequities are also evident in the uneven rollout of the COVID-19 vaccines. Thus, Black Americans face the compounded risks of underlying health conditions and comorbidities linked in part to health inequities, which make them more vulnerable to COVID-19 while having less access to lifesaving vaccines.

As mentioned, another group that has been exhibiting vaccine hesitancy is white, rural conservatives. Polls conducted by NPR, PBS *NewsHour*, and Marist revealed that rural, white Republicans, and in particular male Trump supporters, were amongst the least likely groups to get the vaccine. Similarly, of the 41 million white evangelicals, 45% stated they wouldn't get a COVID-19 vaccination according to a recent Pew Research Study in February 2021.

In comparison to Black Americans, white conservatives offer very different reasons for not wanting to get the vaccine, which bely a fundamental mistrust in science and government. They also fundamentally believe that their freedom is paramount and surpasses public safety. This makes them especially susceptible to disinformation campaigns seeking to sow suspicion about the government, vaccines, and science, itself.

Months after the initial announcement about the vaccine's arrival, there was a noted increase in interest to receive the shot, which seemed to be in response to multi-pronged outreach efforts targeting Black communities. According to a recent Pew survey in February 2021, 81% of Black Americans saw the pandemic as a major public health threat and 49% saw it as a threat to their own health. And according to the Kaiser Family Foundation, 55% of Black Americans said they would be or have been vaccinated, which shows shifts in perspectives amongst Black Americans on getting the COVID-19 vaccine.

While Federal agencies and public health leaders belatedly began instituting public information campaigns targeting marginalized populations, including Black Americans, what has been particularly notable is the concerted outreach on the ground in Black communities by trusted community organizations.

The African American COVID-19 Educational Outreach initiative, a breakthrough collaboration by Kaiser Permanente, East Bay Community Foundation (EBCF), and twelve community partners across the country was created to "prevent disproportionate death and infection rates in high risk communities of color, to dispel misinformation about COVID-19, provide support to community-based organizations on the ground who have the knowledge, expertise, and relationships with the community, and capture learnings to inform future legislation," explains Sachi Yoshii, EBCF's Vice President of Strategy & External Affairs. Yoshii goes on to note how this initiative "highlights how vaccine access is a racial justice issue." The range of activities includes educational outreach, "come to you" vaccination clinics which are mobile and in trusted spaces including churches and barbershops, messaging campaigns and PSAs featuring local Black health care workers, and social media campaigns featuring local cultural personalities.

Preston DuFauchard, CEO of West Oakland Health Council (WOHC), one of the local partners of EBCF, acknowledges that when the clinic started offering COVID-19 testing and the vaccine, some patients expressed concerns about getting the virus from testing based on misinformation, while others were worried about how rapidly the vaccine was developed and its possible side effects. But given the history of racism and inequity in the health system and the politicization of the vaccine, he says these fears are "completely understandable" and he doesn't think the phrase "vaccine hesitancy" applies to the Black community. "Black people want to take control of their own bodies . . . that control involves being informed consumers about medical services," said DuFauchard.

DuFauchard notes that WOHC has seen shifts in attitudes for both testing and vaccination. "We have found good responsiveness in our patient population for acceptance of the vaccine,"

DuFauchard explained. And this is likely due to the fact that WOHC has built its outreach and vaccination efforts around the needs of the community, from having walk-in hours, to proactively reaching out to their patients to scheduling testing and vaccinations, to having their health care providers, who are part of the community, offer their own testimonies about their vaccine experience. It's worth noting that WOHC has not lost a single patient to COVID-19 throughout this pandemic.

Meanwhile, despite the fact that vaccines are now more accessible, rural counties whose populations are overwhelmingly white and conservative are having trouble convincing this population to get vaccinated. Given the size of this community, their reticence may threaten the country's return to safety and normalcy. A targeted information campaign addressing white conservatives and Evangelicals might offer a possible remedy but faces an uphill battle since their mistrust in science and government is deeply rooted in their conservative beliefs.

The stark contrast we see in the reasons for hesitancy in these two communities as well as their respective reactions to vaccination outreach efforts reflects the historical and present-day story of racism in America. When it comes to Black Americans, despite this group's justified fears and mistrust of the health care system due to historical and ongoing systemic racism, they are taking the advice of experts in their communities by getting vaccinated, protecting themselves and others. Meanwhile, white conservatives, who have not had to endure struggles against a racist health care system, behave as if their beliefs are more important than the nation's public health and collective safety. In truth, their vaccine hesitancy is willful vaccine resistance, risking lives and prolonging the pandemic. Theirs is a virulent privilege, rooted in delusions of white supremacy masquerading as faith and ideals.

In a recent *Rolling Stone* article bioethicist and professor of public health, Dr. Faith E. Fletcher noted the impact of unfair scrutiny on Black Americans around vaccine hesitancy. "To advance health equity, we must actively resist and challenge existing narratives that portray communities of color as risky, irresponsible, and incapable of behavior change, and shift the responsibility to structures that disadvantage some members of society." Notably, what's missing is a corresponding scrutiny for rural white conservatives and the risk they pose as they continue to resist the vaccine not out of circumstance but choice.

As people herald the end of this global crisis and the return to pre-pandemic life, there is an opportunity to recognize and acknowledge that while COVID-19 disrupted lives, it didn't disrupt the systemic racism built into American healthcare. Instead, it painfully underscored it.

■

A VIRULENT PRIVILEGE
by Kavita Das

I.

Carmen slumped into the chair across my desk with a deep sigh. As the manager of immunization at the American Academy of Pediatrics, she had just reviewed and updated the Academy's immunization website, including an immunization schedule dictating which vaccines children should receive and at what age they should receive them based on years of evidence accepted by the medical establishment.

She recounted how every time she checked the site, there were more comments from anti-vaccinators who questioned not only the validity of the schedule but of immunization itself. Anti-vaccinators, she explained, had pointed to the inexplicable rise in autism diagnoses and conjectured a connection to vaccines, or, more specifically, the preservatives used in certain vaccines.

Deadly diseases were not an abstract concept to either of us. Both of my immigrant parents are doctors who deal with disease as a profession, and both Carmen, the eighth of eight children of Mexican-American parents, and my father, who was born in Bangladesh and migrated to India, had contracted dengue fever; she as a Peace Corps volunteer in Jamaica and he as a medical student in Calcutta.

More than ten years after my conversation with Carmen, there was a measles outbreak in the very place that epitomizes American childhood: Disneyland. The episode was like a subplot in a dystopian novel—a warning knell of outbreaks to come. A harmful disease that had long been under control through effective vaccination programs saw a resurgence in many states due to exemption laws that value anti-vaccinators' personal beliefs over community safety.

II.

In her book *On Immunity* (Graywolf Press, 2014), Eula Biss brings together different strains of thought and varied perspectives—artistic and scientific, personal and philosophical—to examine our society's fear of contagion and suspicion of vaccines. In order to do this, Biss draws upon her own research and the research of others, including leading physicians and scientists and science historians, and displays brilliance as a thinker and a writer. But probably her most admirable traits in this endeavor are her honesty and vulnerability as a new mother trying to understand how best to protect her young son.

As you read *On Immunity*, Biss introduces you to some of the key concepts and controversies surrounding vaccines. One of the first concepts we're introduced to is one that is central to the effectiveness of vaccinations: herd immunity, the collective immunity acquired when a certain number of individuals in that community, or "herd," have been vaccinated against a disease.

"It is fair to think of vaccination as a kind of banking of immunity. Contributions to this bank are donations to those who cannot or will not be protected by their own immunity," Biss writes.

Therefore, in order for a vaccine program to be most effective, members of a community must value public health over individual well-being and, ultimately, must prioritize the greater good over personal choice. A prerequisite for any effective vaccine program is to provide vaccines that are much less dangerous than the diseases they protect against.

Despite reams of data from countless studies showing that adverse effects of vaccines are rare and minimal, these fears persist, stoked by a few stalwarts at the center of the anti-vaccine movement. They persist even after the movement's singular study was debunked and its author, the key physician in the movement, was discredited. Why?

"Our fears are dear to us," Biss contends, writing about the historical, cultural, and personal origins of that entrenched emotion. "When we encounter information that contradicts our beliefs . . . we tend to doubt the information, not ourselves."

In order for someone to value public health over individual health, they have to see themselves as part of the broader public. This is not the case when people view public health programs as programs for people other than themselves, and, more specifically, people "less" than themselves. Biss herself confesses, "The belief that public health measures are not intended for people like us is widely held by many people like me. Public health, we assume, is for people with less—less education, less health habits, less access to quality health care, less time and money."

Another notion that Biss introduces us to in the vaccine debate is the implication that natural equates with purity, and that man-made equates with contamination. "What *natural* has come to mean to us in the context of medicine is pure and safe and benign. But the use of natural as a synonym for good is almost certainly a product of our profound alienation from the natural world."

As biological agents made by man and administered by physicians, where do vaccines fall? Are they natural or man-made, benign or toxic?

Biss explores both the appeal and the peril of applying the notion of natural to vaccines. "Allowing children to develop immunity to contagious diseases naturally without vaccination is appealing to some of us. Much of that appeal depends on the belief that vaccines are inherently unnatural. But vaccines are of the liminal place between humans and nature . . . The most unnatural aspect of vaccination is that it does not, when all goes well, introduce disease or produce illness."

I was disabused of any romanticizing of the natural from a very early age. First, growing up in an immigrant family, I was among people for whom everyday life was somewhat unnatural, given that they were separated from their homeland. And yet, the abundant opportunities I had were a direct result of this migration.

As a child, I received experimental growth hormone treatment because of a hereditary insufficiency, which put me at risk of not reaching puberty and other health complications. So the notion that *natural* is always better is not one to which I innately subscribe.

What's more, the value of the natural is not universal; rather, this value is arbitrated by forces that outwardly look global, but inwardly seem neocolonial. My household, like many other South Indian households, regarded coconut oil as a staple. We cooked certain specialties in the oil because of the unique flavor and smell it imparted, and we rubbed it into our skin, scalp, and hair as an emollient, especially during New York's long winters. Similarly, coconut water was an inexpensive treat bought on the side of the road during summers in India from a vendor who lopped off the top of a tender coconut to reveal the nectar within.

But within a few years all that stopped. In the 1980s, flawed scientific information made the rounds claiming that coconut oil, high in saturated fat, was extremely harmful to heart health and cholesterol. So, despite their medical knowledge and their cultural understanding of its significance, my parents, like so many other Indian-Americans, all but abandoned coconut oil. Meanwhile, teased at school for my long shiny braids, I stopped using it for hair care.

Three decades later, coconut water and coconut oil have come roaring back: they're all the rage amongst yoga practitioners and hipsters alike. But its current iteration has been relabeled a premium product: at Walmart, it costs nearly twice as much per ounce as orange juice. It seems like every week, a beauty magazine "discovers" the soothing properties of coconut oil, lauding, as *Allure* put it, "Unexpected Beauty Uses" for the substance. But worse yet are the unfounded claims that it can serve as a natural alternative to medical treatment for everything from hair loss to heart disease.

In many ways, popular attitudes towards coconut oil and vaccines are two sides of the same coin: just as devotees of the "natural" lionize coconut oil for unproven health benefits, anti-vaccinators demonize vaccines for unproven toxicities. In the latter case, the consequences are truly hazardous to public health.

A recent research review featured in *The Journal of the American Medical Association* concluded that "A substantial proportion of the US measles cases in the era after elimination were intentionally unvaccinated. The phenomenon of vaccine refusal was associated with an increased risk for measles among people who refuse vaccines and among fully vaccinated individuals." In reaction to the research review, a pediatric researcher told *Reuters*, "What this latest comprehensive review illustrates is that individuals who refuse vaccines not only put themselves at risk for disease, it turns out that they also put others at risk too—even people who have been vaccinated before, but whose protection from those vaccinations may not be as strong as it used to be."

However, given that I first learned of the anti-vaccine movement back in 2003 (almost fourteen years ago), I wonder why such a virulent movement has been allowed to exist and grow to the point where herd immunity has eroded, putting at risk those who are vaccinated and those who aren't. Why are their personal beliefs prioritized by state and national health agencies above the health and well-being of the rest of our citizens?

To understand this, I view the anti-vaccine movement through the lens of our societal attitudes on race and class. Biss speaks to our society's inherent and outsized fear of contagion being brought into our borders from those regarded as foreign, deemed as *other*.

She notes the historical context for this fear: "Avoidance of outsiders, of immigrants, of people missing limbs, or people with marks on their faces is an ancient tactic for disease prevention. And this has fed, no doubt, the longstanding belief that disease is a product of those we define as others."

Biss goes on to underscore the impact of our fear of contagion from "others": "Our tendency towards prejudice can increase whenever we feel particularly vulnerable or threatened by disease . . . The more vulnerable we feel, sadly, the more small-minded we become."

We have only to look at the response by many, including the media, to some recent events. For example, when children fleeing violence-ridden Central American countries arrived in droves across the American border two years ago, right wing media raised concerns about the diseases they were bringing with them and portrayed them as "anchor babies." Even mainstream media outlets, like NBC News, referred to these children using such sterile terms as "unaccompanied alien children," and other outlets like CNN and BBC discussed these children being "caught" and "apprehended" rather than rescued. Similarly, when the Ebola epidemic was rising amongst countries in Africa, many called for a lockdown of flights to those countries, even forgoing sending aid and aid workers, stating that the risk of bringing back the disease was too high. Ebola, but not its victims, saturated our 24/7 media cycle. Our paranoia overwhelmed our humanity. Thankfully, science and compassion eventually won out and our fickle attention span turned to the next crisis, real or perceived.

By contrast, the anti-vaccine movement has remained relatively uncovered by the mainstream media for years, hiding in plain sight. Their members have been viewed as more bohemian and eccentric than threatening or harmful. Anti-vaccine moms are cast as misguided but well-meaning rather than neglectful or selfish. Biss provides some useful insight into the demographics of the unvaccinated: "Unvaccinated children, a 2004 analysis of CDC data reveals, are more likely to be white, to have an older married mother with a college education, and to live in a household with an income of $75,000 or more . . . Unvaccinated children also tend to be clustered in the same areas, raising the probability that they will contract a disease that can then be passed, once it is in circulation, to undervaccinated children. Undervaccinated children, meaning children who have received some but not all of their recommended immunizations, are more likely to be black, to have a younger unmarried mother, to have moved across state lines, and to live in poverty."

What is especially telling about this data is the stark contrast between the race and class of unvaccinated and undervaccinated children. It underscores dual narratives: one of choice, one of circumstance. It also begs the question: would this movement have been allowed to grow, endangering the lives of all children, if it was largely populated by poor families of color rather than driven by middle-class white families? Would its members have been generously perceived as misguided but well-intentioned rather than misinformed and dangerous? Ultimately, these individuals working to undermine the protection offered by vaccinations to our nation's children have been protected by their own race and class privilege—benefiting from another type of herd immunity.

III.

As I arrived at the college health center, I was proud at not having gotten lost during my first day on this beautiful but expansive campus. I stepped into the office, pulled my medical and immunization records from my bag, and handed them to a nurse behind a desk. As I waited for her to look them over and approve them, I thought about my class schedule and how ingenious it would be for me to sign up for microeconomics instead of General Chemistry, thereby thwarting my parents' plans for me to pursue pre-med. Suddenly, her voice interrupted my scheming.

"Your immunization records are incomplete."

"What?!" I was shocked, even incredulous.

"According to your records, you haven't had a TB test and it doesn't look like you completed your MMR."

"Oh! I'll make sure to get it done over fall break." I was surprised that my parents had overlooked these holes in my immunization schedule but I wasn't worried about getting it taken care of during my next visit home.

"Oh no! I can't let you register for classes until you get these done. We can do them here, if you'd like, but you'll have to pay for them."

I wanted to object but I knew that resistance was futile. "OK," I said dejectedly.

"Take a seat and I'll call you when we're ready for you."

As I turned to take a seat in the waiting area, I saw a young white woman in dungarees with untamed curls, the kind I've always envied. Her arms were crossed in front of her and her expression captured perfectly how I felt.

With nothing else to do, we struck up a conversation. She told me she was from Kentucky and I told her I was from New Jersey. She told me that she was the first person in her family to go to college and I told her about my scheme to not become a doctor. We shared our frustrations at having to get on-the-spot vaccinations, especially since tonight was the Freshman Dance Party. When I asked her which vaccinations she was here to get, she responded, "all of 'em," and gave a laugh.

Later that night, we ran into each other at the dance party. She showed off all her vaccination marks like they were badges of honor. Over the next four years, we would wave to each other across campus. I lost track of my classmate from Kentucky, but my scheming was successful—I'm the only person in my family who isn't a doctor. When I think back to that moment, I'm thankful that vaccination wasn't a choice, because I've been able to make so many more.

■

LA OTRA, ADAPTED FROM
ORDINARY GIRLS
By Jaquira Díaz

1985. These were the days of Menudo and "We Are the World," the year boxer Macho Camacho gave a press conference in a leopard-skin loincloth as Madonna's "Like a Virgin" blared from radios across the United States. In one month, the space shuttle *Challenger* would explode while all of America watched on television, entire classrooms full of kids, everyone eager to witness the first teacher ever launched into space. My mother had just turned 22, and a week later Levy turned 8. By then, Mami had three children. She'd already been a mother for more than a third of her life.

In those days, Mami teased her blond hair like Madonna, traced her green eyes with blue eyeliner, applied several coats of black mascara, apple-red lipstick, and matching nail polish. She wore skin-tight jeans and always, no matter where she was going, high heels. She dusted her chest with talcum powder after a bath, lotioned her arms and legs, perfumed her body and her hair. My mother loved lotions, perfume, makeup, clothes, shoes. But really, these were just things to her. The truth was my mother loved and enjoyed her body. She walked around our apartment butt-ass naked. I was more used to seeing her naked body than my own. *You should love your body*, my mother taught me. A woman's body was beautiful, no matter how big, how small, how old, how pregnant. This my mother firmly believed, and she would tell me over and over. As we got older, she would teach me and Alaina about masturbation, giving us detailed instructions about how to achieve orgasm. This, she said, was perfectly normal. Nothing to be ashamed of.

While my father only listened to salsa on vinyl, Héctor Lavoe and Willie Colón and Ismael Rivera, my mother was all about

Madonna. She was American, she liked to remind us, born in New York, and she loved everything American, including her music. She belted the lyrics to "Holiday" while shaving her legs in the shower, while making us egg salad sandwiches for lunch. She talked about moving us to Miami Beach, where most of our *titis* and Grandma Mercy lived, about making sure we learned English.

On New Year's Eve, she made me wear a red-and-white-striped dress and white patent leather shoes. It was hideous. I looked like a peppermint candy. When she styled my hair in fat candy curls, she said she wanted me to look like Shirley Temple. I had no idea who Shirley Temple was, but I hoped she didn't expect me to be friends with her. I wasn't trying to be friends with girls in dresses and uncomfortable shoes. At 6, I was more of a bare-feet-and-shorts kind of girl.

I knew that these were things meant for girls, and that I was supposed to like them. But I had no interest in my mother's curtains, or her tubes of red lipstick, or her dresses, or the dolls Grandma Mercy and Titi Sandy sent from Miami. I didn't want to be Barbie for Halloween, like my mother suggested. I wanted to be a ninja, with throwing stars and nunchucks and a sword. I wanted to kick the shit out of 10,000 men like Bruce Lee. I wanted to climb trees and catch frogs and play with *Star Wars* action figures, to fight with lightsabers and build model spaceships. I didn't have a crush on Atreyu from *The NeverEnding Story*, like my brother said, teasing me. I wanted to *be* Atreyu, to ride Falkor the luck dragon. When I watched *Conan the Destroyer*, I didn't want to be the princess. I wanted to be fierce and powerful Grace Jones. Zula, the woman warrior. I wanted her to be the one who saves the princess, to be the one the princess falls for in the end.

Years later, would I think of Zula during that first kiss, that first throbbing between my legs? It would be with an older girl, the daughter of my parents' friends. We'd steal my mother's cigarettes, take them out back behind our building, and light them up. She would blow her smoke past my face, stick her tongue in my mouth, slide her hand inside my shorts. How she'd know just what to do without me having to tell her—this was everything, this butch girl, so unafraid, getting everything she wanted. And how willing I was to give it to her.

She arrived in the middle of the night, our new neighbor, carried her boxes from somebody's pickup into her living room, then waved goodbye as it drove away. She arrived in silence, filling the empty space of the apartment next door, where nobody had ever lived as long as I could remember, and hung her flowerpots from hooks in the balcony. She arrived with almost nothing, just those plants and some furniture and her daughter Jesenia, a year older than me.

The morning after, my best friend Eggy and I were outside catching lizards, holding on to them until they got away, leaving their broken-off tails still wriggling between our fingers. She stepped out on her balcony, watering her plants with a plastic cup.

"Guess you have a new neighbor," Eggy said.

La vecina, as we learned to call her, was nothing like Mami. She wore no makeup, a faded floral housedress, and out-of-style leather chancletas like my grandmother's, her curly brown hair in a low ponytail. She had deep wrinkles around the corners of her eyes, although she didn't look as old as Abuela. When she looked up at Eggy and me, she smiled.

"Hola," she said. "Where's your mom?"

"Working," I said.

She pressed her hand to her cheek. "And she lets you play outside by yourself?"

"Sure," I said.

We talked for a while, la vecina asking us questions about the neighborhood, about the basketball courts, about what time the grano man came by on Sunday mornings. Eggy and I answered question after question, feeling like hostages, until my father emerged.

"Buenas," Papi said.

La vecina introduced herself, and Papi walked over, shook her hand over her balcony's railing. They got to talking, ignoring me and Eggy, Papi smiling, the way he never smiled. My father always had a serious look on his face, a look that made him seem angry, even when he was happy. He ironed his polo shirts, always trying to look good, grooming his mustache every morning, massaging Lustrasilk Right on Curl into his afro before picking it out, even if he was just lying around the house on the weekend. The only time my father dressed down—in shorts, tank tops, and his white Nike Air Force high-tops—was when he played ball or when we went to the beach.

La vecina laughed at something he said, and my father patted his afro lightly. When I saw the opening, I tapped Eggy on the shoulder and we took off running toward the basketball courts.

Sometimes, when Mami was at work and Levy at school, Papi took me to Abuela's house for lunch. Abuela lived in the next building over. Her kitchen always smelled like fried meat and café, her bedroom a blend of Maja soap, bay rum, and Bal à Versailles perfume. The second bedroom belonged to my tío David, who was a priest at the Catholic Church in the city and only came home occasionally.

In Abuela's apartment, where he'd lived before he and Mami got married, before we were born, Papi was at home. He had a special bookcase there, and some books I was not allowed to touch—expensive, signed first editions on the top shelf, stories not meant for children on the second. That bookcase was his refuge, where he sometimes went when Mami was yelling or flinging plates across the room. He'd sit in Abuela's kitchen, turning pages, always with his café. I would do the same, take a book off the lower shelf, sit at the table trying to make out which words I knew, as if this would transfer a sort magic to me—secrets only Papi knew.

Abuela always said I was like Papi's tail, that when he came into a room, I was usually not far behind. *You are just like your father,* she'd say, knowing how much I loved hearing that. She'd tell me stories about Papi as a kid. Cano, my father's nickname, given to him by my tío David when he was a baby, meant "light." When he was born, my father had been a light-skinned baby with very light hair, and my uncle, three years older, found that hilarious. *La vecina introduced herself, and Papi walked over, shook her hand over her balcony's railing. They got to talking, ignoring me and Eggy, Papi smiling, the way he never smiled.*

Cano, Abuela told me, would climb guayaba trees to steal fruit, sneak out of the house to run through the cañaverales with the street kids. He was always getting in trouble. Cano throwing down with the school bully to defend my tío, the quiet, Jesus-loving kid who refused to fight. Cano getting whooped with a belt by the assistant principal for smacking another kid upside the head. Cano, who'd spent a short time in the Army. Cano the prankster, the papichulo with a girlfriend in every other town, always finding trouble. Cano, who—before any of us were born—had taken off to New York for a couple of years after trouble finally found *him.*

Every time I ran into la vecina, she wanted to talk. She lived alone with her daughter, Jesenia, she told me. Jesenia wasn't in school yet, but she would be starting in a couple of days. Jesenia was shy. Jesenia loved to watch TV. *Do you want to watch a movie with Jesenia? Do you want to jump rope with Jesenia?* I hadn't seen this Jesenia yet, but I was already done with her.

One morning, with Mami at work and Papi asleep on the couch, la vecina caught me leaving our apartment. She was sweeping the front steps when I came out, and called after me when I tried to sneak past her. "Jaqui, wait!" She leaned the broom against her door and sat on the stoop, tapping the space next to her.

I exhaled dramatically, then plopped down on the step.

"Where were you headed?" she asked.

"Out."

"Is your brother at school?"

"Yes."

"Is your mom at work?"

"Yes."

"When does she come home?"

"I don't know."

"Does she come home at night?"

I rolled my eyes. "Yes, she comes home at night."

"Is your father home?"

"He's sleeping."

"Does he take care of you when your mother's not home?"

I studied her face, trying to figure out why all the questions about my parents. "Sometimes Abuela takes care of us."

"Who makes dinner for you?"

"Abuela," I said. "And sometimes Papi."

"What do you like to eat?"

"Ice cream."

She laughed. "What about your father?"

I shrugged. "He likes arroz con pollo, I guess."

At first it felt like being interrogated, but after a while I was so happy to have a grown-up listening to me talk about myself, I let it all out. I told her about the kioskos on the beach where Papi took me to eat ensalada de pulpo. I told her all about how Levy almost died when he was born, how they kept him in the hospital for two months because he was so little, how he'd had machines to help him breathe. I told her how Levy and I were always fighting, how I wasn't supposed to go to the plaza, but I still snuck over there sometimes. She listened to every word I said, *really* listened, even laughed when I made a joke. Then, I don't know what made me do it, but I told her about the tecato who came up to our balcony and pulled out his dick.

"Do you know who he was?" she asked.

"No, but I've seen him before."

"Did you tell your father?"

"No."

"You know," she said, "if you ever need to, you can talk to me."
She looked right into my eyes and waited.

"Okay," I said. And I believed her.

Levy, Alaina, and I shared a cramped bedroom—linoleum covering the concrete floors, aluminum persianas, spiderweb cracks on
cinder block walls. Levy's twin bed against one wall, mine against
the opposite, Alaina's crib in the middle. The thick smell of something burning in the air, wafting from the cañaverales, from the
nearby mills where they made sugar and guarapo de caña.

I woke up sweaty, Levy still snoring, Alaina sitting up, crying
softly, her chubby fingers in her mouth, brown curls stuck to her
moist forehead. Pedro Conga's "Soy Peregrino" blared from the
record player in our living room.

I could hear Mami and Papi arguing in the kitchen. My mother
slamming plates and silverware in the sink, asking over and over
about la otra, a dirty fucking whore she could smell all over him,
this woman who had taken the money *she* worked for, the money
she brought home to take care of her children while my father was
chillin' with his homeboys in la plaza.

My father denied everything. There was no smell on him.
He had not spent the night with another woman. He'd gone out
with friends and was too drunk to drive home. She was imagining things. She was making shit up. How could she think that he
would ever do something like that? It was ridiculous. It was *crazy*.

"Don't you call me crazy!" my mother yelled. Then she started
screaming, like she really *was* crazy, the sound of it threatening
to crack the cinder block walls around us. I would remember this
moment when, a few years older, I'd listen to my mother screaming, wailing, during another one of their fights. All of us already
living in Miami Beach, Levy, Alaina, and I hiding in the bedroom,
our parents hurling coffee mugs and ashtrays at each other, yank-
ing the phone off the wall, turning over the dining room table.
My father already so fed up with Mami, with all of us, he would

accuse her of making shit up, call her foolish, ridiculous, *crazy*. And my mother, not even 30 and already in the snares of schizophrenia and addiction and three kids at war with each other, with themselves, Levy pounding on me, depression already like a noose around my neck.

Another day, la vecina's apartment door wide open, she caught me as I was coming home from the basketball courts, sweaty and breathless, my face hot from the sun.

"Hey, Jaqui!" she called after me, "come in and play with Jesenia!"

I didn't know how to say no to her, and I didn't think she'd like it if I told her that Eggy and I always avoided Jesenia when we saw her riding her bike out front. Jesenia and her Jesenia dresses, one in every color of the rainbow, and her folded-down ankle socks. Jesenia with ribbons in her hair. Jesenia and her stupid pigtails. She was everything I wasn't. I had a mass of sunburned frizz that stood straight up and I liked it that way. Whenever Mami put ribbons in my hair, they ended up on the floor, or stuffed between the couch cushions, or in one of Abuela's planters.

She led me into her kitchen, where her only table was a child-size plastic one with two small red chairs. Jesenia sat there, a plate of chocolate chip cookies in front of her, getting crumbs all over her purple dress. Her pigtails were perfect, each plaited into a tight, long braid and secured with a ribbon. La vecina pulled out the other chair and set a small plate for me.

"Jesenia, say hello to Jaqui."

Jesenia barely looked at me. "Hola."

I nodded, took a cookie, and instead of playing with Jesenia, I answered more questions for la vecina.

"Where does your father work?"

"He goes to the university," I told her, even though I could not remember the last time my father took any classes.

"Really? What does he study?"

"Books," I said, which made her laugh.

Jesenia got up, pushed her chair aside, and left the room.

La vecina poured a cup of milk, set it on the table, then wiped her hands on her dress. "So what's your mother like?"

I studied her for a minute, not sure what she was asking. La vecina was nothing like Mami. My mother would never wear a dress like my abuela's, would never smell like fried plantains and pine oil, would never ask question after question before getting to the point. My mother was direct and she took no shit. She got right to it. We got to a party and right away she was dancing. She was small but scared of nothing, a foulmouthed chain-smoker with a hot temper, who drove a stick shift Mazda Rx-7, who never set foot outside without makeup, without her door-knocker earrings, her heels. As petite as she was, my mother owned every room she walked into. She eclipsed the sun with her confidence, took the world by the throat and shook it until it gave up what was hers. You crossed her and she was ready to throw down on the spot, taking off earrings and heels and tying up her hair. She was curvy, with a swing in her hips, and everywhere we went she had admirers, leering men asking her name, asking for her phone number, calling after her, *Mira, mami!* But she didn't give any of them the time of day. My mother was utterly and completely in love with my father. Hers was the blazing, frenzied love of Puerto Rican novelas, the kind of love that drives you mad. She loved her children, the three of us—Levy, Alaina, and me—even more so. And she never let us forget it.

La vecina waited for me to respond. This woman. I just couldn't picture her in red stilettos and a fishnet dress, dancing like Madonna in front of her TV.

"She's blonde," I said finally, "with green eyes like my brother. And she likes Madonna."

Jesenia came back into the room, dropped a bunch of dolls on the table. "Do you like Barbies?" she asked.

"Sure," I said, which was not entirely true. I had Barbies, dolls Mami had given me for my birthday or Christmas, or that my titis had handed down to me. But I didn't exactly *like* them. They were like reminders of everything I wasn't—blond-haired, blue-eyed. They always made me feel ugly, the brown kid who would never look like her white mother. They'd end up on the floor, tossed aside, with their heads bald. Later, when I learned about sex, I started posing them strategically: Barbie and Barbie facing each other, kissing, their stiff arms sticking up, naked Barbie on top of naked Barbie.

"Do you want to take your father some lunch?" la vecina asked.

"Okay," I said.

She sent me home with a platter of arroz con pollo, some red beans on the side. It was so heavy I almost dropped it walking through our front door, but Abuela took it off my hands.

Hours later, after Abuela was already gone, Levy watching TV, and Alaina in her crib, Mami walked through the door, tired from work. She sat at the kitchen table, rubbing her feet.

"Did you eat?" she asked. "I'll make you something."

"I already ate," I said. "Had some of la vecina's arroz con pollo."

"La vecina?" my mother asked.

"She sent a big platter of food for Papi."

Suddenly, my mother got up, slamming her fist on the table. I jumped back, almost falling over.

My mother shut her eyes tight, brought her hands to her face. Then, without warning, she stomped out of the kitchen.

My father, again, denied everything. He followed my mother as she came back to the kitchen.

"It's not true, Jeannette," he said. "I don't know what she's talking about."

My mother opened the refrigerator, searching, opened the freezer, the oven, lifted the lid to our trash can. She inspected the dishes in the sink, opened and closed all the cabinets, searching and searching. When she didn't find what she was looking for, she came over and took me by the arm.

"Show me," she said. "Where is it?"

I looked for la vecina's platter everywhere, opening drawers and checking the fridge again, but nothing.

"I don't know," I said, tears starting to sting my eyes.

"I'm telling you," my father said, "it never happened."

I looked to my father, trying to understand, searched his face, tried to look in his eyes. But there was nothing there that could clear things up. I burst into tears.

Mami looked back and forth from Papi to me then Papi again. She finally turned back to me, leaning down so her face met mine. "Are you lying?" she asked me.

I couldn't get any words out. My mother was mad as hell, standing there, breathing hard, the stink of her cigarette on my face.

"It never happened," Papi said again.

My mother did not move, did not say a word. She was waiting for me to break. I kept crying, looking at my father for answers. He looked at my mother, beads of sweat collecting at his temple. But he would not look at me.

"I don't know what she's talking about," my father said, looking down at his feet, at the floor, at the wall, at the stove, unable to meet my eyes. And then, finally, I understood.

That night, I would swipe Mami's sewing scissors, cut the hair off every single one of my Barbies, the ones that still had any hair, and flush it in bunches down the toilet. I would pull my father's favorite book off the shelf, Hugo Margenat's *Obras Completas*, slide it under my mattress. And while my parents yelled at each other and threw the rotating table fan across the room and threatened to leave, I would lay my head on my pillow and feel nothing but the sharp sting of my father's betrayal.

Days later, Eggy and I walking back from Abuela's house, where we'd polished off a half dozen mangoes by ourselves, our faces and forearms sticky with juice and pulp, we ran into a mob of people outside my building. Eggy's mom and his brothers, the guy who sold pinchos around the corner from the front gate, a bunch of street kids, some viejas who lived a couple buildings over, everybody rowdy, hollering, shoving each other.

I spotted Pito and Levy and lost Eggy as I pushed through the crowd to get to them.

"What's going on?" I asked.

Pito pointed toward the middle of the group, his face sweaty and red. He elbowed one of the other kids out of the way and pulled me by the arm, trying to squeeze us both through the small space.

"Your mom!" he yelled.

Somebody rammed me right into Pito. I almost fell, but kept moving, struggling through the throng of people, bumping them with my shoulders.

Behind me, my brother shoved me, yelling at the back of my head. "Move!"

"I'm trying!" I hollered back.

When a space opened up, Pito thrust through it until we made it to the front. The crowd was opening up when I saw them: Papi had Mami in his arms, trying to hold her back. Mami was kicking and slapping at my father, trying to get free, her hair windblown and tangled.

Our upstairs neighbor, a six-foot-six basketball player everybody called Gigante, was holding la vecina, her curly hair pulled out of its ponytail and torn to shreds. La vecina swung both arms blindly, aiming for anything she could hit.

When Papi tried to carry Mami toward our front door, she slid down and got loose, and all the street kids exploded, Pito and Levy and Eggy calling out, "Light her up! Knock her out! Préndela!" It was the same kind of shouting we heard in our living room during boxing matches, my father and his friends knocking back Medallas in front of the TV, everybody jumping to their feet when Macho Camacho started wailing on José Luis Ramírez, hollering, *Knock him out! Light him up! Préndelo!*

La vecina was nothing like Mami. My mother would never wear a dress like my abuela's, would never smell like fried plantains and pine oil, would never ask question after question before getting to the point. My mother was direct and she took no shit.

My mother tangled her hands in la vecina's hair, pulled her down out of Gigante's arms and onto the ground, and started kicking. My father got a hold of Mami again, picked her up in the air, my mother red-faced and shrieking, arms flailing, spit flying out of her mouth. He carried her inside.

Gigante helped la vecina get up. She had three long, bloody scratches over her nose and mouth, like claw marks.

Just then, as la vecina was getting to her feet, my mother burst through the front door, a steak knife in her hand, the crowd moving back, opening up more space between themselves and my mother. Everything seemed to slow down, Pito and Levy and Eggy, all of them, disappearing until it was just me and my mother and my mother's knife, the three of us echoing through the years, propelled forward in time, and because I am my mother's daughter more than I have ever been my father's, it will be this moment I think of when I'm a 14-year-old hoodlum tucking razor blades into the sides of my Jordans, brass knuckles and Master combination locks and pocket knives in my backpack; when I am 15 and getting jumped by five girls at the bus stop; when I am 16 and trying to decide how to deal with a friend who has betrayed me; when I am 17 and fighting with my brother. How I would always come back to this, my mother and her knife and all that rage, la vecina leaping back out of her way. And then my father, my father's face, my father's hands, my father's voice, *Jeannette, let go of the knife*, how he took both of her hands into his, saying it over and over, *Suelta el cuchillo, suelta el cuchillo, suelta el cuchillo.*

But my mother would not let it go. Instead, Papi lifted her hands above her head, trying to pry it from her fingers, and Mami bit his shoulder, kicked him. He leaned her up against the doorway, pressing his body against hers until she couldn't move, subduing her, and when he was finally able to get the knife, some of the onlookers rushed to help. It took three grown men to get Mami, kicking and slapping and hurling insults at them, back inside our apartment.

Outside, as the crowd split—while la vecina was still fixing her hair and clothes, limping around looking for her chancletas—I saw Jesenia. She saw me, too. Standing on the front lawn, outside the crowd's perimeter, Jesenia in one of her Jesenia dresses, a white one with big yellow flowers, her hair parted down the middle, braided. How she stood there, alone, her face stained with tears, how nobody else seemed to see her, how nobody stopped as they headed back to their apartments or the basketball courts or la plaza, how nobody asked if she was OK, if she needed help, anything. I'd like to say that when I saw her, Jesenia looking back at me, yellow ribbons in her hair, that we had a moment, that as we looked into each other's eyes, we both understood that we had been lost, that we had been lucky to find each other in a crowd, and we both thought, *Here is a girl who sees me. Here is a girl who understands.*

The truth is we did have a moment, Jesenia and I, seeing each other, knowing each other, and it was clear: We were the same. I hated her, and she hated me. Because we were our mothers' daughters. Because we could not turn back time to the days when our mothers were just girls, or forward, when we would finally break free of them. Because back then we could not see what either of us would become.

■

THE SCHOOL-TO-PRISON PIPELINE IS GETTING WORSE FOR BLACK AND BROWN GIRLS

By Jaquira Díaz

In the US, black and Latinx girls are disproportionately punished and assaulted by school administrators for simple infractions such as showing emotions.

More than 20 years ago, when I was a 12-year-old queer kid coming to terms with her sexuality, I ran away from home. It was after school had let out for the summer, and I spent two weeks in the Florida Keys, joyriding with neighborhood boys, sleeping under a stilt-house restaurant and smoking cigarettes. I was an angry, depressed girl who had spent her childhood pretending to be someone else—except when I found myself in my school's music room. I took guitar and voice lessons, sang in the school chorus and Christmas musical, played the piano. I spent hours writing song lyrics in composition books, choreographed song-and-dance routines for school talent shows. If there was music involved, I was there.

After two weeks in the Keys, I returned home, and was immediately taken to the Miami Beach police department for questioning. Who had I been with? How did I get to Key Largo? Why did I run away? Was there trouble at home? These were all questions I had expected, meant to help the police determine if someone had taken me, if I was being abused. But then the questioning changed course. When exactly had I broken into my elementary school in South Beach? Why had I vandalized the music room? I hadn't, I insisted. What a ridiculous idea! I loved our music teacher, Ms Amor. She had known me for most of my life.

Even though the cops had verified my alibi, had confirmed that I had spent two weeks three hours from Miami, they insisted I had done it. They were convinced I was a delinquent, that I had stolen equipment from Ms Amor's music room and tagged my nickname all over her office. The most painful part was how the information had come to them: Ms Amor, they said, had called them to report me herself.

In the United States, black and Latinx girls are disproportionately punished, criminalized and even physically assaulted in their schools by their teachers, administrators and school police officers. Often they are suspended, expelled or arrested for infractions such as falling asleep in class, talking back to school officials or simply for showing what are considered acceptable emotions when it comes to their white classmates.

On 15 January this year, four black and Latinx 12-year-old girls were strip-searched at East middle school in Binghamton, New York. After interacting with the girls in the hallway, the principal, Tim Simonds, found that they seemed to be on drugs. He suspected that they were concealing prohibited substances under their clothes, so he took the girls to the school nurse's office where, for over an hour, they were questioned and given sobriety tests. No one called their parents for consent. Instead, as instructed by the principal, the school nurse and the assistant principal, Michelle Raleigh, told the girls to remove their clothes while they watched. The one girl who refused to disrobe was suspended, and no drugs were found.

Why did Simonds suspect the girls of drug use? According to the NAACP Legal Defense Fund, which is now representing the students' families, the principal called three of the girls' parents after the search to say that they had been sent to the school nurse because they had appeared "hyper and giddy" after lunch. The school board now denies that the strip-search happened.

The racial disparity in punishments enforced at and by American schools is staggering: a 2015 report by the African American Policy Forum and Columbia Law School's Center for Intersectionality and Social Policy Studies has found that black boys are three times more likely and black girls six times more likely to be suspended than their white counterparts. Black girls, according to the report, have even been punished for wearing their hair naturally.

The cases in point are endless. In 2015, a South Carolina school police officer grabbed a 16-year-old girl named Shakara by the neck, violently slamming her backwards (while her body was still in her seat), and dragging her across the classroom floor, allegedly because she had been "disruptive" and argued with her teacher. Her classmate, Niya, who yelled at the cop, calling him abusive, was arrested too. In 2013, 16-year-old Kiera Wilmot, an honors student, was arrested and taken to a juvenile detention center in Florida after a science experiment she had been working on reacted badly and caused a cloud of smoke to erupt from a bottle. The small explosion didn't damage any property or hurt anyone, but she was charged with possessing and discharging a weapon. In Hoover, Alabama, 16-year-old Ashlynn Avery, who suffered from diabetes, asthma and sleep apnea, fell asleep in class and was hit with a book by a teacher. Later, the police were called to remove her from the classroom because she kept falling asleep; she was beaten and arrested. In Avon Park, Florida, six-year-old Desre'e Watson was arrested for throwing a tantrum in her kindergarten class. She was handcuffed and taken to central booking at the county jail.

Although many of these stories make national headlines, and in some cases videos of the incidents go viral, the very real problem of the school-to-prison pipeline is getting worse, particularly for black and brown girls. The Juvenile Detention Alternatives Initiative found that in 1992, black girls comprised 29% of all girls with juvenile court cases; in 2002, the number was 30%; and by 2009, it was 40%. By all accounts, this increase is not due to a rise in the criminal activity of black girls. It comes down to decisions made by white school officials and police officers—the choice to arrest and detain black girls when their white counterparts are not punished similarly.

These decisions, according to an extensive study conducted by the Georgetown Law Center on Poverty and Inequality, the Human Rights Project for Girls, and the Ms. Foundation for Women, have been "shown often to be based in part on the perception of girls having violated conventional norms and stereotypes of feminine behavior, even when that behavior is caused by trauma." In other words, black and brown girls are typically marginalized at school in these ways because officials judge that they aren't feminine enough, or the right kind of feminine. Black "giddiness" is considered suspect, black hair is "distracting" and any black girl who expresses unchecked emotion, even a six-year-old, can be sent to the county jail.

Teachers might de-escalate situations rather than involving the police, prioritizing their black and brown students' emotional wellbeing and physical safety, as they do with white children. School authorities and police officers could make choices that protect black and brown girls, that support them, rather than choices that lead to their assault and arrest, increasing the risk that they will end up pushed out of the school system and into the juvenile justice system. School policies could, and should, emphasize counseling rather than punishment.

I don't have to tell you that Ms Amor—whose name I have changed to protect her anonymity—was white. That even though we had spent many hours together over the years she had been my music teacher, even though I loved her and trusted her and felt safe with her, it was easy for her to believe that I had vandalized her property. When she saw the damage done to the music room, to her office, she didn't think of the Whitney Houston-loving child who dreamed of one day being in Broadway musicals, which was how I saw myself. What she imagined was a brown girl capable of vandalism, breaking and entering, stealing. She thought I would destroy the one place that had brought me joy.

And I don't have to tell you that the principal, the assistant principal, and the school nurse at East middle school—who saw these black and brown children's excitement and decided it was criminal—were all white. Would they have assumed that white children laughing and playing were on drugs? Would they have demanded that white children who seemed hyper, or happy, or silly, remove their clothes to prove they weren't guilty of a crime? Would they have called their parents first? After the incident, when community members heard that the four girls were strip-searched, more than 200 people showed up at a local school board meeting to call for the termination of the involved school officials. So far, nothing has been resolved.

I never saw Ms Amor again. The police eventually dropped the breaking and entering charges, but I was, from that day onward, deemed a delinquent. I lived under a kind of surveillance, with cop cars constantly pulling me over for random searches, and I eventually became exactly what they expected. I wound up dropping

"Everything We Possess." From Notes from Black Wall Street:
Everything We Possess. © 2021 Crystal Z Campbell.

out of school, moving through the pipeline to the juvenile justice system. But I was lucky: I'm a light-skinned Latina in addition to being black, and in school was rarely read as the latter. If I had been visibly black, all the statistics suggest, things would have been much worse for me. Of this I am sure. Ask any black woman.

■

99 YEARS AFTER THE TULSA RACE MASSACRE, AN ARTIST REFLECTS
By Crystal Z Campbell

D ear Tulsa,
Recently, a youthful physician's assistant used a medical-grade version of a hole punch to extract layers of tissue from my right arm. My skin, the largest organ on my body, now features a gaping hole, clumsily held together by two meager stitches. Despite this invasive procedure, my body is expected to make the repairs on its own.

A biopsy reminded me of you, Tulsa. I thought about how we can grow new skin, but the scar remains. Scars are histories written upon our skin.

Steps from my front door is the site of the 1921 *Tulsa Race Massacre*. This land was once called Black Wall Street. Imagine over thirty-five bustling blocks of mostly Black homes and businesses being firebombed, in one of the wealthiest Black communities in the United States. Imagine being one of hundreds detained, shot, or worse—killed blocks from your home or place of business. Imagine a city ordinance forbidding you to rebuild on your own land. Imagine a century of silence, with little to no trace of your relative, neighbor, friend, or partner. Imagine the bounty of fear and rumor.

Despite coming of age in this state and taking mandatory classes on Oklahoma history, I had never heard of the 1921 Tulsa Race Massacre until I turned 30. By chance, an artist I met in New York City mentioned the massacre in passing. Just shy of a century after-the-fact, the massacre is now a mandatory part of the curriculum in Oklahoma schools, though the massacre was referred to by many Oklahoma state officials as "The Tulsa Race Riot" as recently as 2018. In archives, some newspaper articles about the "riot" are literally punched out, missing from record.

Who imagined someone in the future would search for this? Who omitted bits of evidence surrounding the massacre from the archive? What stake did they have in doing so? I search archives for shelved witnesses while fast-forwarding past land grabs, urban renewal, and gentrification. I wonder about Black residents who resisted during the Tulsa Race Massacre—a resistance omitted by popular media.

Tulsa, I have a complicated relationship with you, and to you, but there is also love. It is the kind of love—like familial love—which you didn't quite ask for, nor choose, but that you know will always be the haint of your existence.

In my creative research, I have made several attempts to think through these historical gaps shrouded in silence. In 2013, I was an artist-in-residence in Lake Como, Italy. A week upon arrival, I made the first of many works I still make around the Tulsa Race Massacre. "Paradise" is an installation that poses questions about the idea of a Black utopia. Who is accountable for such racially motivated destruction, and who might be accountable for reparations, for healing, for the absence of this narrative in public memory? A minimal gesture, the installation featured a large, empty room bathed in blue light. Within closed doors, viewers were immediately immersed in the smell of burning wood. The smell was more of a phantom—no visible objects were burned, nor was there any source of fire.

In "Notes From Black Wall Street," I have been compiling one-hundred archival images from Greenwood before, during, and after the 1921 Tulsa Race Massacre. As we reflect on the recent centennial of other instances of racially motivated domestic terrorism, such as the *Red Summer*, and approach that of the Tulsa Race Massacre, I meditate on these images through the application of tactile layers of paint, like scars, atop archival photographs.

I offer these works as prompts to meditate on the future of our complicit fictions, suppressed memories, and united histories.

> *Walk with me.*
> I am in search of an elevator. A black man. A white woman.
> Escaped goats.
> *Walk with me.*
> I am in search of traces of a former community thriving in exile because of segregation.
> *Walk with me.*

I am in search of pennies, melting together by fire.

To be truthful, for most of my youth, I planned to escape this arid, open plain. This was not because I did not find your red dirt beautiful. This was not because I was not enamored by your rose rocks, your sweeping wind, or your thunder. My father, who chose to retire here from the military, later claimed the most racist experiences he's had in his sixty plus years of living have been in Oklahoma. When he returned from war, my parents moved us from a mostly Black township to a *sundown town*: Norman, Oklahoma. Traces of racial segregation littered my childhood bus rides through the countryside, tainted my impressions of cowboys, and instilled a perpetual anxiety about open land. I grew up here, but this has never been a place of comfort.

Recently, my work rooted in the massacre was pulled from a high-profile exhibition in Oklahoma. Another potential collaboration regarding the massacre was cancelled, with an explanation that Tulsa's sensibilities were "peculiar." I wondered if support for the organization would be revoked; if my work would create discomfort, if it didn't align with the politics of the institution, if it was a history they didn't want to be affiliated with, if it would prompt a conversation they did not want to have.

I am not particularly concerned about my work being shown. I am concerned about critical narratives of this city, this state, this nation, being omitted from history. I am concerned about the culture of silence and censorship that has forced many to try to heal themselves, even if such wounds are beyond repair.

Narratives are skins.
Narratives are tools.
Narratives are weapons.
Narratives are scars.

Rooted by your central Council Oak Tree, Tulsa, you are a place that was founded by Creek Indians following forced removal; they named this "old town" Talasi in 1836. This area of Indian Territory became home to both forced Indigenous migrants and actual "outsiders" (yes, the namesake film was shot here), attracting outlaws and freed slaves who migrated here in search of land of their own.

Amid the ongoing coronavirus pandemic, I have been investigating my own rootedness. Ancestry.com searches suggest that my father's family was rooted in Indian Territory (prior to Oklahoma statehood in 1907), and were Creek Freedmen descendants. I am left to imagine if they had any connection to Black Wall Street, or where they would have landed, were it not for waves of racial intimidation. I am here now, by choice, because I want to unearth these narratives.

Oklahoma's history is riddled with pioneers on Indigenous land, land grabs, oil extraction, boomtowns, unchecked privilege, and waves of settler colonialism. I never imagined as a child that some parcels of Oklahoma would be someone's version of utopia. However, I find comfort in picturing the over fifty Black townships that Oklahoma boasted after the Civil War.

I have always found this state beautiful—and ugly too. I ask, in 2020: How can we be truthful? How can we revisit history in a reparative way? How can we move closer to the impossibility of this utopian vision?

Dear Tulsa, you are famous now, as much as you've ever been. Will *oil be slick enough* to preserve our futures? Ask Larry Clark if *his pictures of hard-lived Tulsa* still hold true. Ask viewers of *HBO's Watchmen* how a graphic novel adaptation can instantly amplify otherwise hushed, historical transmissions? Ask the Supreme Court if the reclamation of Indigenous land should proceed. Ask if art can reframe one of our state's greatest public secrets. And while all of this is happening: Where do you want us to look?

Let's begin by scanning holes, historical omissions, and instances of deliberate extraction. Following the current mayor's suggestion, let's reckon with history and acknowledge that the Tulsa Race Massacre was a crime. If the past is a lesson, a crime cannot be placated by gifting survivors with medallions in lieu of reparations. Justice extends beyond a *pending excavation of mass graves.* Justice requires that the identification of victims be paralleled by the identification of perpetrators. Justice is a prerequisite to healing.

Dear Tulsa, today marks the ninety-ninth anniversary of the Tulsa Race Massacre. Will justice take another hundred years?

The Tulsa Race Massacre, formerly known as the 1921 Tulsa Race Riot, took place from May 31 to June 1, 1921 in the Greenwood District of Tulsa, Oklahoma.

CHAPTER 5

STAKING A CLAIM

Writing Opinion Pieces (Op-Eds)

Writing opinion pieces, or op-eds, has been a long-standing approach to raising awareness and changing minds on social issues. The term *op-ed* derives from "opposite the editorials" and refers to opinion pieces taking on issues of the time written by outside writers, which would appear on the opposite page from editorials, or opinion pieces, written by staff editors, in print newspapers. This was a way for national and local newspapers to bring in the perspectives of people outside of the publication on burning social issues, including topical experts, celebrities, and even everyday citizens.

A typical op-ed gives an opinion in support of or against an issue—gun rights or gun control, for example—written by a topical expert or leader in the field. These op-eds revolve around making an intellectual case for their point of view through facts, data and statistics, and the power of logic and argument. An intellectual op-ed can be useful in countering misinformation or misunderstanding by pointing to corrective information or by revealing flaws in the logic of the opposing view.

In contrast are op-eds written by those who have a deep personal stake in an issue that revolves around the writer's personal experience, insight, and feelings. What makes personal op-eds powerful is while people can argue with logic and the interpretation of data, they cannot argue with someone's personal experience of an issue or their feelings about it. It takes the discussion of the issue beyond the abstract and intellectual and forces readers to consider the impact of the issue on real people.

Readers who use facts and logic to form their views are more likely to be attuned to intellectual op-eds while those who value personal narratives and insights will be moved by op-eds offering an emotional, personal perspective. For example, a newspaper might publish two op-eds that make appeals for greater gun control—one written by a gun violence researcher who cites research, their own and that of others, about how the violence and death caused by guns is tragic yet preventable, the other written by someone who has lost a family member to gun violence and believes stricter gun regulations might have saved their life.

Then, there are those op-eds written by an individual who is both a topical expert and personally impacted by the issue. These are especially powerful because the author has both the authority to make the intellectual case as well as the personal experience to make an authentic emotional appeal. Jose Antonio Vargas is a Pulitzer Prize–winning journalist, and he is also an undocumented immigrant who revealed his immigration status and how he was brought to this country with false documents as a child in a courageous piece for the *New York Times Magazine* in 2011.[1] Just days after Trump was elected president, in November 2016, Vargas wrote an op-ed for the *New York Times* in which he captured how terrifying Trump's xenophobic, anti-immigrant rhetoric was and the fear that gripped him and other undocumented immigrants once Trump was elected president given Trump's fervid promise to "build the wall" along the US's southern border with Mexico.[2] In the op-ed, Vargas appeals to ordinary American citizens and asks what they will do to protect undocumented immigrants in their communities.

While debates around immigration rage on along with questions of what is the path forward for undocumented immigrants, including Dreamers, brought to the US as children, Vargas, through his op-ed, is able to speak with authority not only as an award-winning journalist who covers immigration issues but as someone who has navigated life as an undocumented immigrant. He humanizes the fraught issue of immigration with the details of his circumstances and his feelings about it. Some readers may disagree with Vargas's positions on immigration, but they cannot discount his own lived experiences. Despite the constant debates around immigration and the fate of undocumented immigrants, we have rarely heard from undocumented immigrants themselves, which made Vargas's op-ed so crucial. Furthermore, this erasure of undocumented perspectives from media coverage allowed Trump to paint undocumented immigrants as criminals and terrorists, so Vargas's piece worked to counter this dangerous rhetoric.

Interestingly, after being credited with coining the term and being an early pioneer of op-eds, the *New York Times* recently announced that it was changing the name of its Op-Ed section to Guest Essays. In its official announcement, the storied newspaper noted that the Op-Ed section was first launched with the intent to offer "a welcome mat for ideas and arguments from many points on the political, social and cultural spectrums from outside the walls of The Times—to stimulate thought and provoke discussion of public problems."[3] But recent shifts to digital media necessitated a change in terminology:

> That important mission remains the same. But it's time to change the name. The reason is simple: In the digital world, in which millions of Times readers absorb the paper's journalism online, there is no geographical "Op-Ed," just as there is no geographical "Ed" for Op-Ed to be opposite to. It is a relic of an older age and an older print newspaper design.[4]

The OpEd Project is an indispensable organizational resource for individuals seeking to write and publish op-eds, particularly those who might not be professional writers. Their stated mission is "to change who writes history," and they do this "by accelerating the ideas and impact of underrepresented thinkers, including women of all backgrounds."[5] More specifically, they offer classes, coaching, and guidance on conceptualizing, writing, pitching, and publishing op-eds at local and national outlets.

According to the OpEd Project, typical op-eds follow this outlined format:

- *Lede*—compelling introduction, which is tied to a newshook.
- *Thesis*—statement of position on the issue.
- *Argument*—reasons for your position.
- *First Point of Evidence*—lay out first point of evidence and show how it supports your argument.
- *Second Point of Evidence*—lay out second point of evidence and show how it supports your argument.
- *Third Point of Evidence (if necessary)*—lay out third point of evidence and show how it supports your argument.
- *"To Be Sure" Paragraph*—acknowledge any issues with your argument.
- *Conclusion*—your conclusion connects back to your lede.[6]

Beyond this grounding guidance on the format of op-eds, the OpEd Project offers these excellent questions to consider as you conceptualize and write your op-ed:

- *Why should we readers trust you?* What knowledge, authority, or experience do you bring to this issue?
- *Can you back up what you say?* What evidence have you presented to support your argument?
- *What's new?* What new information or perspective have you presented on this issue?
- *So what?* As marketing and communications director for Race Forward, a racial justice organization, whenever I wrote any promotional material, I would ask myself whether it passed the "so what" test. Why should anyone outside of our organization care about this racial justice issue? Why should they take the actions we are asking of

them? What is at stake? I've continued to use the "so what" test whenever I write an op-ed to ensure I've communicated why the issue matters and what is at stake.

- *What's the difference between being "right" and being "effective"?* Have you written the piece in a way that clearly articulates your argument but doesn't dehumanize those with opposing views, thereby creating the possibility of dialogue?
- *How will your ideas and arguments contribute to the conversation, and be helpful to your audience?* What do you want your audience to take away from reading the piece? Having greater awareness? Taking prescribed action?[7]

In her book *Writing to Persuade: How to Bring People Over to Your Side*, Trish Hall, former editor of the *New York Times* Op-Ed page shares insights and tips on what it takes to write and publish persuasive op-eds. Hall starts off by giving us her own cogent definition of op-eds: "Opinion pieces are not like news stories. They have facts that must be verifiable, but they do not need to be balanced or give equal time to various points of view. There is always a conclusion or a solution."[8]

Hall also offers incisive tips on how to write and pitch an op-ed:

- Know what has run and find a different angle.
- If it's timely, you've got to be fast.
- Make an argument and offer a solution.
- Focus.
- Get to your main idea quickly.
- Think about order.
- Clichés and jargon will doom you.
- Avoid the obvious.
- Don't be blatantly self-promotional.[9]

Can op-eds really change hearts and minds? Towards the end of *Writing to Persuade*, Hall presents us with both sobering and encouraging insights about the potential impact and influence of op-eds. First of all, she discusses how people tend to cling to their ideas and beliefs and this "makes it hard to change opinion."[10] A major reason for this tendency is *confirmation bias*—"we seek out information that confirms what we already believe," and therefore, "our opinions tend to get stronger over time."[11] While we assume facts are irrefutable and can change people's minds, this isn't always the case because as Hall points out research shows we start out with a belief and then find the reasons or facts to support what we already believe.[12]

Why do we stick to our beliefs, even when they run contrary to seemingly obvious and overwhelming facts and logic? Hall notes the reasons range from avoiding the complications and burden of trying to reconcile opposing views to not wanting to admit to our mistaken beliefs.[13] Although it's difficult for people to change their minds, and it often takes time and persistence, we know from history that it is possible. We need only look at how views on race, women's rights, and gay rights have evolved to know that changes in attitudes and beliefs, even those rooted in culture and religion, are possible, albeit gradual.

I share this not to dissuade or demotivate you from seeking to use your crucial perspective to craft an op-ed about an issue for which you are passionate. Rather, I seek to manage your expectations around how and what it takes for people to change their beliefs or positions on social issues. A reader who holds an opposing view is unlikely to change their mind after reading your op-ed. But your piece can be one of the voices in the chorus that helps people understand your position on the issue, and at the very least, provoke them to consider a different perspective. Since change is often slow and challenging, we have to be willing to play the long game.

Hall does, however, offer some tips on how to connect with readers who have opposing views. She cites research that suggests grounding your arguments in the moral values of your opponent:

> People have strong feelings about what makes a good life and a good society, and they support viewpoints that confirm those

feelings. If you don't understand the moral framework of your audience, you can't be convincing. You can't expect someone to change their basic values, so you have to make your argument in a way that fits with their values.[14]

In truth, you don't necessarily have to write your op-ed to opposing audiences with the aim of seeking to change their minds. Given today's antagonistic and toxic climate, where many are clinging to misinformation and conspiracy theories rather than facts or evidence, where many conservatives have traded their patriotism for racist, classist, and autocratic screeds, it might be a bridge too far for your integrity or sanity to try to appeal to values that are anything but moral or to identify with truly abhorrent points of view. Instead, in some cases, it might make more sense to write to the undecided or uninformed. Or you might write to those who share your beliefs, galvanizing others in your camp during a pivotal moment of public debate or boosting morale if there's been a crucial policy setback. You might write because the specific perspective you bring to the issue through your own experience and authority is sorely missing from the public conscience and conversation. The issues matter but so does your own integrity as a writer and you have to decide what makes the most sense for you and the issue you're championing.

In this chapter, I share two of my own op-eds, the first about the danger posed by anti-vaccinators during the coronavirus pandemic, written as a typical intellectual op-ed, and the second about the limits of the concept of tolerance in the wake of racial injustice and inequities, written as a hybrid of an intellectual op-ed and a personal op-ed, drawing on my authority and knowledge from having worked in racial justice and my identity and experiences as a woman of color.

I wrote and published "The Anti-Vaxxer Threat amid a Pandemic" in *Newsday* in the early months of the coronavirus pandemic, when the US led the world in coronavirus cases and a vaccine was only a hope on the horizon many months away. As someone who had written pre-pandemic about the perils of the anti-vaccine movement, I sought to sound a warning call to the public about the dangers posed by the lies and misinformation already being spread by anti-vaccine and anti-science constituencies, which would impede our chance to save lives and return to normal, if—or when—a vaccine became available.

The piece takes a clear position that vaccines are lifesaving and our best hope at overcoming this pandemic and urges us to be vigilant and fight back against the false rhetoric of the anti-vaccine movement, which endangers our lives and recovery:

> This moment underscores the lifesaving importance of vaccines and the essentialness of a strong public health system as a safeguard. We can start by ensuring that our local and national public health systems have the expert staffing and resources they need, but also by striking down personal belief exemptions in the many states that allow them to help eradicate the anti-vaccine movement, which has harmed so many lives by prioritizing individual freedom over public safety and by promoting false beliefs over verifiable science.

Sadly, my op-ed turned out to be predictive. A year later, when vaccines were developed and more readily available, many Americans refused to be vaccinated, fueling the spread of the new, more transmissible Delta and Omicron variants of COVID-19.

My second op-ed piece, "Tolerance Has a Fatal Flaw. This Is the Solution," was published by CNN a few weeks following the death of George Floyd, during the ensuing worldwide protests against policy brutality and for racial justice. I was disheartened that it took George Floyd's murder at the hands of a police officer to drive individuals, communities, and even corporations to finally begin to speak meaningfully about race. At the same time, it was clear to me that there was a lack of understanding about how notions of tolerance and diversity fall well short of inclusiveness, equity, and justice, which are what we need to transform into a truly racially just society. As more and more Americans were finally beginning to acknowledge the cruel realities of racial injustice in the US and talk more truthfully about race, I wrote this piece to suggest that the long-peddled ideal of tolerance falls far short of equity.

I focus on explaining how tolerance is inadequate in helping us create an inclusive and equitable America, while also using my own experiences as a first generation Indian American to illustrate how despite being born in this country and my strong ties and contributions to it, I have sometimes been made to feel merely "tolerated" rather than accepted:

> Tolerance—which shaped my childhood and continues to mold how too many Americans talk about fighting for equity—might be an affirming term, but just barely. I know this from experience; as a brown woman I have felt tolerated for much of my life by white Americans, even though I was born and raised in this country and consider myself an American before anything else about me. Any room I've walked into, be it classroom or boardroom, I've remained aware of the ways in which I'm considered different and don't belong. One of the most enduring impacts of teaching tolerance long enough is that it gets internalized.

This piece combines the intellectual authority of a typical op-ed, drawing on my knowledge from working in the racial justice field, with the experience and emotional insights of a personal op-ed. So even if opponents take issue with my intellectual points on the impact of racism and racial injustice, it's hard for them to argue with my own experiences of them.

Also included in this chapter are two op-eds, the first exploring transracial adoption by Nicole Chung, author of the memoir *All You Can Ever Know,* and the second on the pervasiveness of casteism by Yashica Dutt, author of the memoir *Coming Out as Dalit.* Both offer an insider perspective on their respective issues. Chung herself is a transracial adoptee, and Dutt hails from the

Dalit caste, which is highly discriminated against and stigmatized throughout the Indian diaspora.

In her op-ed, Chung challenges the widely accepted tropes in which transracial adoptees are seen as fortunate for being adopted and white adoptive parents are viewed as saviors deserving of their children's undying gratitude. Chung outlines how damaging these narratives are to transracial adoptees, silencing them from talking about experiences of racism or abuse and discouraging them from connecting with their culture or finding their biological family. As Chung shares, her attempts to provide a more complicated and nuanced depiction of transracial adoption, especially of its darker aspects, have sometimes been met by resistance and criticism from white readers and audiences, who seek to paint her as ungrateful and unloving towards her parents:

> For a long time, the weight of other people's expectations made it far more difficult to consider how I really felt about my identity and the meaning of family. I believed I had to be a *good* adoptee: thankful, loyal, content . . . The presumption that transracially adopted people will express nothing but un-qualified gratitude, feel nothing less than total comfort within the white supremacist frameworks we are exposed to, is fully consistent with the pattern of how race is thought about and talked about in this country: in America, it's often considered worse to call someone racist than to say or do something that is actually racist.

While the public might debate the merits of transracial adoption, the personal insights shared by Chung in this op-ed ensure that we hear the voice and perspective of someone most impacted yet often silenced: a transracial adoptee.

In her op-ed, Dutt uses the recent lawsuit brought on behalf of a Dalit American employee against Silicon Valley technology giant Cisco for discrimination based on caste to highlight the fact that caste discrimination is not restricted to India but is pervasive throughout the Indian diaspora. Much like in cases of race, gender, or sexual identity discrimination, victims of caste discrimination are harassed and passed up for promotions and other career opportunities. Many Americans might not know about caste and how it operates and underpins interactions in Hindu society so Dutt explains by providing some cultural and historical context.

Dutt acknowledges that her own authority comes from the fact that she has a personal stake in Dalit rights because she herself is a Dalit. She discusses how despite fear of reprisal and being shunned by higher caste Indians, she "came out" as a Dalit in 2016. So the Cisco discrimination case holds particular significance for her and fellow Dalit Americans because it highlights discrimination that has been underacknowledged and unchecked:

> Almost every Dalit person I spoke to in the United States, after California filed the lawsuit against Cisco, requested to remain anonymous and feared that revealing their identity as a Dalit working in the American tech industry filled with higher-caste Indians would ruin their career.
>
> Those words also governed my life until 2016, when I decided to publicly reveal my caste identity and "come out" as Dalit. Growing up "passing" as a dominant-caste person in India while hiding my "untouchable," caste I lived in the same fear that stops most Dalits from articulating their harassment and asserting their identity in India and the United States.

Notably, Dutt's op-ed in the *New York Times* underscores that caste discrimination should no longer be viewed as an Indian problem but a global one.

These op-eds are particularly powerful because Chung and Dutt are both topical experts and personally impacted by their respective issues, given their identities. While some might disagree with their views on transracial adoption and caste discrimination, they cannot question their lived experiences and the authority derived from them.

There's no denying that even with dizzying changes wrought by digital media and constant noise from social media altercations, opinion pieces remain a powerful way to have our position and perspective on a social issue heard widely. While it is challenging to change people's minds since we tend to hold tenaciously to our beliefs and opinions, we might provoke them to acknowledge some of the merits of our argument or open their eyes to the personal impact of the issue. Ultimately, we have to decide if we are writing to convince our opponents, to bolster our fellow believers, or to reach the undecided. Regardless, our opinion pieces are part of the crucial, long-held democratic tradition of engaging in debate and dialogue in the public square about pressing social issues.

■

THE ANTI-VAXXER THREAT
AMID A PANDEMIC
By Kavita Das

The explosive spread of the coronavirus in the United States has pointed to state-of-the-art health care and public health systems now buckling under the weight of the number of infections, especially in our densest cities.

Much of America is on lockdown, and we boast the most number of coronavirus cases in the world. Yet, even after local and state governments advised residents to socially distance, many continued to congregate and travel, believing themselves to be immune to the virus and failing to see themselves as vectors for its spread. We're seeing mounting deaths of mostly older individuals and those with underlying conditions but also some young and seemingly healthy people.

Meanwhile, most of us sit in our homes wondering when we will resume our normal lives, and what the new normal will look like. Our greatest hope lies in the development and distribution of a vaccine against COVID-19. But despite the misleading chatter from President Donald Trump, a vaccine is likely many months off, if not more. As a society, many of us don't understand what goes into developing and distributing a vaccine; we take them for granted. Worse yet, we've allowed a virulent anti-vaccine movement to grow and cause harm, especially to those who are immune-compromised.

Many states have threatened the greater good by permitting parents to refuse vaccinations for their children through personal-belief exemptions. This has led to the spread of diseases that were mostly eradicated, including the resurgence of measles and whooping cough. The anti-vaccine movement's false rhetoric also has helped erode our appreciation of our public health system and our responsibility to uphold herd immunity on behalf of our fellow citizens.

Eula Biss' seminal 2014 book, "On Immunity: An Inoculation," examining the emergence of vaccines and the rise of the anti-vaccine movement, notes that when it comes to society's support of its public health system, "the belief that public health measures are not intended for people like us is widely held by many people . . . Public health, we assume, is for people with less—less education, less health habits, less access to quality health care, less time and money."

As part of a larger trend of bucking science and evidence-based guidelines, anti-vaxxers have popularized horrific practices like "measles parties" and "chicken pox parties" to promote the spread of these diseases, mischaracterizing them as normal and harmless. I increasingly hear people say in casual conversation, "I'm not getting the flu shot; the shot is worse than the flu." Meanwhile, the flu kills tens of thousands of Americans every year.

Our own president has expressed anti-vaccine sentiments with no scientific bases and appointed avowed anti-vaxxer Robert F. Kennedy, Jr. as head of a commission on vaccine safety. So, it is hardly surprising that upon taking office Trump disassembled the National Security Council's Global Pandemic Team, which would have spearheaded our national response to this pandemic, and has allowed countless positions to remain vacant in the Centers for Disease Control and Prevention, the key agency overseeing our public health response to infectious disease.

This moment underscores the lifesaving importance of vaccines and the essentialness of a strong public health system as a safeguard. We can start by ensuring that our local and national public health systems have the expert staffing and resources they need, but also by striking down personal belief exemptions in the many states that allow them to help eradicate the anti-vaccine movement, which has harmed so many lives by prioritizing individual freedom over public safety and by promoting false beliefs over verifiable science.

■

TOLERANCE HAS A FATAL FLAW. THIS IS THE SOLUTION
By Kavita Das

As a first-generation Indian American who grew up in 1980s Reagan-era New York City shaped by efforts at multiculturalism, I had social studies classes that were filled with lessons about America's guiding principle of tolerance. My teachers pointed to the Statue of Liberty as this virtue's crowning symbol, asking us to bring in pennies to help underwrite efforts to restore Lady Liberty marred by decades of pollution. When we learned about Martin Luther King Jr. and his fight for civil rights for Black Americans, "tolerance" also took on the tacit assumption that we had now achieved his dream, even if it had cost him his life.

According to the Merriam-Webster dictionary, the primary definition of tolerance is the "capacity to endure pain or hardship," followed by secondary and tertiary definitions, "sympathy or indulgence for beliefs or practices differing from or conflicting with one's own;" or "the act of allowing something." However, its primary definition most closely aligns with how it operates in American culture. For example, when we talk about pain, we talk about how much we can "tolerate." And if someone described an experience as "tolerable," would you rush out to experience it for yourself? Probably not.

Tolerance—which shaped my childhood and continues to mold how too many Americans talk about fighting for equity—might be an affirming term, but just barely. I know this from experience; as a brown woman I have felt tolerated for much of my life by white Americans, even though I was born and raised in this country and consider myself an American before anything else about me. Any room I've walked into, be it classroom or boardroom, I've remained aware of the ways in which I'm considered different and don't belong. One of the most enduring impacts of teaching tolerance long enough is that it gets internalized.

Tolerance is an underwhelming goal for a truly vibrant and just American society because, like diversity, it is satisfied by the mere presence of those with different experiences and perspectives. Instead, we should strive for inclusion, where people are accepted, welcomed and valued. We should prioritize equity, where opportunities are distributed based on an accurate understanding of our sociocultural history. Recent events make painfully clear how much further we have to go. To get to a better place, we must use the power of our imagination, compassion and intrepid spirit to look past tolerance and manifest what an inclusive and equitable America would look like across every sector of our society.

Underlying America's guiding principle of tolerance is a presumption of who's entitled to do most of the tolerating (white Americans) and who is relegated to being tolerated (everyone else). While some watered down history books would have us believe tolerance is what built America's multicultural society, it is in part responsible for our current deep divisions. Adopting tolerance as a guiding principle does nothing to challenge the power structures or systemic racism at work in American society.

In fact, we need only flip the script on tolerance to see that it is Black Americans who are being forced to tolerate much more. Just in the last few months alone, we have seen Black men and women killed while doing everyday things that white Americans take for granted, like going for a run to sleeping in their own bed.

Meanwhile, the pandemic has highlighted how unequal freedom is in this country. Protesters against police brutality and racism are accused of being reckless and face further brutality for attempting to peacefully gather (many while masked), but white rallygoers advocating for ending shelter-in-place policies have been permitted to endanger the general public by protesting free of masks, sometimes with weapons strapped to their backs and with little to no police intervention. Despite verified photos showing white New Yorkers crowding the city's parks, 68% of arrests for failure to social distance were of black New Yorkers, while just 7% were white. Given the hateful rhetoric from the President and other lawmakers referring to the coronavirus as the "Chinese virus," Asian Americans have been experiencing a rise in hate crimes.

In a 2017 article titled "America is Stuck in the Purgatory of Tolerance" veteran journalist and TV news anchor, Dan Rather said of tolerance, "We often hear about how we need to be more tolerant: to make room for people, ideas, and actions with which we may not agree. This is a prerequisite for a functional democracy. But tolerance alone is not sufficient; it allows us to accept others without engaging with them, to feel smug and self-satisfied without challenging the boundaries within which too many of us live." Rather goes on to aptly note that tolerance is merely a "way station" to the "much grander destination" of true inclusion of people of diverse backgrounds and experiences.

I'm no longer content just being tolerated. I want more for Black Americans, for fellow Americans of color and for my country. In order to stand up for this nation and its potential, I'm rejecting tolerance, the notion that the people who have historically had and abused their power and privilege should feel like they are benevolently putting up with people who have just as much claim to this country and its true ideals. I want to be included, why not even welcomed?

Tolerance, like this virus and the ongoing pandemic of racism in America, has kept us shut in our respective homes and silenced us from engaging with each other for fear that we may have differing opinions. In this moment we must choose to close the distance between us by acknowledging our interdependence and our respective and inherent value as well as the fact that we are made stronger and more dynamic by inclusion. The alternative is intolerable, hence the desperation and rage we see playing out in the streets of city after city across America.

■

STORIES OF TRANSRACIAL ADOPTEES MUST BE HEARD—EVEN UNCOMFORTABLE ONES
By Nicole Chung

As a Korean American adoptee, the strength of my connection to my white family is what makes me feel safe, relatable, approachable to some.

It's not necessarily the first question I get, but it always comes up. On tour for my book, published in 2018, an audience member asked if I, a Korean American adoptee, am "still close" to my adoptive parents. When I said yes, they followed up, as if in disbelief: "So, you and your family are really *OK?*"

An interviewer wanted to establish right off the bat that I had "never felt unloved" by my white family "in spite of" my race. Another inquired as to how often we see each other. I've had people tell me they were "relieved"—even "pleasantly surprised"—to find that my book is "not angry or bitter." At a reading, someone wondered if my parents were offended by any of the sentiments I had expressed around my transracial adoption: feelings of racial isolation and confusion, exacerbated by a childhood spent in overwhelmingly white spaces; a suppressed but stubborn curiosity about my birth family; the slow-to-evolve conviction that I needed to find a way to grasp for more knowledge, more truth about my personal history, than my adoptive family could offer me. (Before I could answer, my mother, who was sitting in the front row, piped up heroically: "*No*, we weren't offended!")

Sometimes, when I confirm that my family and I are not estranged, the person questioning me will visibly relax, as if consoled to learn that I genuinely love the people who raised me. But what if I had another kind of story to tell? Suppose we had conflicts we couldn't reconcile, as many families do? Suppose I *was* angrier; suppose we *weren't* in contact; suppose I didn't even think of them as my family any more?

I now recognize some number of these exchanges for what they are: requests for reassurance, little tests I have to pass if I want to be perceived as anything other than a resentful adoptee, an ungrateful daughter, an angry person of color. My esteem for my white family, the strength of my connection to them, is what makes me feel safe, relatable, approachable to some. This, it turns out, is the price of admission, the prerequisite for whatever authority they are willing to grant me when it comes to talking about my own experience.

Not long ago, a woman who had read my book emailed to tell me to face the facts: my birth parents hadn't wanted me. That I had complex emotions about my adoption, she said, was "an insult" to my adoptive family. "I feel so sorry for your good parents," she wrote.

That word, "good," and all that it implies, is fascinating to me. As an adoptee, I've been asked to make this distinction over and over: only one family can be "good." Only one family can be "real." So I must choose between the white adoptive parents that have been regularly portrayed (by others) as selfless saviors, and the Korean immigrant family that, by default, has been relegated to illegitimacy, selfishness, otherness. And if I am not prepared to choose and love only my white family and forswear all others, then I am unworthy of any family's love.

For a long time, the weight of other people's expectations made it far more difficult to consider how I really felt about my identity and the meaning of family. I believed I had to be a *good* adoptee: thankful, loyal, content. This pressure transracial adoptees might feel to be "good" can be directly linked to the belief that people of color should shrug off damaging, dehumanizing racism rather than call it out—that it's our responsibility to not show anger, to reassure white people at any cost, to place their comfort over our own humanity. The presumption that transracially adopted people will express nothing but unqualified gratitude, feel nothing less than total comfort within the white supremacist frameworks we are exposed to, is fully consistent with the pattern of how race is thought about and talked about in this country: in America, it's often considered worse to call someone racist than to say or do something that is actually racist.

Because I moved in entirely white circles as a child, I acquired a kind of instinctive understanding of whiteness, if not white privilege itself. I was in my late 20s before I really began to interrogate the ways in which I had been uniquely positioned, as a transracial adoptee, to adapt and make myself more palatable to white people. I started to wonder who I might have become otherwise, and how my adoption and subsequent proximity to whiteness could be used to bolster the pernicious racism at the heart of the colorblindness myth—how it could even be wielded against other people of color.

It took so long for me to realize that love for my family didn't have to mean staying silent, that I had a right to my anger. I am still not always confident in owning it, but now, at least, I can recognize when it is just, even necessary.

When I was in my early 20s, a white man told me that transracial adoptions like mine were "the best way to fight racism." I was in the midst of my own "good adoptee" campaign at the time, but I still found his statement shocking. I knew that I'd experienced plenty of racism as a Korean American adoptee, and that having a white family was no kind of inoculation—usually it just meant that I faced those battles alone. As much as they loved me, my family could not always understand or help me fight a form of prejudice they had never experienced.

I still meet a lot of people who want the story of transracial adoption to be a simple, comforting one: it's an antidote to racism; proof that love conquers all. When you grow up being told how lucky you are to have been adopted, how "blessed" you are that your parents "took you in" and "brought you up as a Christian, in a country that actually values girls and women," how freely can you talk about your feelings of abandonment or anxiety, your deep curiosity about your lost heritage, your encounters with bigots, the losses and pain you carry?

There is, of course, no singular, universal adoption experience: some of us are very close to our adoptive parents and some of us aren't. Some of us might want to connect with our birth families and our cultures of origin, and some might not. We need to complicate the stories and notions around transracial adoption: what adoptees go through and how we are allowed to feel about our experiences, how race is relevant to our lives. We must listen to transracial adoptees and make room for their perspectives, including the ones that make some uncomfortable— because when it comes to the wellbeing of adopted people and their families, the truth will serve far better than even the most comforting of lies.

THE SPECTER OF CASTE
IN SILICON VALLEY
By Yashica Dutt

On June 30, California's Department of Fair Employment and Housing regulators sued Cisco Systems Inc., for discrimination. The cause was not, like most workplace discrimination lawsuits, based on race, gender, age or sexual orientation. It was based on caste.

The lawsuit accuses Cisco, a multibillion-dollar tech conglomerate based in San Jose, Calif., of denying an engineer, who immigrated from India to the United States, professional opportunities, a raise and promotions because he was from a low caste, or Dalit, background. The lawsuit states that his Indian-American managers, Sundar Iyer and Ramana Kompella, who are described as high-caste Brahmins, harassed the engineer because of their sense of superiority rooted in the Hindu caste system.

Many Indian-Americans reacted with disbelief that a giant corporation in Silicon Valley could be mired in caste discrimination. For Dalit Americans like me, it was just another Wednesday.

Dalit, which means "oppressed," is a self-chosen identity for close to 25 percent of India's population, and it refers to former "untouchables," the people who suffer the greatest violence, discrimination and disenfranchisement under the centuries-old caste system that structures Hindu society.

Caste is the gear that turns every system in India. "If Hindus migrate to other regions on earth, Indian Caste would become a world problem," B.R. Ambedkar, the greatest Dalit leader and one of the architects of the India Constitution, wrote in 1916. He was prophetic.

Caste prejudice and discrimination is rife within the Indian communities in the United States and other countries. Its chains are even turning the work culture within multibillion-dollar American tech companies, and beyond. The Cisco engineer, whose complaint led to the lawsuit and who identifies himself as a Dalit, has not been named in the lawsuit.

From the mid-1990s, American companies, panicking at the feared "millennial meltdown" of computer systems, were hiring close to 100,000 technology workers a year from India. An overwhelming majority of the Indian information technology professionals who moved to the United States were from "higher castes," and only a handful were Dalits.

Over the Fourth of July weekend, I participated in a video call with about 30 Dalit Indian immigrants. A Dalit information technology professional on the video call spoke about moving to the United States in 2000 and working at Cisco between 2007 and 2013. "A large percentage of the work force was already Indian," he told us. "They openly discussed their caste and would ask questions to figure out my caste background."

Higher caste Indians use the knowledge of a person's caste to place him or her on the social hierarchy despite professional qualifications. "I usually ignored these conversations," the Dalit worker added. "If they knew I was Dalit, it could ruin my career."

According to the lawsuit, Mr. Iyer, one of the Brahmin engineers at Cisco, revealed to his other higher-caste colleagues that the complainant had joined a top engineering school in India through affirmative action. When the Dalit engineer, the lawsuit says, confronted Mr. Iyer and contacted Cisco's human resources to file a complaint, Mr. Iyer retaliated by taking away the Dalit engineer's role as lead on two technologies.

For two years, the lawsuit says, Mr. Iyer isolated the Dalit engineer, denied him bonuses and raises and stonewalled his promotions. Cisco's human resources department responded by telling the Dalit engineer that "caste discrimination was not unlawful" and took no immediate corrective action. Mr. Kompella, the other Brahmin manager named in the lawsuit, replaced Mr. Iyer as the Dalit engineer's manager, and according to the suit, "continued to discriminate, harass, and retaliate against" him.

In 2019, Cisco was ranked No. 2 on Fortune's 100 Best Workplaces for Diversity. The technology giant got away with ignoring the persistent caste discrimination because American laws don't yet recognize Hindu caste discrimination as a valid form of exclusion. Caste does not feature in Cisco's diversity practices in its operations in India either. It reveals how the Indian information technology sector often operates in willful ignorance of the terrifying realities of caste.

In "The Other One Percent: Indians in America," a 2016 study of people of Indian descent in the United States, the authors Sanjoy Chakravorty, Devesh Kapur and Nirvikar Singh estimated that "over 90 percent of migrants" came from high castes or dominant castes. According to a 2018 survey by Equality Labs, a Dalit-American led civil rights organization, 67 percent of Dalits in the Indian diaspora admitted to facing caste-based harassment at the workplace.

In the backdrop of caste supremacy in the Indian diaspora in the United States, when higher-caste Hindus often describe and demonize Dalits as "inherently lazy/ opportunistic/ not talented," even apparently innocuous practices like peer reviews for promotions (Cisco and several other tech companies operate on this model), can turn into minefields, ending in job losses and visa rejections for Dalits.

Almost every Dalit person I spoke to in the United States, after California filed the lawsuit against Cisco, requested to remain anonymous and feared that revealing their identity as a Dalit working in the American tech industry filled with higher-caste Indians would ruin their career.

Those words also governed my life until 2016, when I decided to publicly reveal my caste identity and "come out" as Dalit. Growing up "passing" as a dominant-caste person in India while hiding my "untouchable" caste I lived in the same fear that stops most Dalits from articulating their harassment and asserting their identity in India and the United States.

The overwhelmingly higher-caste Indian-American community is seen as a "model minority" with more than an average $100,000 median income and rising cultural and political visibility. But it has engendered a narrative that is as diabolical as it is in India: insisting that they live in a "post-caste world" while simultaneously upholding its hierarchical framework that benefits the higher-caste people.

Ranging from seemingly harmless calls for "vegetarian-only roommates" (an easy way to assert caste purity), caste-based temple networks that automatically exclude "impure" Dalits, and the more overt and dangerous arm twisting of American norms—right-wing Hindu activist organizations tried to remove any mention of caste from California's textbooks in 2018—caste supremacy is fiercely defended, almost as a core tenet of Indian Hindu culture.

Yet after decades of being silenced, Dalit Americans are finally finding a voice that cannot be ignored. I was able to come out as Dalit because after moving to New York and avoiding Indian-only communities, for the first time, I was not scared of someone finding out my caste. Finding comfort and inspiration in movements like Black Lives Matter and Say Her Name and the tragic institutional murder of a Dalit student activist in India, I was able to understand and acknowledge that my history was a tapestry of pride, not shame.

Most Dalits in America still live with the fear of being exposed. But the pending California vs. Cisco case is a major step in the right direction.

CHAPTER 6

ARE YOU THE RIGHT STORYTELLER FOR THIS STORY?

*Understanding Cultural Sensitivity
and Avoiding Cultural Appropriation*

Every few months, it seems there is an eruption over cultural appropriation in the literary world. Writers and readers who share an identity take issue with the portrayal of their community by a writer from outside of their community. Fellow writers, especially those from outside of this community come to the defense of this writer, decrying their artistic freedom is in danger from cultural censorship. A raging debate ensues, with writers and thinkers divided between these views. Rinse and repeat.

Cultural appropriation is amongst the most fraught social issues in the literary and broader artistic arena and one for which there isn't always a simple, straightforward answer. Given the controversy and complexity of cultural appropriation, I turn to fellow writers and academics who have interrogated cultural appropriation in ways that go beyond the binary debates we tend to hear.

Instead of giving you sample texts as in previous chapters, I reference three related books. I also include four pieces that explore cultural appropriation with nuance and offer some guidance: (1) the introduction ("Appropriation and American Mythmaking") and conclusion ("Business as Usual") of Lauren Michele Jackson's *White Negroes: When Cornrows Were in Vogue . . . and Other Thoughts on Cultural Appropriation*; (2) Kaitlyn Greenidge's "Who Gets to Write What?"; (3) Alexander Chee's "How to Unlearn Everything: When It Comes to Writing the 'Other,' What Questions Are We Not Asking?"; and (4) my piece "Who Gets to Write About Whom: Examining Authority, Authenticity, and Appropriation in Biography." However, before we attempt to parse this thorny topic and how to navigate it, since it is in itself a social issue, it helps to take a few steps back and begin by examining our understanding of the craft of literature.

In his crucial book *Craft in the Real World*, Matthew Salesses examines literary craft and its elements, revealing that craft is not wholly objective but instead has been shaped by forces, which often go unacknowledged:

> What we call craft is in fact nothing more or less than a set of expectations. Those expectations are shaped by workshop, by reading, by awards, and gatekeepers, by biases about whose stories matter and how they should be told. How we engage with craft expectations is what we can control as writers. The more we know about the context of those expectations, the more consciously we can engage with them.[1]

The expectations that undergird literary craft and how it is taught, Salesses points out, are "never neutral," and have been shaped largely by white men, who have historically played the dominant roles in literature, as writers, scholars, and critics.[2] Similarly, there has been a tendency to view issues of identity and how they shape writing (and the interpretation of writing) as separate—and less important—to craft. But Salesses corrects this by noting "craft is inseparable from identity"[3] and "race, gender, sexuality, etc. affect our lives . . . Real-world context, and particularly what we do with that context, is craft."[4]

I opened *Craft and Conscience* by urging that before we even begin to write we need to examine our own motivations for writing. By setting down our motivations and hopes for our writing, we prioritize them above the expectations placed on us by the powers that be, whether it be to adhere to traditional and narrowly defined ideas of craft or to be salacious and sensational in order to attract the most readers. As Salesses notes, "In the world we live in, and write in, craft must reckon with the implications of our expectations for what stories should be—with, as [Audre] Lorde says, what our ideas really mean."[5] Our expectations of our work and our responsibility to our subjects are not only as important as craft but should be seen as crucial elements of the craft of writing about social issues.

"If writers really believe that art is important to actual life, then the responsibilities of actual life are the responsibilities of art," Salesses says, removing the supposed ideological divide between our responsibilities as individuals out in the world and our responsibilities as writers on the page.[6] We must ensure elements of craft do not supersede our ethics and integrity in writing about issues of injustice and inequity. Ultimately, when writing about social issues, conscience should be integral to craft, and craft should be inseparable from conscience.

Just as craft cannot and should not be separated from identity and conscience, we cannot ignore the impact of culture on craft because, as Salesses explains, "craft, like the self, is made by culture and reflects culture."[7] Therefore, if we believe craft is impacted by culture, then issues of cultural sensitivity and cultural appropriation should be approached not as matters of political correctness but as matters of craft, explored and taught with just as much rigor as any other elements of craft. Two books that do precisely this are writer and academic Lauren Michele Jackson's *White Negroes: When Cornrows Were in Vogue . . . and Other Thoughts on Cultural Appropriation* and writer, poet, and academic Paisley Rekdal's *Appropriation: A Provocation*. While Jackson provides a

broad sociocultural exploration of cultural appropriation especially of Black cultural elements, Rekdal offers an in-depth interrogation of appropriation in the literary realm.

Jackson begins by pointing out that though appropriation has
become a loaded term, the word itself has a fairly innocuous origin
and history. "*Appropriation* gets a bad rap. The word, centuries old,
denotes an act of transport—some item or motif or a bit of property changing hands." But today, Jackson notes:

> appropriation is everywhere, and is also inevitable . . . So long
> as peoples interact with other peoples, by choice or by force,
> cultures will intersect and mingle and graft onto each other . . .
> The idea that any artistic or cultural practice is closed off to
> outsiders at any point in time is ridiculous, especially in the age
> of the internet.

So, if appropriation is inevitable, why should we concern ourselves with it? "The answer, in a word," Jackson keenly observes,
"power." She points to the limitations of the conversations we've
been having about cultural appropriation:

> Leading discussions about appropriation have been limited to
> debates about freedom and choice, when everyone should be
> talking about power. The act of cultural transport is not in it-
> self an ethical dilemma. Appropriation can often be a means of
> social and political repair. The foil to assimilation for so many
> people America puts in danger is the appropriation of normative
> values with a twist . . . When the powerful appropriate from the
> oppressed, society's imbalances are exacerbated and inequalities
> prolonged.

Beyond the immediate offensiveness of cultural appropriation
to those whose culture has been appropriated are its lasting harm
and consequences:

When appropriative gestures flow to the powerful, amnesia follows. When culture is embraced and its people discarded, it's easy to trick the country into believing somebody white started it all. Nor does the American Dream offer incentive to investigate the possibility that it might be otherwise.

Meanwhile, in *Appropriation: A Provocation*, Rekdal offers this characterization of appropriation in the artistic realm: "Appropriation in art changes the object's meaning by changing the context through which the viewer sees, hears, or reads the object itself."[8] Rekdal goes on to dissect what cultural appropriation means and its impact on the literature of yesterday, today, and tomorrow by examining what lies at the heart of cultural appropriation:

> Because what we're really talking about with cultural appropriation . . . is identity, and while we all have identities, few of us are prepared to unravel the Gordian knot of social realities, history, and fantasy that constitute a self and its attendant ideas of race, ethnicity, gender, sexuality, or even physical or mental ability, let alone discuss what an accurate representation of any of these selves might look like on the page. And the more you and I think about identity, the more we might discover that cultural appropriation is less a question of "staying in one's lane," as one of your classmates put it, than an evolving conversation we must have around privilege and aesthetic fashion in literary practice.[9]

And like Jackson, Rekdal acknowledges appropriation is a matter of power, and the tangible ways in which it exacerbates existing inequities in our society:

> The fact is . . . people's actual bodies, identities, and artifacts have been commodified by powerful groups and institutions. For these readers, the question of creativity will always take

second place to the enduring history of colonialism, which means that for them appropriation is an inherently political, not only literary, practice.[10]

When writers seek to write about individuals and communities outside themselves, it is critical they approach this with not just curiosity but compassion. As Rekdal urges, "when it comes to writing about or through the lives of others, we have to begin with the desire to respect each other's dignity and difference from ourselves, and this requires an understanding of the history of the individuals we wish to represent."[11]

And while empathy for our subjects is important, as Rekdal explains, empathy can be limiting and problematic, especially when used as a singular lens:

> One of the most dangerous side effects of empathetic desire when it appropriates another culture's trauma is that it conflates the underrepresented community with its marginalization and pain. These in turn risk becoming the community's authenticating narratives both for readers outside and within the community.[12]

In her *New York Times* opinion piece, "Who Gets to Write What?," novelist and essayist Kaitlyn Greenidge, like Jackson and Rekdal, acknowledges power is at the heart of the debate around cultural appropriation. While she champions the artistic right of fiction writers to write characters whose identities are different from their own, she takes issue with writers who bristle when held accountable for their lack of cultural sensitivity. As Greenidge notes:

> A writer has the right to inhabit any character she pleases—she's always had it and will continue to have it. The complaint seems to be less that some people ask writers to think about cultural appropriation, and more that a writer wishes her work not to be critiqued for doing so, that instead she get a gold star for trying.

In pushing back against arguments made by writers who misconstrue any valid criticism over lack of cultural sensitivity as political correctness and censorship, Greenidge cites the literary great Toni Morrison, who noted that the backlash stems from marginalized writers taking back the power to define the terms of their own literature.

This belated movement to rebalance power and prioritize cultural sensitivity in literature is welcome by many, especially writers of color and other historically marginalized writers, but has led to a "paranoia about nonexistent censorship," as Greenidge notes, especially amongst some white writers who have never been burdened by the harms of cultural insensitivity or appropriation and who feel their rights as artists supersede others' humanity.

Given all of this, how does a writer with good intentions navigate writing about subjects outside of their experience and identity? What steps can writers take to ensure they are not perceived as culturally insensitive or appropriative? What does cultural sensitivity actually look like and entail? While issues of cultural sensitivity and appropriation can be murky and complex, there are some guiding principles writers can follow. In *Appropriation*, Rekdal offers some probing questions writers should ask themselves:

- Whose desire animates your text?
- Does this desire expand or contract historical memory, and in what ways does this desire encourage you to investigate your own racial meaning?
- Is your understanding of your own identity at the margin or the center of the story?
- Does your identity need to be at the margin or the center of this story?
- What kinds and types of interactions have you had with the communities you wish to represent?
- In what small and large ways have those interactions informed your research, your perception of [the people whose stories you're telling], and your writing?

- What are the reasons your particular project needs to be written and published by you?
- Which audience is your project ultimately suited for, and how does your text signal that?[13]

In his incisive article "How to Unlearn Everything," Alexander Chee, author of *How to Write an Autobiographical Novel*, discusses being confronted by a question at the core of the debate around cultural appropriation: "Do you have any advice for writing about people who don't look like you?" Chee is skeptical of the intent of this perpetual question:

> The question is a Trojan horse, posing as reasonable artistic discourse when, in fact, many writers are not really asking for advice—they are asking if it is okay to find a way to continue as they have. They don't want an answer; they want permission. Which is why all that excellent writing advice has failed to stop the question thus far.

Like Rekdal, Chee responds to this query with a set of insightful questions for writers:

- Why do you want to write from this character's point of view?
- Do you read writers from this community currently?
- Why do you want to tell this story?

While Chee's first question applies most directly to fiction, it also applies to nonfiction written by a writer from outside the community they are portraying. Chee points to the cultural history of storytellers and their importance to their communities. "The traditional role of the storyteller is to tell the stories of a community, or stories that have inscribed the values of that community, or both." Just as importantly, Chee notes how stories shape our perspectives from an early age. "How you grew up, who you grew up with, how you know them. All of this affects what you think is real, and whom you think counts as human—which, in turn, affects how you write stories." Ultimately, Chee rightly observes, "If you're not in community with people like those you want to write about, chances are you are on your way to intruding." One way to be in community with those you are writing about is to read and engage with the literature of that community as Chee notes in his second question. You cannot be trusted by a community when you have not taken the time to be informed by stories told through their own voices.

When it comes to his third guiding question, "Why do you want to tell this story?," Chee suggests, "I think every writer needs to ask themselves this question. But the urgency of it takes on a different shape when we think about other cultures." Chee reveals that he asked himself all of the above questions when he was contemplating writing about a subject outside of his own identity and experience and that he probed even further by asking himself the following questions gleaned from conversations with fellow authors Kiese Laymon and Chinelo Okparanta:

- Does this story contain a damaging stereotype of a marginalized group?
- Does the story need this stereotype to exist?
- If so, does the story need to exist?

Ultimately, Chee notes how the perpetual fixation on whether white writers can write about other communities and identities distracts already marginalized writers from focusing on "how do we write our own literature?"

When I was immersed in writing my biography, *Poignant Song: The Life and Music of Lakshmi Shankar,* I noticed how woefully undiverse the field of biography was, both in terms of authors as well as subjects. As the debate about cultural appropriation raged on, I wondered how it related to writing biographies, stories of other people's lives. I was an Indian American woman writing the life story of an Indian American woman musician. What did I think of white biographers writing the life story of marginalized subjects? What was gained and lost by this?

I parsed my thoughts about this question in my essay, "Who Gets to Write About Whom: Examining Authority, Authenticity, and Appropriation in Biography." Although I focused on the field of biography, my exploration applies broadly to nonfiction writing. I observed that issues of authority, authenticity, and appropriation kept bubbling up in the literary realm in terms of "Who is permitted to tell whose story?" and the more specific question "Should non-marginalized writers write about marginalized people?" As I note in my piece, these questions seem especially important to biography, "a genre specifically tasked with telling other people's real-life stories." But before we answer these questions, we have to acknowledge the context for these questions. The realm of biography has long been biased towards the life stories of white individuals, most often white male figureheads, told by white authors, also most often male. This context is significant because as I state in my essay, it "results in a reinforcement of cultural erasure," which in turn impacts the way history is told, whose contributions are credited and whose are left out.

When I came to the question of who should be writing the life stories of marginalized individuals, I reflected on my own experiences and observations as a woman of color writer writing the life story of an overlooked woman of color artist. Here are my guiding observations:

First, I believe, in theory, most anyone can write about most anyone else.

Second, if the biographer doesn't share the same racial, cultural, or other marginalized background as their subject, it is incumbent on the biographer to address this through extensive and immersive research.

Third, in addition, the biographer who does not share identity or experience with their subject must also spend much time and energy reflecting on how their own identity relates to that of their subject and consider how it shapes or colors the lens through which they are viewing their subject's life. This element, I believe, is most at risk of being absent from biographies by "outside" biographers.

Finally, even with all the research and self-reflection, ultimately, a skilled biographer who shares the same identity or background as the subject will be able to yield certain insights that are unavailable to the biographer who doesn't share these attributes.

Some in the literary world believe writers should keep identity—their subject's as well as their own—out of the scope of their work. This is falsely framed as being objective but instead is an attempt to mitigate the fact that they do not share an identity, community, and experiences with their subject. I don't see how an author can plumb the depths of a person's life story without addressing their identity, even in instances where the subject might not have publicly identified with their identity, which in itself reveals something about them that should be investigated in the telling of their life story. Just as importantly, I don't believe an author can truly convey a person's life story without reflecting on how their own identity shapes their approach to telling this story. Who are they relative to their subject? How do/did their respective identities shape their lives? How does their identity affect the way they view their subject's life, judge their actions? It is crucial to reflect on whether there are power dynamics at play that impact how the writer views their subject and the ways in which this is reflected in the approach to and writing of their life story.

Writers who believe themselves to be objective and colorblind are usually not, and as Rekdal incisively noted, they are not "prepared to unravel the Gordian knot of social realities, history, and fantasy that constitute a self and its attendant ideas of race, ethnicity, gender, sexuality, or even physical or mental ability."[14]

As much as I believe just about anyone can write about anyone else, I also believe writers who share an identity, community, and set of experiences are more able to understand the nuances and traits specific to that culture and community in a way that outsiders cannot. No amount of research is guaranteed to provide an outside writer with access to intangible yet indelible elements, as I note in my final observation.

When writing the lives of those from marginalized backgrounds, it's crucial they are rendered in ways that are well researched, are nuanced and fully embodied, and avoid stereotypes. This cultural sensitivity is a matter of respect for cultural identity but also a matter of good writing craft. When you think of the most compelling stories you have read about people, fictional or nonfictional, those characters are vibrant because they are detailed, fully embodied and nuanced, not rendered with broad strokes or reliant on tired (and possibly biased) stereotypes.

The farther the writer is from the community they are writing about, the more research they need to do, and this research needs to be immersive. This means that the writer must interrogate their sources of information. Who are the sources of information they are primarily referencing about this community? Are they from within or outside of this community? And in the writer's vision for their piece, how often will voices from within the community be heard? Is it important to acknowledge that there may be multiple viewpoints within this community?

Writers writing about a subject or community outside of their identity or experience should consider having an individual from within that community who is familiar with the topic read their work to ensure their rendering of the community is accurate and culturally sensitive. Informally, writers who already know each other professionally and personally might do this work as a favor or in exchange for other tasks. However, this has bred a tendency by writers to assume that writers from marginalized communities will do this for free, instead of recognizing that this is, in fact, labor and should be compensated.

In response to the growing recognition of the importance of cultural sensitivity, formal resources and networks of cultural sensitivity readers have developed. *Conscious Style Guide* is an online resource offering guidance on a host of stylistic issues around identity and other areas. Two networks of sensitivity readers, including Writing Diversely and Writing with Color, list sensitivity readers according to their areas of expertise and services offered. Other useful resources include People of Color in Publishing, Editors of Color Database, and Black Editors & Proofreaders.

In truth, even when writers share a similar background to their subject, it is still important to probe the assumptions shaping their approach to writing about their subject because no identity or community is monolithic. For example, in the South Asian diaspora, caste wields a strong influence even though it often goes unremarked upon. Therefore, a South Asian writer should consider how caste may be at play in the dynamics of a South Asian community they are covering and they should reflect on how their own understanding and experience of caste influence their perceptions and interactions with their subject. Meanwhile, when a Black writer is writing about a Black subject, issues such as class or education can influence their perspective. Similarly, immigrant journalists should be conscious of tendencies of some in the media and in their own communities to harmfully frame documented immigrants as good and deserving and undocumented immigrants as criminal and undeserving.

While cultural insensitivity and cultural appropriation are fraught and complicated issues and the prospect of avoiding them might seem daunting to writers, hopefully, this chapter offers a range of insight and guidance. One key aspect of avoiding cultural insensitivity and appropriation is to make conscious and informed choices about how to depict our subjects, especially if we do not share an identity or community with them. And while there are no guarantees that every reader will accept those choices as culturally sensitive, there is something to be said for taking the issue head on, just as we would any other aspect of craft, thereby demonstrating that others' humanity takes precedence over our desire for unfettered artistic freedom.

■

INTRODUCTION AND CONCLUSION FROM WHITE NEGROES: WHEN CORNROWS WERE IN VOGUE . . . AND OTHER THOUGHTS ON CULTURAL APPROPRIATION

By Lauren Michele Jackson

INTRODUCTION: APPROPRIATION AND AMERICAN MYTHMAKING

Conscience, it has been said, makes cowards of us all.[15]

"Appropriation" gets a bad rap. The word, centuries old, denotes an act of transport—some item or motif or a bit of property changing hands. An artist might appropriate an ancient symbol in a painting or a government might appropriate monies through taxes to fund public education. Taking only the root of the word, the meaning seems clear. To *make something appropriate* for another context. In some circles, the word is still used this way. But colloquially? Not so much.

The debate over cultural appropriation rages on. It was not too many years ago that a certain former Disney star suited in unicorn pajamas rattled her waist in an online video that went viral, prompting America to find language and meaning for what exactly was happening, the language with which to encounter this white girl who so loved black dance.

Versions of this debate have risen up repeatedly. The practice of repurposing culture is as old as culture itself, and America has been *making* other cultures *appropriate* to its amusement and ambitions since the very beginning. "You've taken my blues and gone," Langston Hughes laments in the opening of his 1940 poem "Note on Commercial Theatre."[16] In the 1920s, the poet, playwright, and author observed the great promise in the recognized gatherings of Negro artists making Negro art. Nearly two decades later, he frets over the problem that Negro art no longer needs Negroes to sell, those ole blues sung "on Broadway" and "in Hollywood Bowl."[17]

I recall a similar anxiety emanating from the pop music takeover of Eminem. At the 2000 MTV Video Music Awards (VMAs), the rapper, sporting close-cut bleached-blond hair, entered the theater in a white "wife beater" (offensive, if not inaccurate) and loose gray sweatpants, trailed by dozens of white close-cut bleached-blond look-alikes. The performance was simple, yet clever and effective, and still memorable within the history of an awards show that only recently has failed to diagnose the culture. At the time, Eminem appeared to be the portent of hip-hop's future—artists, critics, and other protectors of the genre worried about the next coming of Elvis, worried that Eminem might catalyze a transformation of rap similar to what long ago happened to rock and roll, and to jazz before that. They weren't so wrong. Thirteen years later, the VMA for Best Hip-Hop Video was awarded to a white anti-hip-hop rap duo from Seattle named Macklemore and Ryan Lewis. Those same 2013 VMAs invited Robin Thicke and Miley Cyrus to jerk and jive to the riff of a song that would later pay court-ordered royalties to Marvin Gaye's estate for borrowing without permission.

National dialogue on appropriation extends beyond the boundaries of popular music. From Halloween costumes to Cinco de Mayo parties to the Washington Redskins to decorative bindis and other music festival fashion, the new millennium and an avowedly more conscious generation of people is tasked with taking seriously all kinds of cultural masquerade. Yet the more popular—and accusatory—the word "appropriation" has become, the fewer people seem willing to understand the meaning behind it. Where it briefly seemed obvious that dressing up as a person of another race to the point of stereotype is *not okay*, as I write this, the country is in the midst of forgiving and actively forgetting the surfaced photograph of a state governor costumed in either blackface or Klan robes. (The governor refuses to disclose which partygoer in the photo is he.) After years of being chastised for wearing sombreros and Native-like headdresses, white people feel indignant. They are paranoid that people of color see appropriation in everything.

Appropriation is everywhere, and is also inevitable. Appropriation, for better and worse, cannot stop. So long as peoples interact with other peoples, by choice or by force, cultures will intersect and mingle and graft onto each other. We call hip-hop a black thing and it is, indeed, *a black thing*, that *also* emerged in neighborhoods where black and brown people homegrown and from the South, from the islands, melded together to produce the music of their experiences in shared poverty and community. Early rap was itself an appropriation of another generation's sound—funk, soul, disco—repurposed for something different and new. Rap also revolutionized the lively form of appropriation known as sampling, a means of incorporating the past, the recent past, and other genres to make timeless music. "I have all of Billy Joel's shit in my iPod," said the legendary Grandmaster Caz in a 2007 interview with RapReviews.com, also citing Simon and Garfunkel as lyrical influences.[18] The idea that any artistic or cultural practice is closed off to outsiders at any point in time is ridiculous, especially in the age of the internet.

Most everyday acts of appropriation, done unconsciously, escape our notice: the word that works itself into your speech because your best friend sprinkles every other phrase with it and where they got it from they don't even know; a new style you have grown into without thought, without a specific icon in mind, by just going with the flow of fashion; some recipe from Pinterest or your favorite food blog that advertises itself as nothing more than chicken casserole, made with ingredients and techniques that don't, to you, recall any culture in particular; the yoga pose you sink into after a workout; the way you shimmy when your favorite song comes on. Said the eminent cultural theorist Homi K. Bhabha, in an *Artforum* roundtable on the subject, "We can never quite control these acts and their signification. They exceed intention."[19]

Which returns us to the contention at the heart of the matter: If appropriation is everywhere and everyone appropriates all the time, why does any of this matter?

The answer, in a word: power.

Leading discussions about appropriation have been limited to debates about freedom and choice, when everyone should be talking about power. The act of cultural transport is not in itself an ethical dilemma. Appropriation can often be a means of social and political repair. The foil to assimilation for so many people America puts in danger is the appropriation of normative values with a twist. Examples include cakewalking on the old plantation, extravagant realness in the ballroom, poetic verse mastered and improved upon by the descendants of those beaten or worse for the crime of literacy. Ask any book of poems by Paul Laurence Dunbar or Gwendolyn Brooks or Terrance Hayes how insurgently wonderful literature can be when black poets experiment with the forms at their disposal, even the ones that come from Europe. When the oppressed appropriate from the powerful, it can be very special indeed.

And yet.

When the powerful appropriate from the oppressed, society's imbalances are exacerbated and inequalities prolonged. In America, white people hoard power like Hungry Hungry Hippos. "One cannot understand American capitalism either historically or in its current configuration," says political scientist Michael Dawson, "without understanding the profound role that the racial order has had in shaping capitalism in the United States, key institutions such as markets, and the state itself." In the history of problematic appropriation in America, we could start with the land and crops and cuisine commandeered from Native peoples along with the mass expropriation of the labor of the enslaved. The tradition lives on. The things black people make with their hands and minds, for pay and for the hell of it, are exploited by companies and individuals who offer next to nothing in return. White people are not penalized for flaunting black culture—they are rewarded for doing so, financially, artistically, socially, and intellectually. For a white person, seeing, citing, and compensating black people, however, has no such reward and may actually prove risky. "After all," says another eminent critic, the cultural theorist Lauren Berlant, "the American Dream does not allow a lot of time for curiosity about people it is not convenient or productive to have curiosity about."[20]

The disparity in power between white and black in America is more severe than anyone can imagine from their own income bracket. According to a 2018 report by the Samuel DuBois Cook Center on Social Equity at Duke University, "Black households hold less than seven cents on the dollar compared to white households."[21] Framed another way in the same report, "A white household living near the poverty line typically has about $18,000 in wealth, while black households in similar economic straits typically have a median wealth near *zero*. *This means that many black families have a negative net worth*" (emphasis in original). The research also found

- Black households with a college-educated breadwinner hold less wealth than white families whose breadwinners do not have a high school diploma.
- White households with unemployed breadwinners have a higher net worth than black households whose breadwinners work full-time.
- Controlled for income, black families save at a higher rate than their white counterparts and spend less than whites.
- White single-parent households have over double the net worth of two-parent black households; and single white women with children possess wealth equal to single black women without children.

These figures ought to be staggering. They should be made plain and visible everywhere, as profuse and common as the severe inequality quantified. They should be posted on the sliding doors of every Trader Joe's in the nation, pinned on every campus corkboard, memorized by every magnet school child until members of the next generation of American overachievers know how little merit and achievement matter in this country. Contrary to myths that say *if only black folks did right*—saved money, went to college, got married, started a business—nothing is as predictive of success in America as being born white. In fact, as the report concludes, "There are no actions that black Americans can take unilaterally that will have much of an effect on reducing the racial wealth gap." Another report, published by the Institute for Policy Studies in 2016, found that if current trends continue, the average black family won't reach the amount of wealth white families own *today* for another 228 years.[22] This is reality. This is America.

The enormity of this wealth gap is exacerbated by the gap between who is allowed to thrive off intellectual property and who is prevented from doing so by this nation's hysterical, driving compulsion to own and regulate all things black. From dabbing to "squad," collards to street wear, babywearing to voguing to EDM, jazz to "lit" to "slay" to durags; from Timbs to Kimberlé W. Crenshaw's "intersectionality," it is destiny that black insights will be grasped by white hands, passed along from the edgy to the not-so-edgy, till everyone joins in, even the racists. This can take a long time, decades even, though the internet lights a fire under the timeline. When it's time to pay the piper, however—that is, give credit where it's due—somehow the accolades land in the lap of somebody white, or at least someone who is not black. The contradiction is what's meant by the adage made famous by Paul Mooney: "Everybody wanna be a nigga, but don't nobody wanna be a nigga," an ambivalent turn of phrase. Everybody wants the insurgence of blackness with the wealth of whiteness. Everybody wants to be cool without fearing for their lives. They want blackness only as a suggestion, want to remain nonblack, keep centuries of subjection and violence at bay with the prefix *non-* firmly in place. When appropriative gestures flow to the powerful, amnesia follows. When culture is embraced and its people discarded, it's too easy to trick the country into believing somebody white started it all. Nor does the American Dream offer incentive to investigate the possibility that it might be otherwise.

This is a book about black aesthetics without black people. Each of the following essays takes up an area of popular culture, each curious in its own way about the desire for black culture by people who are not black. It's a strange half-life indeed, blackness in decay without its people. There's the dead black boy made art at the 2017 Whitney Biennial, the fall of a Southern cuisine queen named Paula Deen, there's Marc Jacobs, Christina Aguilera, the Kardashians, the Women's March. Mostly, though, the figures exposed are us, consumers of culture regularly bamboozled by the tireless process of American mythmaking.

To anyone confused about it all, I hope that I may be of service in enlightenment.

To those who count themselves allies, may these essays make you a little less sure of yourselves.

To those *who been knew*, may you revel in the wonder of what people like us have made out of this dull, dull world.

CONCLUSION

BUSINESS AS USUAL

"Come on up, Dr. Miller," called Evans from the head
of the stairs. "There's time enough, but none to spare."

In an essay published by the *Chronicle of Higher Education* in 2017, literary theorist Walter Benn Michaels argues against the existence of cultural appropriation, calling it, per the essay's title, a "myth." His reasoning does not begin with his disbelief in the ordering power of racism—a position netting him a fair amount of notoriety within and outside academia—but with his disbelief in the existence of culture, period. "The problem is that the whole idea of cultural identity is incoherent," he writes, too incoherent to draw lines around, too slippery to hold, too capricious, too rhetorical to lay any sort of meaningful claim to.[23] Naming several of the prestigious greatest hits of the great appropriation wars—Dana Schutz, "Kenny" Goldsmith, Sam Durant, and, *well*, AncestryDNA—Michaels believes it was false propriety and fictive kinship, not racial science or anti-blackness or bad art, that "got them in trouble."* Even if white privilege "enabled them to treat something that didn't belong to them as if it did," that quandary can only be a quandary if another kind of privilege, genetics, enables people of color to treat something, culture, that does not belong to them as if it does. In short, investment in cultural difference gives appropriation life, Michaels says, lobbing the ball back across the net.

I don't wholly disagree with Michaels—culture *is* incoherent and confusing and borderless just as much as it is shared and trenchant and guarded and intuited. The same way that I share language and traditions with white friends who also grew up in the Midwest and have stayed in the Midwest, I have language and traditions that they don't share, that I better share with strangers who are black and grew up in the South, in England, in the West Indies, or in Canada. And they, too, have language and traditions better shared with others around them, of whatever race, than with a black American from the Midwest. Culture is contradictory, not mythical.

Lost in an elaborate whodunit, Michaels (along with less intelligent critics) deeply misreads the terms of grievance, pinning the propriety impulses on the language of the oppressed. However, the initial ownership claim is not made by the person who notices the disparity between who labors and who profits, but by the entity who declares the right to claim and profit in the first place. "No stories belong to anyone," may be true in spirit—in law and capital it is quite another matter. Ideas and practices and art

---

*"Trouble" here seems to mean embarrassment and a few impassioned opinion pieces.

and appearances accrue value the whiter they become, the whiter they are perceived as being all along. Underwriting is a money matter. And black people have been underwriting white capital for centuries.

Binding the disparate cultural touchstones in this book, appropriation runs on desire more than hatred, inattention more than intention. I've made my case out of cases, making the commonplace exceptional by default, but I cannot overstate the regularity of appropriation, how often it is, for most, a nondilemma. Appropriation is impossible to delaminate from our most basic appreciation of what it means to create and share something, whether or not that something was ever intended to be for sale. Appropriative gestures are devilish in their contortions, every bit as convoluted as they make you feel by sussing them out.

Complex problems often deserve complex solutions, but in the case of power and appropriation the answer is quite simple when looked at from a bird's-eye view. Equality is too tame. Fair compensation is too modest. Our world deserves reordering. Only under a transformation on that scale could I ever imagine a version of society in which black people have options instead of destinies, options instead of statistics. Reorganizing the terms of what counts and who counts on planet Earth and beyond is only fathomable by minds more creative than my own.

At a humbler level, in the here and now and the everyday, we are alone together with our desires and our gestures. We are all of us tainted by the forces that order our world—capitalism, anti-blackness, imperialism—and saying so is not the same as license to roll over and accept come what may. On the contrary, if there is a call embedded in this book—and even at this stage, I am not sure if there is—it is a call to more alertness, more intensity, more care, and more fluency in the racial dramas performed as part and parcel of business as usual. "There's time enough, but none to spare."

There is time enough, but none to spare.

■

WHO GETS TO WRITE WHAT?

By Kaitlyn Greenidge

When I was in graduate school, I remember a fellow writer bringing to a workshop a lynching scene. The writer was not black. He was, in fact, a Chinese-American man named Bill Cheng, who would go on to write a novel of the blues called "Southern Cross the Dog."

In class that day, we hemmed and hawed over discussing the scene until our professor slammed the table and shouted at the room, "Does Bill have the right to write this scene?"

"No," one of my classmates answered, one of the other writers of color in the room, who was also, like Bill, not black. I remember being furious, spitting mad. Of course, of course, I thought, he has a right to write this scene. At the time, I don't think I could have said why I felt so strongly, was so offended by the fact that our white professor would ask this of a room of mixed writers.

Now I look back and I can say I felt so strongly that Bill had a right to write that scene because he wrote it well. Because he was a good writer, a thoughtful writer, and that scene had a reason to exist besides morbid curiosity or a petulant delight in shrugging on and off another's pain—the fact that a reader couldn't see that shook my core about what fiction could and couldn't do.

And yet the question was worth asking: Had he "culturally appropriated" an experience—an experience of pain, no less? He hadn't been lynched, and when most people think of lynching in this country, they do not think of people who look like him. Should everyone get to create the art they feel called to make?

Some would have you believe that if you're a serious writer, you are not allowed to add questions about who is telling what story and why to the list of things we ask of a piece of fiction.

It can be hard to come up with real answers to those questions. It's especially difficult if you aren't doing the work of creating fully human characters, regardless of your or their identity. And it can be really, really, hard to come up against your own blindness, when as a writer, you are supposed to be a great observer. It can be terrifying to come to the realization that it is totally possible to write into this blind spot for years. Whole books, in fact whole genres of fiction, make their home in this blind spot, because of writers' publishing community's biases.

When I was writing my first novel, I was determined to include a section in the voice of an 80-year-old, white, Yankee heiress. The character is deeply racist, but the kind of racist who would consider Donald J. Trump vulgar and never use the ugliest of racial epithets. Bone china and lace tablecloth and genteelly rusted Volvo parked at the family home in Concord, Mass. kind of racist. Her inability to honestly acknowledge her racism leads to her complicity in a large, very awful crime against a community of people, one she spends a chapter of the book attempting to apologize for, without ever admitting guilt. She desperately wishes for black Americans' approval while still being unable to imagine us as humans with a full emotional range like hers.

It was a personality I thought I knew well, growing up going to the prep schools of the wealthy and connected as a scholarship student. I wrote a draft in this voice, tucked it into my manuscript like a stink bomb, and smugly sent it off to my agent and my professor, waiting for their reactions.

"It doesn't work," I was told. "She's not believable as a character. She doesn't work." "Damn white readers," I jokingly said to my friends. But once I got over myself, I took apart that section piece by piece. I rewrote and failed and rewrote and failed. As much as this character had begun as an indictment of all the hypocrisies of my childhood, she was not going to come out on the page that way, not without a lot of work. I was struck by an awful realization. I would have to love this monster into existence. The voice of this character had been full of scorn and condescension. I rewrote it with those elements in place, but covered with the treacly, grasping attempts at affection of a broken and desperately lonely woman.

Five years or so after I came to that realization, I wrote to Bill Cheng after reading the novelist Lionel Shriver's *keynote* on "Fiction and Identity Politics" at the Brisbane Writer's Festival. Wearing a sombrero, Ms. Shriver spoke out against "cultural appropriation" as a valid critique, arguing that it censored her work as a writer, that she would not have free rein to fully imagine others' perspectives and widen her world of characters. "Did you hear about this?" I typed into our chat window, and Bill wrote back, "Hold on . . ." Then his answer pinged.

"Why do they want our approval so badly?" Bill typed back to me.

This is the question, of course. It's the wish not so much to be able to write a character of another race, but to do so without criticism. And at the heart of that rather ludicrous request is a question of power. There is the power of rendering another's perspective, which is not your own. There is the adage "Don't punch down," which sits like the shiny red lever of a fire alarm, irresistible for some writers who wish to pull it.

We writers, in the United States at least, have a peculiar, tortured relationship with power. We want it both ways. We talk about the power of the written word to shift whole levels of consciousness while constantly lamenting the death of publishing, the death of the novel, the death of the reader. Those first concerns are valid, but the last become questionable, especially in the face of numerous studies to the contrary that say that people are reading at similar rates as a few years ago. Readership has also grown in certain groups—according to analysis of recent data, the demographic group most likely to have read a book in the last year is college-educated black women.

The anxiety about a shrinking audience is accompanied by a dull realization that writing from the perspectives of those who have traditionally been silenced in "great literature"—the queer, the colored, the poor, the stateless—is being bought, being sold, and most important to writers obsessed with status (and we are all obsessed with status), winning awards and acclaim.

Claudia Rankine, when awarded the MacArthur genius grant this past week, noted that the prize was "the culture saying: We have an investment in dismantling white dominance in our culture. If you're trying to do that, we're going to help you." For some, this sounds exciting. For others, this reads as a threat—at best, a suggestion to catch up and engage with a subject, race, that for a long time has been thought of as not "universal," not "deep" enough for fiction. The panic around all of this is driving these outbursts.

It must feel like a reversal of fate to those who have not been paying attention. The other, who has been relegated to the background character, wise outcast, dash of magic, or terror or cool or symbolism, or more simply emotional or physical whore, is expected to be the main event, and some writers suspect that they may not be up for that challenge.

A writer has the right to inhabit any character she pleases—she's always had it and will continue to have it. The complaint seems to be less that some people ask writers to think about cultural appropriation, and more that a writer wishes her work not to be critiqued for doing so, that instead she get a gold star for trying.

Whenever I hear this complaint, I am reminded of Toni Morrison's cool assessment of "anti-P.C. backlash" more than 20 years ago: "What I think the political correctness debate is really about is the power to be able to define. The definers want the power to name. And the defined are now taking that power away from them."

The quote is two decades old, but this debate, in certain circles, has never moved past the paranoia about nonexistent censorship.

This debate, or rather, this level of the debate, is had over and over again, primarily because of an unwillingness on one side to consider history or even entertain a long line of arguments in response. Instead, what often happens is a writer or artist acts as though she is taking some brave stand by declaring to be against political correctness. As if our entire culture is not already centered on a very particular version of whiteness that many white people don't even inhabit anymore. And so, someone makes a comment or a statement without nuance or sense of history, only with an implicit insistence that writing and publishing magically exist outside the structures of power that dominate every other aspect of our daily lives.

Imagine the better, stronger fiction that could be produced if writers took this challenge to stretch and grow one's imagination, to afford the same depth of humanity and interest and nuance to characters who look like them as characters who don't, to take those stories seriously and actually think about power when writing—how much further fiction could go as an art.

It's the difference between a child playing dress-up in a costume for the afternoon and someone putting on a set of clothes and going to work.

■

HOW TO UNLEARN EVERYTHING: WHEN IT COMES TO WRITING THE "OTHER," WHAT QUESTIONS ARE WE NOT ASKING?

By Alexander Chee

"**D**o you have any advice for writing about people who do not look like you?"

I was at the Bread Loaf Writers' Conference this summer, on a panel of writers of color. We talked about our concerns, from supporting the work of other marginalized writers inside of predominantly white institutions to finding ways to create community. Jericho Brown, Ingrid Rojas Contreras, Lauren Francis-Sharma, and I took questions from Cathy Linh Che. It was a good conversation. Near the end of the discussion, we opened it up to the audience, and then we found ourselves at this question.

I realized I had been waiting for it. Dreading it a little. The question has been a mainstay of literary events ever since Lionel Shriver took to the Brisbane Writers Festival stage wearing a sombrero and delivered a defense of writing whatever she wanted, about whomever she wanted. Online, it has become one of those fights with no seeming end.

Before Shriver, this was a topic for difficult and meaningful pedagogical conversations, often led by writers of color in YA and sci-fi and fantasy, like speculative-fiction author Nisi Shawl, whose book *Writing the Other*, co-written with Cynthia Ward, is considered a go-to guide. As the writer Brandon Taylor wrote on Lit Hub, there is no shortcut to putting in this work, and yet the problems that arise from authors' not giving it the necessary thought mean there is now what he calls "a cottage industry of minor fixes," from sensitivity readers to freelance editors, who work with this focus.

Given all the excellent writing about the challenges of rendering otherness, someone who asks this question in 2019 probably has not done the reading. But the question is a Trojan horse, posing as reasonable artistic discourse when, in fact, many writers are not really asking for advice—they are asking if it is okay to find a way to continue as they have. They don't want an answer; they want permission. Which is why all that excellent writing advice has failed to stop the question thus far.

I don't answer with writing advice anymore. Instead, I answer with three questions.

1. Why do you want to write from this character's point of view?
We write what we believe a story is, and so our sense of story is formed by the stories we've read. But for most of us, the stories we hear are the first stories that teach us. Stories from family. Stories in the news. Stories we're taught at school. Gossip, trash talk, and jokes, which are the shortest, complete form of narrative. How you grew up, who you grew up with, how you know them. All of this affects what you think is real, and whom you think counts as human—which, in turn, affects how you write stories.

The traditional role of the storyteller is to tell the stories of a community, or stories that have inscribed the values of that community, or both. Modern fiction works differently. It's less overtly connected to any idea of a debt to a community, but there's always a relationship back to that role. I do believe that much of the shape of an idea for a piece of fiction depends on what you think the word *community* means, and how you experience it at an unconscious level.

I once advised a young white writer who believed that because she had loved a novel written by a writer from a certain background that she, too, could write about a family from that background. Her country had colonized this country, but a condition of being a colonizer is that you do not know the country you are taking possession of, or the culture—you don't have to. I knew the questions this student still had to answer because I knew people from this community. I had to draw her attention to everything she didn't know. She seemed resentful throughout. Her previous adviser had believed she could write this novel, too.

But if you're not in community with people like those you want to write about, chances are you are on your way to intruding.

2. *Do you read writers from this community currently?*
People don't often know their blind spots until they do a simple audit of their bookshelf. When I go to literary parties at editors' homes, I experience the shelves upon shelves of white writers like a rebuke. Most of what has survived to us thus far is literature written by white male writers. The last three decades especially have seen a struggle to revive the books we've lost—books by women, people of color, and queer writers—and to then try and write out of that recuperation a new tradition. But most of us writing now were not educated by that expanded canon.

I teach roughly seven writing workshops a year, and have since 1996. For the 24 years I've been teaching creative writing, the stories I see have predominantly been about white people, or characters that mysteriously don't have any declared ethnicity or race at all. This is true no matter the number of students of color in the class, and no matter the amount of writing I assign by writers of color, and even, to my surprise, no matter the declared radical politics of the students. In general, the beginner fiction that writers produce is what they think a story *looks like*. Those stories are often not really stories—they are ways of performing their relationship to power. They are stories that let them feel connected to the dominant culture. There was one day last year when two queer Korean-American students both submitted stories about queer Korean-American characters, and it felt like the dawn of a new era.

This brings me to the flip side of this question, a question for the rest of us who aren't white men: How do we write our own literature? I am thinking of when I interviewed Ursula K. Le Guin and she told me she had to teach herself to write as a woman. Or my own first stories, when I did much the same as these students. In the 1980s, I had to learn how to write myself and people like me onto the page. My own life on the page felt impossible to explain in any detail when I was a student writer. I had to ask myself why I was embarrassed to mention that I was Asian-American, much less to center it in a story. Strangely, it took finding writers like Mavis Gallant and Gregor Von Rezzori, whose works described characters who had lived among several cultures, as they were writing about Europeans. Reading about someone who was of Austrian and French heritage may not feel like a mix of cultures, but I unexpectedly found permission there—white writers teaching me how to write mixed-race Asian-American characters like me.

3. Why do you want to tell this story?

I think every writer needs to ask themselves this question. But the urgency of it takes on a different shape when we think about other cultures.

A few years ago, I was on a train, headed out to Portland, Oregon, and I met a retired British couple, a man and a woman, at dinner. They were both white. She looked like Camilla Bowles and he looked like James Bond's dad, complete with a black eye patch over his left eye and striking, swept-back silver hair. The woman was more social, intent on drawing me out. When she learned I was a writer, she asked me what kind of writer, and I told her. She apologized for only being interested in mystery novels. I know that it was just her being polite—people who only read mystery novels believe they are a superior form of writing. Her husband seemed uninterested in our conversation, until he learned I taught writing, and then he seemed to light up.

"Do you believe writing can be taught?" he asked. I said I did, unlike some writing teachers. He told me about his desire to write mystery novels. He was a retired police detective. His wife rolled her eyes as he talked about how crimes aren't solved in real life the way they are in mystery novels, and eventually, she brought the conversation to a halt, saying, "I just don't want him to be embarrassed."

Later, as I wrote in my journal, I had the idea to write a novel about a police detective who has just retired, who wants to write mystery novels, and his wife, who only reads mystery novels and doesn't want him to. He has spent a career solving crimes he can't talk about. He begins writing about two unsolved cases, and while the writing isn't going well, he is drawn eventually into trying to solve them. I even wrote 100 pages of it and sent it to my readers, who then began a process like the one I use with students, asking me questions.

Everyone liked it. But there were questions. *Does this have to be set in London? Is there some way it can be set in the United States?* One reader told me foreign editors typically dislike Americans writing about Europe and the U.K. because of how little the average American writer knows about these places. And while one of my most enthusiastic readers had been raised and educated in the U.K. and provided me with a library of books to help with finishing it, I questioned myself.

I wasn't stealing the story of the retired detective I'd met—the novel I would write would never resemble his—but I was trying to use my idea of him and his wife as the main characters. I was interested in the crisis a retirement can be within a long marriage. I was also interested in writing a thriller. But I realized that it required a level of work I wasn't sure I was willing to do—hire the equivalent of a British sensitivity reader, for example, since I would be almost colonizing the colonizer, as it were.

In trying to figure out if I should write the above story or not, I asked myself these first three questions, and then three more, which I got from conversations with the writers Kiese Laymon and Chinelo Okparanta:

4. Does this story contain a damaging stereotype of a marginalized group? Does the story need this stereotype to exist? If so, does the story need to exist?

A stoic white retired British police detective and his wife did not at first glance seem like damaging stereotypes. But even in thinking about this, I had to ask myself why I wanted to write the novel. Other questions grew from that. Did I really want my next novel to be set in London? Wasn't there enough to write about in America? What was I doing writing about a white man? Even if I wanted to write a meta–murder mystery, wasn't there some other way to do it? The long-standing Anglophilia I had developed when the first queer books, films, and music I found came out of the U.K. in the 1980s was something I had come to watch out for.

I eventually figured out how to set it here in America, though it has taken a back seat, joining the five other ideas for novels and another book of essays all lurking in my files.

These discussions distract me increasingly from the conversations I'm interested in. If I'm helping students cross boundaries, I urge them to look at the ones they find within. I also urge them to set them for themselves. I'm more interested in how there's another literature possible when people who belong to the status quo challenge it from within. I'm thinking of Jess Row's novel *Your Face in Mine*, a story that explores taking on an identity you weren't born into, literally, when the narrator discovers a white Jewish friend from high school has had surgery to "turn" himself black. Row, who is white and Jewish, pursues the peculiar turns that are possible when someone with white privilege seeks to rid himself of his guilt—not through restorative justice but through camouflage and counterfeit. Or the inimitable Ocean Vuong's *On Earth We Are Briefly Gorgeous*, an autobiographical novel set in the second person. The narrator writes the novel to his mother, who is unable to speak or read English and will never read it. This direct address to her—Asian-American refugee to Asian-American refugee—is drawn out of that history and intimate proximity. It uses the Japanese literary form *kish tenketsu*, a dramatic structure that refuses to deploy conflict. No rising arc, no "climax." Vuong was influenced by canonical works like *Moby-Dick*, but he uses them to feed his daring, to write something entirely new.

I was with him recently at NYU for a night of readings. He said two things that night that I still think of. "What is pretentious but to have the pretense to the assumption that you belong here?" And, "If you are an Asian-American writer, artist, poet, or painter, prepare to be unfathomable, inconceivable."

These are two polestars, a North and South. One was what I perhaps still needed to lay down, and the other was something to pick up. In my reluctance for my retired detective narrator, I could finally see how tired I was of the idea of having to pretend to be a white man, or be like one. Better to catch the energy that rises when I fling myself at everything I fear writing.

Increasingly, this question is a trick question. A part of a game where writers of color, LGBTQ writers, women writers, are told to write as white men in order to succeed, and thus are set up to fail. While white men are allowed to write what they think the stories of these people are, and are told it is their right. This game is over.

So when I meet with those beginner students to discuss their first stories, I ask them to think of stories only they can write. Stories they know but have never read anywhere. Stories they always tell but never write down. That's what this question is really about. Or could be. If the questioner asked it of themselves more often than they asked other people.

■

WHO GETS TO WRITE ABOUT WHOM: EXAMINING AUTHORITY, AUTHENTICITY, AND APPROPRIATION IN BIOGRAPHY

By Kavita Das

Earlier this year, the official portraits of President Barack Obama and First Lady Michelle Obama were unveiled. These portraits were particularly momentous because they were of our country's first Black president and first lady. But also of importance was that both the president and first lady chose Black artists—Kehinde Wiley and Amy Sherald—to paint their portraits.

Upon the unveiling, President Obama reflected on the significance of his choice of artist on Instagram saying, "Today, @KehindeWiley and @ASherald became the first black artists to create official presidential portraits for the Smithsonian [. . .] Thanks to Kehinde and Amy, generations of Americans—and young people from all around the world—will visit the National Portrait Gallery and see this country through a new lens." First Lady Michelle Obama echoed similar sentiments in her own Instagram post.

For his part, the magnitude of his dual role as the portrait artist for the first Black president and as the first Black presidential portrait artist was not lost on Wiley. "We can't not recognize the important significance of representation in art and the decision that this president and first lady have made in choosing artists like ourselves," Wiley told CNN. "[T]hey're signaling to the rest of the world that it is OK to occupy skin that happens to look like this [. . .] on the great walls of museums in the world."

This artistic choice made by President and First Lady Obama about who would see them and who would translate their vision into an artistic portrait also bears consideration in the realm of literature and most particularly in biography, where the lens of the biographer can be compared to the lens of the portrait artist.

Meanwhile, in the broader literary world, across nonfiction and fiction genres, questions of authority, authenticity, and appropriation keep bubbling up. The key question debated time and again is: "Who is permitted to tell whose story?" And at the root of this question lies the deeper question: "Should non-marginalized writers write about marginalized people?"

These central questions are batted back and forth in literary panels and articles, as writers with marginalized identities claim that non-marginalized writers, usually white and heterosexual, have no right to write about their communities, and that their work is inauthentic and culturally appropriative. Meanwhile, the non-marginalized view their work as imaginative, not transgressive, and justify it by voicing concerns about censorship and artistic constraints, declaring that nobody should be able to dictate to anyone else who and what they can create art about.

In 2016, the *New York Times* explored "Who Gets To Tell Other People's Stories" in its series, Two Writers on this Topic. Anna Holmes took the position that writers should have the freedom to write beyond their scope of experience, but noted that it is important that they are driven by a motive of "empathy" rather than of "exploitation" in telling other people's stories. "I am not of the opinion that [. . .] artists cannot, or should not, attempt to tell the stories of people unlike themselves—and I am resistant to claims that, for instance, men are by definition unable to paint honest portrayals of women. (Or Koreans of Latinos, or African-Americans of, say, the white Amish.)" Pointing to a related essay by James Parker, Holmes suggested that there is "a robust, if uneasy, coexistence between the idea that identity is part of experience, and that experience (or the absence of such) should not preclude anyone from telling other people's stories."

Holmes's counterpart in the column, writer James Parker essentially agreed with Holmes but spoke less of the identity of the writer or their subject, instead focusing on what it takes for the writer to reach a deep understanding of the humanity of their subject. "If you don't open your heart to somebody, feel the weight of his individuality, expose yourself to his predicament, how can you possibly hope to understand him?"

A few months later, in an opinion piece also in the *New York Times* entitled "Who Gets To Write What," Kaitlyn Greenidge, a Black writer, defended the right of writers to write about things outside their experience, "A writer has the right to inhabit any character she pleases—she's always had it and will continue to have it." But Greenridge tempered this with the caveat that writers shouldn't presume that they are exempt from criticism if their portrayals are inaccurate or lack depth or nuance. "The complaint seems to be less that some people ask writers to think about cultural appropriation, and more that a writer wishes her work not to be critiqued for doing so, that instead she get a gold star for trying."

Moreover, Greenidge addresses the "paranoia about nonexistent censorship" amongst writers seeking to write what they want while also remaining above reproach, by pointing to this quote from lauded Black writer Toni Morrison: "What I think the political correctness debate is really about is the power to be able to define. The definers want the power to name. And the defined are now taking that power away from them."

This conversation about authenticity, authority, and appropriation is especially crucial and relevant to the genre of biography, which can be regarded as the literary cousin to portraiture, a genre specifically tasked with telling other people's real-life stories. For the past five years I've been working on a biography about Lakshmi Shankar, a Grammy-nominated Hindustani singer who played a key role in the movement that brought Indian music to the West in the late 1960s. Last year, I participated on a panel at the 2017 Biographers International Organization (BIO) conference entitled, "Whose Lives Matter, and Who Should Be Writing Them." On this panel, which was mostly made up of writers of color writing about people of color, we talked about the challenges of writing about subjects who've been marginalized by history in various ways.

In terms of considering the panel's first question—"Whose lives matter?"—in a 2016 piece I wrote for the *Los Angeles Review of Books* entitled "Biography: Where White Lives Matter," I observed that the field of biography is overwhelmingly biased towards publishing and promoting biographies about white subjects, which results in a reinforcement of cultural erasure. I went on to attribute this in part to the fact that like the biographies that are most often published, the realm of biography—from publishers, to editors, to agents, to organizations—is overwhelmingly white. Therefore, through their composition, structure, and actions, irrespective of their rhetoric, the publishing sector articulates whose life stories they believe matter. In the piece, I predicted that the end of Obama's presidency would usher in several biographies, and I pondered about how his racial identity would be treated by presidential biographers, who are overwhelmingly white. If the racial identity of President Obama's portrait artist holds significance, isn't the racial identity of his biographer relevant to how his story might be told?

The second question our panel considered—"Who should be writing them?"—is a fraught, complicated question, and my thoughts on it are necessarily layered. Essentially, my perspective can be summed up in four parts:

First, I believe, in theory, most anyone can write about most anyone else.

Second, if the biographer doesn't share the same racial, cultural, or other marginalized background as their subject, it is incumbent on the biographer to address this through extensive and immersive research.

Third, in addition, the biographer who does not share identity or experience with their subject must also spend much time and energy reflecting on how their own identity relates to that of their subject and consider how it shapes or colors the lens through which they are viewing their subject's life. This element, I believe, is most at risk of being absent from biographies by "outside" biographers.

Finally, even with all the research and self-reflection, ultimately, a skilled biographer who shares the same identity or background as the subject, will be able to yield certain insights that are
unavailable to the biographer who doesn't share these attributes.

My thoughts on who can and should write whose stories have
been shaped by my own work on Lakshmi Shankar's biography—a
biography about an Indian American woman by an Indian American woman. For several years I was too intimidated to take on the
responsibility of relaying Shankar's life story because I felt I lacked
the necessary credentials as a historian or as an ethnomusicologist.
The sheer research required—to tell the story of a Hindustani
musician necessitated relaying the story of Hindustani music—
made me want to quit before I even started. Ultimately, it was the
potential loss of her story to the world, given her advanced age at
the time, and the cultural erasure of yet another woman of color,
that urged me ever forward against all doubts. I realized that I had
been focusing on all the ways in which I wasn't qualified to tell her
story, rather than on the ways I was.

First, my family had a close relationship with Lakshmi Shankar
for most of my life. This both gave me access and a close perch
from which to make observations of her both as an artist and a
person. But I also knew that my close relationship could also be
a hindrance, if I let the biography slip into hagiography. Second,
Lakshmi Shankar was a South Indian woman who married into a
Bengali family and who became a lauded singer of North Indian
music. Not many people, Indian or non-Indian, can understand
the significance of the cultural, geographical, and gender barriers she transcended through her life and music. However, I was
born to a Bengali father and South Indian mother and grew up
steeped in both North Indian and South Indian music so I inherently understand the regional and cultural insularity of these
worlds, the invisible barriers erected to both protect culture while
keeping outsiders out. My own grandmother is of comparable age
to Lakshmiji, as I deferentially called Lakshmi Shankar, and they
both were married as teenagers, yet their lives were so different. In

many ways, my grandmother served as a reference point for what Shankar's life might have been had she not taken the artist's path.

Then there is the fact that I'm a writer who, before coming to writing, spent 15 years working on social change issues, including racial justice. So, in addition to depicting the key professional and personal moments within the narrative of her life, I have the ability to understand their significance in context to sociocultural history. I can illuminate some of the forces that worked in her favor as an artist, and the many forces that worked against her— including her cultural identity and gender.

While there can be other biographies of Lakshmi Shankar, my biography of her could only be written by me. Those with greater training and expertise in music might yield more nuanced musical insights while others who are historians might bring other historical facts to bear on her story. But there are certain insights and observations, given my shared cultural background and personal experience with Lakshmiji along with my own voice as a writer, that only I could have gleaned. Ultimately, it will be for readers and critics to decide the particular value of my role as narrator of Lakshmi Shankar's story.

Some of the tension in recent conversations about authority, authenticity, and appropriation in writing comes from the emergent reality that many writers who for so long have been viewed, and have viewed themselves, as "inside" writers, now suddenly find themselves, for the first time, regarded as being on the "outside." Where once there was no topic that was considered beyond their scope, they are encountering constraints in the form of questions about their authority and authentic tie to those narratives. Meanwhile, marginalized authors who have long been mining the life stories of descendants and figures in their communities often overlooked by history books only to now be "discovered" by the mainstream publishing sector, are justifiably defensive.

However, it is in itself problematic to have the starting point for this conversation be, "Who is permitted to write about what?" or "Why can't I write about her?" Instead, it needs to start from

234 | KAVITA DAS

a broader set of questions about the inequities in the publishing realm. "Who is permitted to write and be published? Whose stories are seen as important and elevated?" Beyond whether already empowered writers have permission to write about those outside their communities, the more critical questions are: "What is the particular value of a biographer who shares an identity or experience with their subject? What is the importance of authentic stories and voices in biography?"

If the current conversation were a story, it would be centered on the moment the writer walks into a room, leaving out any background on how they got there, who built that room, who else gets to walk into that room, who doesn't, and why not. Ultimately, any lover of literature or history shouldn't be satisfied with a story that is half-told and pre-ordained.

Beyond these ideological debates, the question of "Who has *permission* to write about whom" has ethical implications. In his book, *Vulnerable Subjects: Ethics in Life Writing* (Cornell University Press, 2004), G. Thomas Couser examines the issue of writing about others, especially those more vulnerable in society, through bioethical and anthropological lenses. He notes that, "What is at stake in the ethics of life writing is the representation of the self and of the other, which is always at once a mimetic and political act." Couser goes on to state, "Such writing should not be beyond criticism, especially when it concerns issues of public moment . . ." He observes that rather than labeling valid criticism aimed at writers of others' stories as "policing," we should be concerned by the "policing" by "cultural gatekeepers" in the publishing sector who reinforce whose stories get told and who gets to tell them. Ultimately, Couser believes there needs to be "greater diversity in life writing, in two distinct respects: more kinds of *lives* represented and more kinds of *representation*."

Speaking of Wiley's unique artistic vision in rendering the subjects of his portraits, President Obama said Wiley "would take extraordinary care and precision and vision in recognizing the beauty and the grace and the dignity of people who are so often invisible in our lives and put them on a grand stage, on a grand scale, and force us to look and see them in ways that so often they were not." It is evident that in portraiture, as in biography, who does the seeing affects who gets seen and how they are portrayed.

CHAPTER 7

RIPPLE EFFECTS
OF MAKING WAVES

Implications (Good and Bad)
of Writing About Social Issues

I started *Craft and Conscience* by asking you to identify your motivations for writing about a social issue and I shared essays, my own and those of others, including George Orwell and James Baldwin, who reveal their own motivations for writing about social issues, like fascism and racial injustice, respectively. Motivation serves as both catalyst and compass, helping us navigate our way through the sometimes challenging and lengthy writing process, carrying us across rejection and revision.

Most of the best writing about social issues is informed by deep research and knowledge but also by motivation, opinion, and perspective. It is our motivation and perspective that make our work that much more compelling and uniquely ours. As readers, we immediately grasp that the writer wants us to care about this issue because they themselves care about it, and we connect to them through a shared sense of empathy and curiosity. Yet, there continues to be a debate around the idea that journalism and narrative nonfiction must be objective and neutral in order to be of substance.

When it comes to covering issues of social justice, I believe the field of journalism needs to reckon with why objectivity and neutrality are prioritized and prized above conscience. Are these the traits we most want from chroniclers of social issues that have moral quandaries at their core? As noted in chapter 1, lauded journalist Christiane Amanpour observed how, in the wake of the 2016 election of President Trump, "it appeared much of the media got itself into knots trying to differentiate between balance, objectivity, neutrality, and crucially, truth." And she went on to explain how in her approach to journalism, "I believe in being truthful, not neutral. And I believe we must stop banalizing the truth." And she's not alone.

In their August 2021 essay in the *New Yorker*, Russian-American journalist Masha Gessen poses the question that serves as the title of the piece, "Why Are Some Journalists Afraid of 'Moral Clarity'?" Gessen acknowledges the ongoing debate in the media and asks, "What is so terrible about moral clarity?"[1] They and other journalist colleagues are raising concerns about the recent tendency by journalism outlets to publish writing that is morally reprehensible under the misguided assumption that this is necessary in order to appear balanced by providing multiple perspectives on an issue. One example that Gessen and others have pointed to is the *New York Times*'s regrettable decision to publish an unconscionable op-ed by Republican senator Tom Cotton that called for the use of military force to quell the largely peaceful racial justice protests in the wake of George Floyd's murder at the hands of police. It is worth noting that the *New York Times* felt compelled to add an editor's note to the piece, acknowledging it had received strong internal and external criticism and discussing the ways in which its editorial process fell short in publishing the piece as it is.

Gessen delves down to the foundations to seek a definition of "moral clarity" in order to illustrate how critical it is to journalism. Citing the words of a fellow journalist, Gessen notes that journalism grounded in moral clarity begins with "objective facts" rather than any presumed agenda, and they go on to explain, "moral clarity is a quest, guided by clear values and informed by facts and context, and clearly aligned with the original concept of journalistic objectivity."[2] These ideals, Gessen points out, used to be at the heart of journalism but have given way to narrow and conservative notions of objectivity and neutrality:

> Objectivity in journalism came to mean presenting both sides of an argument from a position of neutrality. But not every argument has two sides: some have more, and some statements should not be the subject of argument. There cannot be arguments about facts.[3]

Perhaps the rise of a more rigid practice of journalism, with an overemphasis on objectivity and neutrality above moral clarity, helped spark the creation of "solutions journalism" and "advocacy journalism." Solutions journalism is essentially journalism that focuses on the solutions to a social problem in lieu of just presenting the social problem, which is often the case in media coverage of social issues. Perpetual focus on the social problems rather than on individuals and organizations working towards possible solutions is not only demoralizing to those working to address those issues but gives the public a skewed sense that the problem has no potential solutions or advocates. This can leave readers believing that there is nothing they or anyone else can do, which may be false and also a lost opportunity to shed light on people and organizations working to address the issue that might need the attention and support of interested readers.

According to the Solutions Journalism Network (SJN), which works to change the culture of journalism by training more than eighteen thousand journalists, solutions journalism is effective for the following reasons:

- it enhances knowledge and accountability
- it strengthens audience engagement
- it helps restore trust[4]

In terms of how solutions journalism enhances knowledge and accountability, SJN explains that "when incorporated into broader coverage of an issue, it offers a more accurate account of the state of play than does a dystopian ticker tape of corruption and failure. It also strengthens accountability by raising the bar and removing excuses for inaction."[5] SJN goes on to note that the goal of solutions journalism is to "provide society with the information it needs to correct itself."[6]

According to SJN, evidence from studies demonstrates that solutions journalism strengthens audience engagement by bringing in new audiences and retaining the existing audience's attention. Furthermore, solutions journalism seems to help restore readers' trust in journalism and public institutions "by showing that the system can work to solve society's most pressing problems. Some studies have uncovered a kind of 'halo effect' in which solutions journalism strengthens the perception of a newsroom's trustworthiness."[7]

There is particular skepticism and scrutiny around journalism being done by advocacy organizations working to raise awareness and change policies around a specific social issue. The June 2018 *Columbia Journalism Review* (*CJR*) article "Advocates Are Becoming Journalists. Is That a Good Thing?" explores this debate. While it acknowledges that advocacy journalism fills in critical gaps in media coverage of social issues, especially those specific to countries and regions in the Global South, it questions the legitimacy of journalism embedded in advocacy organizations:

> But these groups are not fundamentally journalistic in nature. Although they may look and behave like modern media organizations, they are advocacy groups, and have an explicit agenda; they are looking for impact. That agenda may coincide with the news, and they may use traditional journalistic techniques to advance it, but in most cases the larger goal of this work is in service of some kind of policy change or other action, and not information or the public record per se.[8]

The blurring of the line between journalism done by advocacy organizations, even when done by experienced journalists hired into these organizations, and that done by traditional media organizations is cause for concern to some journalism stalwarts. *CJR* talked to the then editorial director of the American Civil Liberties Union (ACLU) Terry Tang, a veteran journalist, whose newsroom was producing fourteen to twenty stories weekly:

> Does the desire to promote a specific viewpoint on an issue or news story ever get in the way of producing this kind of journalistic content? Tang says it doesn't, and that the editorial group makes a point of sticking to a very traditional, fact-based approach. In the end, she says it's a matter of trust—if the organization were to bend the rules, eventually people would stop trusting what it was saying.[9]

In the article, *CJR* cites instances where advocacy organizations crossed journalistic and ethical lines by promoting misleading information because they were more motivated by their mission or by the need to use a sensational story to raise funds for their cause than by truth and accuracy. Ultimately, however, *CJR* concludes that journalism by advocacy organizations is on the whole a positive force:

> In the end, the world of journalism and the world as a whole are probably better off now that there are activist organizations that are trying to use the tools of modern media to tell stories. The more sources of information there are, especially from remote or developing nations, the better. In some ways, that's one of the biggest benefits of a democratized media environment.[10]

While the power brokers of journalism debate the role and ethics of journalism, some journalists, especially journalists of color, are taking back some of the power by creating new systems of journalism, which merge community-based local journalism with digital media, challenging key aspects of traditional media. Unlike traditional journalism and media, where power has been concentrated amongst a small number of wealthy individuals, typically white, and corporations, and the content is created with the aim of reaching a largely white mainstream audience, these new journalism upstarts are hyper-focused on their communities. Beyond this, they are also redefining the role of journalism by blurring the line between the journalist and their community, as well as the line between reporting on events on the ground and responding to them.

After working in senior leadership roles at the *Los Angeles Times* and *CNN Digital*, journalist and media executive S. Mitra Kalita cofounded URL Media with Black journalist and media executive Sara Lomax-Reese, with the aim of supporting a range of community-based journalism outlets by and for communities of color. Kalita also created *Epicenter-NYC*, a digital newsletter and news site for her incredibly diverse Jackson Heights community in Queens, New York City, a microcosm of the world. Soon after it launched, in the midst of the COVID-19 pandemic, *Epicenter-NYC* went from reporting on the challenges and casualties of the pandemic in their particularly hard-hit community to becoming a crucial informational hub for getting thousands of community members vaccinated, especially vulnerable populations including immigrant workers and their families, who might have limited English literacy or face documentation challenges.

Of the crucial work being done by *Epicenter-NYC* on behalf of its community, Kalita said, in an interview with *MIT Technology Review*, "What we're doing now is continuing the route of connecting people to each other and opportunities. There's a lot of matchmaking going on. We can sort through a list of about 7,500 to 8,000 people who said they need help, and then find places in proximity. We've become this wonderful marriage—a centralized operation that also embraces decentralized solutions."[11]

As to the debate about whether this work constitutes journalism, Kalita offers her own convictions. "Inevitably, the question I get is 'Is this the role of a journalism organization?' The essence of what we are describing is [a method] for these people to prove that they are human. In some ways, there is no greater purpose of our journalism."[12] Keeping community at its center focuses and animates the work of community-based digital journalism, even as it is empowered by technology and social media. Unpredictable global events like the COVID-19 pandemic play out on the global stage, but they wreak havoc and traumatize at the local level, offering opportunities for community-based digital journalism outlets, like *Epicenter-NYC*, to not just cover but support the communities they know best. "Maybe never again will we have this opportunity to interface with the public as we are right now with vaccines," says Kalita, before underscoring the powerful lessons of the pandemic and the questions it raises for our society and its chroniclers, "How does that change the delivery of other services? . . . How do you take this moment, learn, and then react accordingly?"[13]

Journalism is certainly due for a reckoning, where it revises its code of ethics to emphasize moral clarity and conscience above objectivity and neutrality; however, the field of personal essays gives me even more cause for concern. Recently, I took a class on the personal essay with Eula Biss, a masterful essayist whom I admire as much for her craft as the range of social issues she's covered in her brilliant essays. However, she confirmed my own misgivings about the personal essay space by acknowledging there is no code of ethics for personal essayists. This is deeply concerning, given that personal essays are where we examine the personal impact of fraught social issues and search for and make meaning of our lives through these explorations. Biss went on to note that while ethics in personal essays is an ongoing conversation, every essayist has to work out their own set of ethics. I have taken many nonfiction and essay-writing classes and workshops across a spectrum of institutions, however, and hardly any of them addressed ethical issues in a meaningful way.

Instead of leaving it up to writers, many of whom are at the mercy of editors and publishers, to develop their own code of ethics, discussions of ethics should be incorporated into every nonfiction and essay-writing class. Ethics are not ancillary to craft but, in fact, critical to the craft of writing. And when it comes to writing about social issues, I will go so far as to say that you cannot write about social issues responsibly unless your work is grounded in ethics. So many problematic essays that have been and continue to be published, sometimes to the regret of the writer and to the distress of many readers, could be avoided by foregrounding discussions of ethics and moral clarity in the work and in the editorial process.

Now that we understand that motivation, perspective, opinion, and ethics are important drivers for writing about social issues, we can acknowledge that we are motivated by the possibility of our writing having an impact. But what do we mean by "having an impact"? Often, when we talk about wanting our work to have an impact, we are talking about wanting to raise awareness and change the conversation, and if we are really fortunate, change hearts, minds, and culture and contribute to policy shifts. So, when we talk about impact, we are usually presuming a positive impact.

However, we need to be aware that our work can also have a negative impact, such as provoking an angry reaction towards our subject or towards ourself, as the writer. Whether the overall impact is positive or negative, there are implications to writing about social issues, which may be felt far and wide, like the ripples from a powerful wave we have set in motion. We should consider and prepare for how these implications may play out in our own lives and in the lives of others.

It is especially crucial to consider the implications of our work when we write about subjects outside of our experiences and communities outside of our identity. Here are some considerations:

- *How might your subjects be impacted, positively, negatively, or both, if this story is published?* Even positive attention for an issue can have negative implications for individuals or communities affected by that issue if it violates their privacy by creating undue scrutiny on their lives.

- *Have you been transparent with your subjects about the intent of your work on this issue and their portrayals in it?* What is their reaction? When possible, writers should be transparent with their subjects about the intentions of their work. This ensures that the depiction of the subjects' circumstances is fair and accurate and, ultimately, strengthens the work as well as the relationship between the writer and their subjects.
- *What can you do to prepare your subjects for any positive and negative attention the piece might attract to them?* It's important to let individuals and communities featured in your piece know the possible positive and negative implications of your piece being published and talk with them about how to handle these potential situations.
- *Are featured individuals dealing with existing stigmas that make them additionally vulnerable?* How will the piece impact their security and well-being? It is critical to think about how the security and well-being of vulnerable subjects might be impacted by your writing. Are they made more or less vulnerable by your work? For instance, if you are writing about individuals who are undocumented or in substance abuse recovery, how will your work impact them, and are they prepared for this?
- *Does the published piece reflect the identities and lives of your subjects responsibly and with integrity?* If not, are you willing and able to make changes and corrections if the writing or editorial process has resulted in mischaracterizations of your subjects? Hopefully, you are familiar and comfortable with your publisher's approach to social issues. Be sure to ask your editor for a clear understanding of what interventions are available to you, as the writer, during and after the editorial process, to mitigate any issues in tone or accuracy.

If you are directly or indirectly connected to the subject you are writing about, be sure to consider the implications, positive and negative, to yourself as the writer. Start by assessing how close you are to the subject. Here are some questions to help in that assessment:

- What is your relationship to the subject/story/issue?
  - Are you part of the community or outside of the community covered in your work?
  - Are you directly or indirectly impacted by the issue?
  - How indirectly are you learning about the issue? How many levels of filters has the story been through before reaching you?
  - How will you be impacted by your coverage of this issue? Who might view your coverage of this issue favorably or unfavorably?

If you are directly or indirectly affected by the publication of your story, you need to consider the impact on yourself. Are you prepared for the possible positive or negative implications for yourself? If you are telling the story of a social issue through your own lived experiences or your eyewitness account, it is critical to feel comfortable with that part of your life being exposed to the public. You have to prepare yourself for the range of possible reactions from strangers as well as people you know, from those who are understanding and supportive to those who are judgmental and critical.

Most of all, you have to be at ease with the idea that once your story is in the public domain, it no longer belongs just to you. Therefore, I encourage writers to carefully consider whether they are comfortable with the loss of privacy that comes with telling your life story.

If you are concerned by personal implications to you if family members, friends, or colleagues learn about this aspect of your life, then consider asking if it is possible to publish the piece anonymously or under a pseudonym. Or consider fictionalizing it.

Bear in mind, every writer has a different threshold for what they are comfortable revealing about themselves and their lives through their writing, so do not feel pressured to share details that other writers share in their work, unless you are truly comfortable with making those details public. This is why I believe it is often worth hitting pause between writing a fraught personal piece and submitting it and publishing it, to give yourself the time and space to reflect on the implications of it being out in the world. Social issues matter, but so does your sense of comfort.

It is important to consider carefully the integrity and tone of an outlet and its editor to ensure you feel secure having your story live there. Emerging writers drawing from their life experiences can feel pressured to publish when they find a publication interested in their work, but they should only do so if they feel comfortable with the publication and the terms of being published (for example, editorial process, payment, rights) since they will have to live with the consequences—potential affirmation and potential stigma—of having their story out in the world. I'm particularly concerned for marginalized writers who might be made further vulnerable due to multiple social and economic factors. Outlets, which for so long have been closed off to these writers, have in recent years shown a growing interest in traumatic stories of marginalization. In the best-case scenario, outlets seek out these stories with the intention of raising awareness and garnering empathy for a social issue, but in the worst-case scenario, they seek to exploit sensational aspects of the story to bring more eyeballs and clicks to their site, without any regard for the impact on the writer.

Several factors in publishing are cause for concern for marginalized writers, from lack of cultural sensitivity given the largely undiverse newsrooms and editorial mastheads of most outlets to the social and financial vulnerabilities these writers face. In my estimation, the rise in interest in social issues has ironically fueled this phenomenon, allowing some outlets to disguise their desire for ever more popularity with a hollow intent to cover a social issue, all while exploiting vulnerable writers and subjects.

Coming to writing full time in 2013 after working in racial justice, I was struck by the lack of diversity and equity in every aspect of publishing, from the leadership of big publishing houses to the editors reviewing and accepting submissions at literary magazines, which are often feeders for publishing houses. It was no mystery to me, an emerging woman writer of color, why so few books and pieces by writers of color and other marginalized writers were being published or publicized. What was a mystery to me was why more writers (and readers) were not talking about this major oversight, at least, publicly. It smacked of lack of imagination and unconscious bias on the part of the very people who were supposed to be the stewards of literature; in broader terms, it was the ongoing manifestation of widespread systemic racism, perpetuating the erasure of certain authors and stories. Given my work in racial justice and my commitment to social change, I felt compelled to respond to it.

When Jamaican writer Marlon James won the 2015 Man Booker Prize, I grew frustrated by fellow writers romanticizing revelations about how he had nearly given up writing and even resorted to destroying his work due to the overwhelming rejection he received from agents and editors earlier in his career. Writing peers wanted to focus on his eventual success and not the fact that he, and many marginalized writers, face daunting obstacles to getting published, and many ultimately do give up, robbing readers and themselves of their writing.

I was motivated to reveal that behind the romantic notion constantly peddled by literary power brokers—that "good writers should persist beyond rejection"—lies an industry rampant with systemic racism, as evidenced by its woefully undiverse staffing at decision-making levels and in the lack of diversity in the authors it publishes. My piece, "Writers Shouldn't Romanticize Rejection," published in *The Atlantic* in 2015, ended up going viral and being discussed in many online spaces about literature and publishing:

> These barriers are steep for all writers, but they are even more daunting for writers of color and other underrepresented writers who write narratives that revolve around themes of identity. Not only is it harder for writers of color to get published, but when

rejecting our work, publishers tell us that what we're writing about is too narrow and niche and won't appeal to mainstream audiences. It's hard not to perceive this as both a rejection of the relevance of our work as well as ourselves. And for many writers of color who face barriers in other parts of their life due to their identity, the rejection is compounded, forcing some to put down their pen and give up their voice.

I was thrilled to see my piece shared widely within my networks and fellow writers using it as a point of instruction and discussion in their creative-writing classes. But I made an error in judgment. In my elation, I read online comments in a *Reddit* thread about my piece. While there were commenters who agreed with me and shared their own experiences and insights, some ugly comments decried me as just another writer of color blaming the system for my own insecurities and limitations.

At first, I was stung by what seemed like a personal attack that went beyond the ideas expressed in the piece. But as someone who has worked in a digital racial justice organization, I was no stranger to the inflammatory responses which inevitably follow any writing that challenges inequities. I came to view the fact that someone felt compelled to respond to my piece, even with a negative comment, as a secondary sign of success; I had struck a nerve. In truth, after some time passed, I channeled my feelings about this episode into a humorous piece for *McSweeney's* about how no time of year is suitable for rejections. I have included my essay for *The Atlantic* here, and I share this context so that you can understand my motivations for writing it and the implications to me, positive and negative, of having it out in the world.

As challenging as it is to write about fraught social issues, such as racism and misogyny, for me, it is easier than examining myself or the personal implications of these issues on my life. I'm more comfortable holding a mirror up to the world than to myself, especially my flaws and insecurities. I had worked in public health for six years addressing various aspects of health disparities, from the need for greater cultural competency in pediatricians to a lack of breast cancer education, screening, and treatment for broad and diverse populations to the demand for mental health services for returning Iraq and Afghanistan veterans who faced the "invisible wounds" of post-traumatic stress disorder and other mental health challenges associated with armed conflict. Yet, I had never shared my own health issues, which had plagued me since birth, or my struggle to become my own patient advocate in a health-care system, which because of my gender and race, overlooked and undermined my bodily agency.

When I began writing about being born with a cleft palate and my medical journey to remedying it and the struggles I endured along the way, I decided to concentrate on the writing process rather than the publishing process. I was conflicted; I wanted to write my truth about being born with a birth defect, but I wasn't sure how I felt about that truth living out in the world, beyond my closest family and friends. Focusing on the writing helped me hone in on what I wanted the piece to be and who it was meant for instead of trying to write it to fit the parameters of a specific outlet. Ultimately, I came to realize I wanted the piece to be as much about what I lost as what I gained—a recovered sense of smell and agency over my own body and health.

"Recovering My Fifth Sense" was published in *Longreads*, a space known for longform essays and journalism, which gave me the latitude to explore various themes in the narrative. I worked with an editor who was sensitive to the nuances of identity in the piece.

> While I emerged from this latest medical fiasco having regained a moderate sense of smell, I also emerged from it resolving to be my own patient advocate, relieving my parents of the burden of trying to be both my parents and my doctors, a burden I'm certain, was both unexpected and trying for them. I recalled the mix of trepidation and determination with which I had moved out of my parents' bedroom as a child. Fear had gripped me after they

had tucked me in, turned out the light, and disappeared into their bedroom. I also recalled the way the sunlight had streamed onto my bed when I awoke the next morning in my own room.

While I felt vulnerable and exposed to have out in the world this personal piece about my health struggles, I was pleasantly surprised by the encouraging response from friends and family. I was particularly moved, however, when strangers reached out to thank me and share their own struggles and journeys with having cleft lip and cleft palate. I had hoped my piece would raise awareness about the challenges faced by people born with these issues, but I never expected to find solace and community. I share this piece here, along with my motivations and misgivings in writing it, to underscore how important it is to take the time and space to consider the personal implications of publishing your personal story about social issues. And to acknowledge that sometimes our writing about social issues has implications beyond our own expectations.

In her essay for San Francisco Museum of Modern Art's *Open Space*, "There Is No One Way," disability rights activist, writer, and editor of *Disability Visibility: First-Person Stories from the Twenty-First Century*, Alice Wong examines the perilous impact of the coronavirus pandemic on people with disabilities. Given the myriad ways in which society, from its infrastructure to its policies, is exclusionary and ableist, Wong rightfully points out how members of the disabled community have long known the lessons our broader society is just beginning to learn through this pandemic— that we can adapt working, learning, and cultural environments to be virtual or hybrid and to suit different modes of being and learning. Furthermore, lack of access to what is important to us and sustained isolation is physically and mentally taxing, but we can view it as an opportunity to innovate ways to maintain connectivity and access. Wong acknowledges, as someone who has long championed adaptations and accommodations on behalf of herself and others in the disabled community that are most often met with perpetual resistance, it is bittersweet to see these changes so quickly embraced and enacted by so many when forced by a pandemic.

The implications of pointing out this hypocrisy of ableism highlighted by the pandemic allows readers, especially ableist readers, to reflect on their pandemic experiences, and reconsider and reenvision ways to make the world more inclusive and accessible to people of all abilities.

> The urgency of this time elicits an impulse in me to tell my own story and amplify the stories of disabled people—to create in the face of overwhelming pain, bigotry, and oppression. I guffaw thinking about how often ventilators, an essential part of my cyborg body, have been in the news. The political and cultural circumstances of this historic time led me to write about my experiences as a disabled vent user and the eugenic implications of healthcare rationing that are happening across the world due to shortages. With my podcast, Disability Visibility, I produced a series of episodes about the impact of COVID-19 on disabled people, in particular disabled people of color who are disproportionately at risk. On my blog, I published a series of guest essays by disabled and immunocompromised people examining fatphobia, ableism, and genocide. All of these activities were unplanned, created in response to the overwhelming fear, sadness, and anxiety I feel in this moment.

Wong's piece is a crucial invitation to all creators to reflect and create not in spite of the pain and obstacles of the pandemic but because of it, something she and other disabled artists and activists have long understood and mastered.

Gabrielle Bellot's searing essay "Stepping on a Star" first appeared in *We Wear the Mask*, an anthology on the phenomenon of "passing," which is defined as the "knowing decision about hiding or omitting one's background to obtain acceptance into a community" by Brando Skyhorse and Lisa Page, the co-editors of the anthology. Bellot's personal essay chronicles her fraught journey to coming out as a queer transgender woman. Her honesty about her struggles on this journey enables the reader to understand how Bellot's decision to come out and inhabit her true self is filled with implications—lack of bodily safety, sexual harassment, psychological and emotional trauma, loss of family and friends, loss of educational and professional networks. We get a clear sense of what is at stake for her, which makes the implications of writing about transition and identity as a queer transgender woman that much more significant:

> Sometimes, it is petrifying, the way it feels that if I do not pass, I will pass, instead, onto the undiscovered country, like so many trans women of colour before me, if the wrong person reads the book of my being. But it is real, being me, being a trans woman, a woman—and I would not give that up for all the wishes an errant genie could grant, even if that genie could have me be born as a cis woman. After all, as much as that would make certain parts of me fit better together, it would also not be me; being trans is who and what I am, and I love it, hate it, and love it, and do not know what to make of it. As we travel, after all, our past changes, as we do in the present; the traveller into the future leaves behind a wake of self as tenuous as seafoam. And perhaps there is nothing that reveals this better—or worse, if such things frighten—than transition.

Bellot's unflinching candor and compassion in unfolding her journey leaves us with a sense of how profound is the impact of living her true identity not just on an existential level but also on a day-to-day basis, just being able to do the ordinary things most of us take for granted, like trying on lipstick in a drugstore.

In this final chapter, I focused on the implications of writing about social issues to encourage writers to consider the implications, both positive and negative, of publishing writing about social issues, and to push forward, with eyes wide open, to how it will impact others and themselves. We write to be seen and heard so why not be clear-eyed and earnest in our assessment of how our work might ripple out into the world, hopefully joining forces with the currents created by others who also seek progress. In truth, this book and the class out of which it grew are implications of my own passion for and commitment to writing about social issues. I'm grateful I have had the opportunity to witness, connect with, and guide others along their own currents, as we collectively create the momentum for sea change.

■

WRITERS SHOULDN'T ROMANTICIZE REJECTION
By Kavita Das

L ast month, the Jamaican writer Marlon James won the 2015 Man Booker Prize for Fiction for his riveting novel, *A Brief History of Seven Killings*. A spate of articles came out documenting his win, noting the fact that the 44-year-old James was the first Jamaican to win the prize. One article by *The Guardian* however, focused on the fact that the manuscript of James's first novel, *John Crow's Devil*, was rejected close to 80 times before finally being published in 2005. It also discussed how James had given up when faced with such vast rejection. "There was a time I actually thought I was writing the kind of stories people didn't want to read," he said, going on to describe how his desperation drove him to destroy his own work. "I actually destroyed the manuscript, I even went on my friends' computers and erased it."

This article was shared among writers on social media with exclamations of, "don't give up!" and "keep at it!" But this reaction reminded me of the exuberance of many when Obama was elected President: To them, his election demonstrated the country had become blissfully "postracial," despite all evidence to the contrary.

Time and time again, the literary establishment seizes on the story of a writer who meets inordinate obstacles, including financial struggles, crippling self-doubt, and rejection across the board, only to finally achieve the recognition and success they deserve. The halls of the literary establishment echo with tales of now-revered writers who initially faced failure, from Stephen King (whose early novel *Carrie* was rejected 30 times before being published), to Alex Haley (whose epic *Roots* was rejected 200 times in eight years). This arc is the literary equivalent of the American Dream, but like the Dream itself, the romantic narrative hides a more sinister one. Focusing on how individual artists should persist in the face of rejection obscures how the system is set up to reward only a chosen few, often in a fundamentally unmeritocratic way.

What are we meant to make of the fact that James's manuscript was rejected 80 times? Sadly, this phenomenon isn't that uncommon. In fact, there's a website dedicated to bestsellers that were initially rejected. Was it lack of imagination on the part of those publishers? Was it unconscious bias against a new and unfamiliar narrative—one that they didn't regard as "mainstream?" Or was it a complex business decision based on multiple factors? As an emerging writer of color, I'm no longer inspired by this narrative. I don't see much cause to celebrate when writers of James's profound talent are roundly rejected in the course of normal business.

I'm weary of articles about beloved novels that almost didn't exist and esteemed writers who almost walked away for good. And while I'm genuinely happy and grateful for the voices that make it through to be published and am thrilled when they receive well-deserved rewards and recognition, I know they are the slim exceptions, and that this is particularly true of writers of color.

In 2012, the writer Roxane Gay wrote a piece entitled "Where Things Stand," which examined how many books by writers of color are reviewed by the pivotal *New York Times Book Review*. She found that in 2011, nearly 90 percent of the books reviewed were by Caucasian authors. Africans and African Americans only accounted for four percent; Asians, Asian Americans, and South

Asians together also only accounted for four percent; and Middle Eastern and Hispanic authors each accounted for a paltry one percent. Gay contrasted this with the fact that according to the 2010 U.S. Census, Caucasians only accounted for 72 percent of the population. Although she acknowledged that her examination was imperfect and limited in scope, Gay noted that it still pointed out glaring disparities for writers of color:

Writers deserve that same fighting chance regardless of who they are but here we are, talking about the same old thing—these institutional biases that even by a count of 2011 data, remain deeply ingrained.

Three years later, I remain perplexed by a system that creates the conditions by which manuscripts that will go on to be lauded are first broadly rejected. While other sectors have certainly overlooked brilliant new ideas and missed opportunities for innovation, this fact isn't usually romanticized or celebrated. In other sectors this level of oversight would be called "a system failure," or "inefficiency," or "failure to innovate." And policies and practices would be put into place to try to prevent this from happening in the future.

But I don't see those kinds of self-critiquing evaluative discussions or major efforts to dismantle such systems in the literary world. Just last month, *Publishers Weekly*'s annual field survey confirmed that 89 percent of the publishing sector workforce is white–exactly the same as the year before. Instead, the focus continues to be on individual persistence against myriad, intangible barriers, rather than on the role of the system in creating and perpetuating many of those barriers, thereby putting the full burden on writers.

These barriers aren't just unique to the American publishing industry. Earlier this year, a report came out about the publishing prospects for writers of color in England. The report, according to an article in *The Guardian*, "found that the 'best chance of publication' for a black, Asian, or minority ethnic (BAME) writer was to write literary fiction conforming to a stereotypical view of their communities, addressing topics such as 'racism, colonialism or post-colonialism as if these were the primary concerns of all BAME people.'" And like the *Publishers Weekly* survey, the report also confirmed the lack of diversity within the U.K. publishing sector.

One of the most curious aspects of this mode of operation is that it gives rise to a secondary narrative: that of discovery. Instead of dismantling these barriers, literary power players emphasize how they "discovered" an author, even though that author was knocking at the door of the literary establishment the whole time, just waiting to be seen and let in.

These barriers are steep for all writers, but they are even more daunting for writers of color and other underrepresented writers who write narratives that revolve around themes of identity. Not only is it harder for writers of color to get published, but when rejecting our work, publishers tell us that what we're writing about is too narrow and niche and won't appeal to mainstream audiences. It's hard not to perceive this as both a rejection of the relevance of our work as well as ourselves. And for many writers of color who face barriers in other parts of their life due to their identity, the rejection is compounded, forcing some to put down their pen and give up their voice.

In a recent NPR article about the need for greater diversity in the publishing sector, the writer Daniel Jose Older describes the formidable obstacle faced by writers of color in getting past gate-keeping publishers and agents, who are predominantly white:

You have to always be conscious of that. Am I going to be submitting something that is going to put the person on the defensive? Is my voice somehow going to be somehow alien or unrecognizable to the person I am submitting it to?

The article goes on to discuss how *Corona*, a novel written by the author Bushra Rehman about a Pakistani Muslim girl from Queens was rejected by major publishers. "That was the one comment that I remember, that there is not an audience for this work." Thankfully, Rehman persisted and Corona was published by a small independent press.

But the impact of this publishing system failure goes beyond the writer. It means readers lose vital stories that make up the broader contemporary narrative. This isn't just unfortunate, but also perilous, as explained by Chimamanda Ngozi Adichie in her TED Talk, "The Danger of a Single Story":

It is impossible to talk about the single story without talking about power. There is a word, an Igbo word, that I think about whenever I think about the power structures of the world, and it is nkali. It's a noun that loosely translates to "to be greater than another." Like our economic and political worlds, stories too are defined by the principle of nkali: How they are told, who tells them, when they're told, how many stories are told, are really dependent on power.

Just weeks ago, the author Mira Jacob was asked to give the keynote speech at a *Publishers Weekly* event. She was speaking about her experience being published as a writer who's a woman of color, but ironically her speech went largely unheard, for technical and non-technical reasons. Adapting her remarks for a *Buzzfeed* post, Jacob said, "American audiences are capable of so much more than some in your industry imagine. And if we can break that down to what I really mean, I mean this: White Americans can care about more than just themselves. They really can. And the rest of us? We are DYING to see ourselves anywhere." Jacob goes on to explain why it makes good business sense to publish books that reach and reflect untapped audiences. "Because all of us are so ready to talk about the world we live in. We are ready to have a publishing industry that is of that world."

So, the next time a brilliant writer wins an award only after being rejected countless times, I will celebrate the writer and their persistence and victory against the odds. But I will continue to hold out hope that the winds of change will shift the odds in favor of more writers, creating a victory for everyone who loves new, untold stories.

■

RECOVERING MY FIFTH SENSE
By Kavita Das

Just two weeks before my birth in November 1974, my parents moved into their first house, a split-level ranch in Bayside, Queens. They had been in America for less than a year, having first emigrated to England from their homeland of India so that my father, a gastroenterologist, could pursue his Ph.D., and my mother, an obstetrician-gynecologist, could receive additional medical training.

While my mother was giving birth to me my father was home raking leaves, because it was fall and leaves need raking, and because fathers were not considered crucial to child birthing in Indian culture. I came into the world around midday, a glowing, healthy baby of six pounds, seven ounces.

In the hospital, after the nurses had brought me to my mother's bedside, she began to give me my first feeding. As soon as I started to hungrily suck on the bottle, milky formula began trickling out of my nose. She wiped it away and began again, but the formula, once again, leaked from my nostril. That's when she suspected that, although I had been spared the perceivable deformity of a cleft lip, nestled between my plump cheeks and hidden behind my rosebud lips, was a cleft palate.

An online search for "cleft," leads me first to the MacMillan Dictionary's definition: "A narrow space in the surface of something," such as "in a rock or in someone's chin." Oxford Dictionaries notes that "cleft" is both the past participle of the verb "cleave," as well as an adjective, meaning "split, divided, or partially divided into two." It also introduces me to a new turn of phrase, "be (or be caught) in a cleft stick," meaning to "be in a situation where any action one takes will have adverse consequences." (The phrase derives from an object of the past, a wooden stick with a partial slit in which one can hold something. References to a cleft stick exist in English literature, including Dickens' *Oliver Twist*, but according to World Wide Words, the first example of its usage in this particular expression was recorded by the *Oxford English Dictionary* dating back to 1782, when, in a letter, 18th-century English poet William Cowper stated, "We are squeezed to death, between the two sides of that sort of alternative which is commonly called a cleft stick.")

When I search for "cleft" on a medical website, however, my search hits closer to home. According to the Centers for Disease Control and Prevention, a "cleft lip and cleft palate are birth defects that occur when a baby's lip or mouth do not form properly during pregnancy." The CDC estimates that each year in the United States around 2,650 babies are born with a cleft palate, a condition where "the tissue that makes up the roof of the mouth does not join together completely," typically occurring between the sixth and ninth weeks of pregnancy, when the palate forms in the fetus. But while science can explain how and when a cleft palate forms, it is unable to explain why. Research suggests they are caused by some combination of genes and other factors, including substances the mother might have come into contact with during pregnancy.

What is known, however, is that orofacial clefts are more common in Asian, Latino, and Native American babies, and curiously, according to WebMD, "twice as many boys have a cleft lip, both with and without a cleft palate," yet "twice as many girls have cleft palate without a cleft lip." Throughout my childhood and even in my teenage years I wondered about the relative significance of being an Asian-American girl, and here, ironically, was irrefutable—even if not positive—evidence of its significance.

My earliest quest for the relevance of my Asian-American identity began in gift shops, where I searched through racks of pastel beaded necklaces that spelled out names. *Karen. Kathryn. Kayla.* No *Kavita.* Strange, because years later there would be three Kavitas in my small women's liberal arts college. In high school, there was my search to find Asian-Americans represented in my curriculum. It would not be until World Literature in 12th grade that I would see the lives of Asian-Americans portrayed in Amy Tan's *The Joy Luck Club*. Sadly, Tan would be the only writer of color we would read that year, because it turned out World Literature meant mostly reading works reflecting different parts of the world, but always through the perspective of a white scribe, as in Shakespeare's *Othello*, E.M. Forster's *A Passage to India*, and Nadine Gordimer's *July's People*.

As a baby, I was coddled by my parents out of much love and concern. I grew into a roly-poly toddler and a rambunctious young child, and yet because of my cleft palate, I was besieged with minor health issues. Eating some solid foods and drinking milky liquids caused my nose to dribble. Like other children with orofacial clefts, I had associated issues with my inner ears, requiring tubes to be surgically inserted and rendering plane travel painful. Yet, I was a well-traveled child, journeying with my parents to Hawaii, Mexico, Japan, and India, cotton balls stuffed in my ears to help relieve the pressure.

My parents' concern grew when I began to speak. I was vivacious, confident in my adorableness, and had much to say. Yet, as words bubbled out of me, not many of them were intelligible to others. I knew what I was saying, but others did not. My questions were often met with dumbfounded expressions or requests for me to repeat myself. "Nanny, Nanny," I ran around the house calling after my beloved Daddy, my cleft palate preventing me from articulating the sounds of a hard "d."

Thankfully, around age 4, I began speech therapy with a friendly but firm young, Midwestern, white woman I only knew as Karen. I have vague, watery memories of Karen and our sessions, which took place at the Bronx hospital in which I was born and where my father practiced. I remember Karen being tall, thin, and having a kind face framed by chestnut brown hair, done up in the waves and feathers of a 1980s hairdo. I also remember lots of machines resembling movie reels and audio tape decks, only bigger. I listened through headphones too big for my tiny head and repeated what I heard over, and over, and over again. I recall feeling frustrated when Karen said "No, not like that. Like this." And when she repeated the desired sound back to me, I wondered, "Isn't that what I just said?"

I have only two mementos from my years of speech therapy with Karen. The first is an oversized stamp of a moose she presented to me as a reward for my efforts, which launched my eventual stamp collection. The second is her unremarkable Midwestern accent, separating me from my Queens classmates, and later leading people to remark, "You don't sound like a New Yorker!"

At age 5, I underwent surgery to repair my palate by essentially closing the gap in it. There was great hope this would resolve my numerous related health issues. When I woke up in my hospital room, I remember pulling a piece of remnant red string from the roof of my mouth and being startled by the realization I could no longer breathe through my nose. While repairing my cleft palate, the surgeon had mistakenly sewn closed my nasal passages. I would never breathe through my nose again. And while this flawed surgery resolved some health issues, it spawned new ones.

My immigrant physician parents couldn't believe how American medicine had failed their daughter. They wondered how a 5-year-old would adapt to suddenly not being able to breathe through her nose. Their new greatest fear became that I would unconsciously shut my mouth, asphyxiate, and die in my sleep. So they moved my twin bed into their bedroom and every night I went to sleep with my mother's death-defying invention in my mouth: a pacifier with a hole cut into the top. At the age when most children were being encouraged by their parents to assert their independence and head out into the world of school and friends, I was pulled back to my parents' side and reminded constantly of how precarious my life was.

The most puzzling side effect of my cleft palate was that my parents began to exhibit a strange, contradictory pattern of panic-inducing overprotectiveness alternating with a laissez-faire attitude, especially when it came to leaving me in the care of others. As a child, I was not permitted to attend sleepovers. So when a friend had a birthday slumber party at her house, I was forced to leave after the cake-cutting and opening of the presents. When family friends hosted an overnight cast party after a rehearsal for an Indian play we were putting on at the local Hindu temple, I was the only child who couldn't stay over, returning home with my parents, my eyes stinging as I cried all the way home in the backseat of the car.

In stark contrast to their typical claustrophobic overprotectiveness, there were several instances when my parents left me in the hands of complete strangers. During a trip to Acapulco, Mexico when I was 5 or 6 years old, my parents left me in the care of a white middle-aged couple who were seated on a neighboring towel on the beach, while they went off to give parasailing a try. I vaguely remember realizing something was wrong when I saw the couple looking at their watches while whispering to each other about what to do, as I pretended to play in the sand to cover up my worry and boredom.

Eventually, my parents showed up, full of profuse apologies, explaining how my extremely near-sighted mother had knocked her eyeglasses into the sea, preventing her from being able to see clearly the signal for when she should pull the string on her parasailing chute. She landed in choppy waters, unable to swim, but fortunately with a life preserver. The couple distractedly listened while quickly packing up their beach gear and making a hasty exit.

My mother and father were clearly unfazed by this episode because just a year later, during a visit to Japan, they did it again. This time we were in a Tokyo shopping mall and I was holding court, ironically in the food court, with several teenage Japanese girls surrounding me and smiling at my every word and antic. I was regaling them with my favorite knock-knock jokes and doing show-and-tell with the ingenious toys I had just purchased, which included a disc on a string that whirred and lit up when you pulled the string on both sides. My parents found endearing my ease in interacting with people I had just met, on the far side of the world, but also saw it as a rare opportunity to take a break, heading back to a jewelry store where my father had tried on a coral ring but had not purchased it due to their own indecision, coupled with my growing impatience.

I was enjoying being the center of attention and being fawned over by these beautiful teenage girls, especially since at least in my experience, American teenagers didn't give 6-year-olds the time of day. At some point, I looked over in my parents' direction and didn't see them. I started to panic and began to break away from the group. Seeing my distressed expression, one teenage girl reassuringly said, "Don't worry, they're coming soon. You stay here, you show me this," pointing to the blue and red plastic disc I held suspended between two strings. Rather than being contrite, when my parents returned, they snapped a few photos of this encounter and pasted them into our family album for everyone to see.

Meanwhile, at home, I began lodging protests against sleeping in my parents' room, insisting that they move my twin bed into my playroom, which I reasoned to them—and to myself—was right next to their bedroom. In truth, I was torn. I wanted to be as independent as my friends at school, yet I was also scared, less so of real dangers and more so of those conjured up by American television, namely the Blob and the Yeti. I no longer worried about asphyxiating in my sleep, and after my parents turned out their bedroom light, I would quietly pull the pacifier from my mouth and place it beside me, where it would lie for the rest of the night.

Although nighttime trips to the bathroom or walks down into the dimly lit basement brought on terrors of what lurked in the dark, I continued to protest, and my parents moved my bed into my playroom. On my first night in my own room, when they turned out the light, I insisted they leave my door and their door wide open, just so they could hear my screams. And then I conducted a test of the emergency broadcast system by calling out to them a few minutes later, to which they replied, their voices laced with impatience, "Now, just go to sleep!" I slept with the covers pulled over my head and tightly tucked all around me. Ironically, if I did asphyxiate, it would not be due to my mouth-breathing, but to the cocoon of bedsheets I'd entrapped myself within, my only protection against sinister forces.

In addition to my curtailed freedom, I wrestled with other results of my failed surgery. I was still hampered by upper respiratory illnesses and was a magnet for colds. When I caught a cold, it was interminable, filled with long, sleepless nights of trying to blow my nose while having no control over my nasal passages. I could now only take in four-fifths of the world: I had all but lost my sense of smell. What does it mean for a 5-year-old to lose her sense of smell? To lose a way of perceiving the world as other children your age soak it all in is to be at a disadvantage. To join your friends in burying your noses in colorful roses during a game of hide-and-seek on a spring day at the Queens Botanical Garden, to hear them sigh blissfully while you have no olfactory reaction, is to be made keenly aware of this disadvantage. Now that I could speak, I was not allowed to smell.

All the senses work in concert and enhance one another, and it was missing out on the interplay of smell and taste that left me most bereft. I was blessed to be part of a family claiming not one but two Indian subcultures—Tamilian and Bengali—which meant two languages, two sets of cultural customs, and best of all, two cuisines, one given to chilies and coconuts, the other to *haldi*, or turmeric, and *gur*, a thick paste of unrefined sugar. Spices are central to Indian cuisine, from the comforting scent of ghee, clarified butter, to the heady aroma of garam masala. As the saying goes, you eat food first, not through your mouth, but through your eyes and nose. By all accounts, my mother is an excellent and inventive cook, and while I grew up loving her dishes, I was always aware that unlike my parents and my two siblings, through my taste buds I was only enjoying a fraction of the flavors. This feeling was compounded when my mother, at the dining table, would ask us, "Can you taste what I put into the dal today? I added a different spice."

■ ■ ■

In defiance of my health challenges I immersed myself in activities: learning to play classical violin, learning to sing Carnatic South Indian music, dreaming up new worlds and identities in one-girl shows I staged in our basement, my stuffed animals playing the role of an obedient audience. What I never got to immerse myself in were my mother's and father's tongues. Early on in my treatment, my parents had been advised by doctors to not speak to me in any language other than English because a child like me would have enough issues learning to properly speak one language. This was yet another adverse outcome of medicine practiced in a country where other languages are not valued, and not taught to children during formative years, when their brains have the greatest plasticity, allowing them to learn several languages simultaneously. Unlike my palate, this cleft could not be repaired.

As my colds, flus, and upper respiratory illnesses persisted, my parents wondered if it was time to seek a surgical solution. The surgeon who had made the error was remorseful and had offered to correct it, but had passed away of cancer soon after. I remember feeling a pang of guilt when, upon hearing of his death, I thought it was God's way of punishing him for his error.

When I was around 12, I traveled with my father to Boston Children's Hospital for a consultation with a supposedly renowned ENT surgeon. My father had put his hopes in this first-rate medical facility and his fellow physician. The physician, along with his ENT residents in training, "rounded on me," which meant he examined me as my father provided him with my medical history while the students observed. Afterwards, he asked to examine me in private. Instead of looking up my nose or into my ears, he peered at my ear and began pinning it to my head with his hand.

"Your ear sticks out. Perhaps we could pin it back, like this?"

I remember being a strange mix of dumbfounded and enraged.

"No thank you. My ear is just fine," I muttered.

Although I had developed a deep fear and loathing of being poked with needles and prodded with medical implements, I was unprepared for this type of violation.

"Fine. Let your ear stick out through your wet hair at the beach," he shot back, in a mocking tone.

It was clear from the way he interacted with his worshipful surgical residents just a few minutes prior that he was unaccustomed to hearing the word "no" uttered by anyone, let alone a 12-year-old patient. During the long drive back to New York, I recounted to my father what had happened. Whether because the surgeon offered no definitive solution or because of what I relayed, my parents closed the door on corrective surgery.

I learned to live with the effects of my ill-repaired cleft palate and so did my parents. In addition to my persistent upper respiratory issues, I needed to get braces twice because my palate and mouth-breathing impacted the growth of my jaw and teeth. Truthfully, these were all secondary to the daily challenges of being an Asian-American teenager in a virtually all-white high school in suburban New Jersey, where we'd moved when I was in 8th grade. My New York City street smarts were no match for passive-aggressive rumors whispered in the hallways and racist notes tucked into my locker. The notes contained unflattering pencil drawings of me accompanied by notes about my "smelly" brown body, "greasy" black hair, and "metal mouth." Still, I survived high school mostly intact, even managing to balance being features editor of the school paper, playing violin in selective youth symphony orchestras, and squeaking by academically to get into a venerable women's college.

It was in college that I thrived, away from the watchful and worried gaze of my physician parents. I lived alternately with roommates and alone, learning to think for myself and rely on my own intuition, and doing so alongside other young women who hailed from all over the country and world. As I got to know them, it became clear that despite their varied backgrounds, each had their own set of struggles against their families, their cultures, or their own deep insecurities.

I lived abroad in Paris for six months. The city was awash in sights and sounds, but although I had nominal olfactory capabilities (10–20%), I longed to immerse myself in its storied smells. I visited a parfumerie, whose cornucopia of fragrances might have been overwhelming to others, but to me, was evocative. I listened carefully to how the purveyor described the perfumes I tried on and settled on L'Eau d'Issey Miyake, precisely because I could only pick up the faintest traces of its light, clean, scent. I looked forward to going to the boulangerie, a new experience for me, and upon entering, I got an inkling of what people meant when they spoke of the rich, yeasty aroma of fresh bread coming out of the oven. And when I drank my first glasses of wine, I mimicked my roomies as they swished the liquid around in their glasses, sticking their noses over the rim, but the wines I could taste best were the ones I liked least—the most robust reds—which burned my nasal passages with the scent of alcohol, reminiscent of high school chemistry lab.

After college, I continued my journey of independence, moving to Philadelphia to work in city government on community development issues. I found an apartment, learned how to cook, and for the benefit of my health, I joined a gym and found a dentist I trusted—not an easy endeavor since as a mouth-breather I found dental appointments triggered much anxiety. So, I was taken aback when on a weekend visit with my parents, they suggested I give surgery one last try to open my nasal passages. My mother would regularly shake her head during meals, saying, "If only you could smell. This would taste even better!" I had become acclimated to being a perpetual patient under a doctor's care, but more than this, I had grown used to being under my parents' constant care. So, despite strides I had made towards reclaiming responsibility for my own health care, I found myself relenting and agreeing to let them look into it.

Over the next few months I would be taken into surgery twice, put under three times, and endured two more surgical errors. During the first surgery, the surgeon made a split decision in the operating room not to go along with the treatment plan of inserting temporary tubes in my nasal passages and instead made incisions in my nasal passages to see if they would suffice. They did not. A few weeks later, I went into surgery again, and he inserted the tubes but left the premises before I had awoken. When I did wake up, I could barely sip water from a straw because of the way he had left the tubes dangling into the back of my throat. I felt like I was being choked. The ENT residents wrung their hands as they decided whether or not to call the surgeon to ask him to return. Meanwhile, my parents whispered to each other in Bengali and finally my father helpfully suggested that instead of trying to move the tubes up, which would require them to be unsutured and resutured, perhaps they could just snip the bottoms of the tubes. The residents nodded their heads vigorously at this revelation and I was put under once more.

The next several weeks were rough. In addition to dealing with increasing pain and inflammation from the chafing of the tubes and a growing nasal infection, I ended one government job, moved, and began another government job. Still, I endured it because I knew it would be worth it in the end. I would finally be able to breathe through my nose, and no longer have to deal with myriad complications.

When the day finally arrived to have the tubes removed from my nose, I felt a strange mix of relief and excitement. Though the fever brought on by the nasal infection had subsided, the painful swelling persisted. Now, I eagerly anticipated the chance to finally do two things most everyone else does without a second thought: inhale and exhale through my nose. After the surgeon pulled out the tubes, my pain immediately lessened. But when I attempted to take a deep breath in, instead of feeling my lungs expand as they filled with air, I felt as if I was trying to drink the thickest milkshake through the thinnest straw. Whatever air I was able to draw in through my nostrils was woefully inadequate. I tried again and again, but to no avail. Since I could only pull a tiny amount of air into my nose, I still had to breathe through my mouth. The surgeon blamed the operation's failure on the proliferation of scar tissue narrowing my nasal passages. Essentially, he was blaming his failure on the physical marks of previous failures. We had never discussed the unlikelihood of success. I was crushed. This had all been for nothing.

Leaving the doctor's office dejectedly, we stepped out into a bright spring afternoon. The air felt fresher and crisper to me than ever before, but I attributed this to spending the last several weeks with tubes shoved up my nose. At dinner that night, when my mother poured a spoonful of ghee over my rice, the steam from the hot rice carried the ghee's buttery, rich aroma up into my nostrils. Throughout the meal, it was like I was tasting each food for the first time—the nuttiness of coconut flakes, the pungent tartness of sambar, the bright spiciness of lemon pickle. I had not regained the ability to breathe through my nose, yet I'd had more of my fifth sense restored.

I came to savor food in new ways, along with the fresh smell of newly cut grass and the heady scent of a bouquet of peonies. I even relished strange smells, like the hearty pungency of boiled eggs and the eerie duskiness of smoke. And my interest in perfume and wine, first piqued in Paris, grew as I now finally learned to grasp the difference between top notes and base notes.

While I emerged from this latest medical fiasco having regained a moderate sense of smell, I also emerged from it resolving to be my own patient advocate, relieving my parents of the burden of trying to be both my parents and my doctors, a burden I'm certain, was both unexpected and trying for them. I recalled the mix of trepidation and determination with which I had moved out of my parents' bedroom as a child. Fear had gripped me after they had tucked me in, turned out the light, and disappeared into their bedroom. I also recalled the way the sunlight had streamed onto my bed when I awoke the next morning in my own room.

■

THERE IS NO ONE WAY
By Alice Wong

In a time of destruction, create something.
—Maxine Hong Kingston

L iving during the coronavirus pandemic means living in separation and intimacy simultaneously. Isolation can happen deep inside of you or result from the built and social environment. Connection and being loved by others can happen without touch, words, or sound. Staying at home and being socially distant is not new to disabled, older, sick, immunocompromised, and housebound people like myself. Many of us maintain rich and fulfilling networks in a world designed to exclude and devalue us. This pandemic is just one of a series of crises we have survived.

As with many other marginalized communities, disabled artists and activists have always figured out how to exist and thrive in ways that may seem atypical or inferior by "normal" standards. I have incredible relationships with friends and colleagues whom I haven't met face-to-face for years—in part because I've worked with fellow activists and writers to build online communities where we can find one another and mobilize collectively. In 2016, I collaborated with Gregg Beratan and Andrew Pulrang in #CripTheVote, a nonpartisan online movement encouraging the political participation of disabled people that has since become a network for discussion about disability issues. Several years ago, after novelist Nicola Griffith tweeted the hashtag #CripLit, we worked with her to host a series of Twitter chats for disabled writers, focusing on publishing, representation, disabled narratives, and storytelling.

Disabled writers and artists have long railed against the difficulties in applying for and then requesting access at residencies, internships, conferences, and events. This does not even include the barriers disabled writers face in having their work considered for publication. Imagine my bittersweet ambivalence over the last two months: suddenly concerts and performances are live-streamed, video conferencing has turned into the default mode of working and meeting, and the concepts of time and productivity have become more flexible after people collectively freaked out and struggled to adjust.

I moved to San Francisco from Indianapolis more than twenty years ago and never looked back. The rich history of disability rights and culture in the SF Bay Area called and welcomed me with open arms. There's nothing more joyful than being in a room filled with disabled people, laughing, gossiping, scheming, and celebrating. The last two major events I attended took place in the fall and winter: a fundraiser for a disability rights organization in Berkeley and a book panel at the San Francisco Public Library. My outings have been less frequent over time, but I learned ways to show up locally and beyond that may be less apparent yet still meaningful.

Having progressive neuromuscular disability means I am considerably weaker than I was five to ten years ago—but I've never felt more engaged and alive than I do now. Is it the virus? Is it the hand sanitizer slathered over my bony fingers and hands? What is clear to me, based on experience and mistakes, is that I know what I want to do with my time and capacity. I wield both like swords, cutting out the shit and carving into the good meaty bits I seek as a creator, shaping it into something new and beautiful.

The urgency of this time elicits an impulse in me to tell my own story and amplify the stories of disabled people—to create in the face of overwhelming pain, bigotry, and oppression. I guffaw thinking about how often ventilators, an essential part of my cyborg body, have been in the news. The political and cultural circumstances of this historic time led me to write about my experiences as a disabled vent user and the eugenic implications of healthcare rationing that are happening across the world due to shortages. With my podcast, Disability Visibility, I produced a series of episodes about the impact of COVID-19 on disabled people, in particular disabled people of color who are disproportionately at risk. On my blog, I published a series of guest essays by disabled and immunocompromised people examining fatphobia, ableism, and genocide. All of these activities were unplanned, created in response to the overwhelming fear, sadness, and anxiety I feel in this moment.

Artists are essential cultural workers. We need media and stories of this time to expose the hypocrisy and flaws, provoke discomfort and reflection, advance our understanding of the human condition, provide sustenance to our spirits, and agitate for a better future. At the beginning of 2020 I imagined I would focus this year on the launch of my book and activism around the Presidential election. With everything in flux and uncertain (something disabled people are familiar with), I am pivoting to maximize access and impact. I want to leverage everything I have to support and bring attention to the communities I'm part of, just as many Bay Area artists and activists are doing right now.

I worried several months ago about how I would promote my upcoming book, *Disability Visibility: First-Person Stories from the Twenty-First Century*, because I do not travel and have limited stamina. Writer, poet, performer, cultural worker Leah Lakshmi Piepzna-Samarasinha wrote in *Guts Magazine* about the toll book promotion and tours take and how she and other disabled, neurodivergent, and chronically ill writers adapt and bend normative capitalist expectations: ". . . if there's one thing disabled people are good at, it's saying *there is no one way it has to be*." This idea, along with other disabled wisdom, is something everyone can learn from.

My one "traditional" book event was going to be at the San Francisco Public Library this July, timed to mark the thirtieth anniversary of the Americans with Disabilities Act. I imagined signing books, giving a reading in front of my family and friends, and getting a chance to thank everyone for supporting me. I decided to cancel it: even if the shelter-in-place order expires after May, I do not anticipate that I will feel safe. Instead, I've organized a series of online book events this summer and fall featuring myself and some of the contributors to the anthology.

It is a privilege to have a book published and yet the pressure to promote can be incredibly difficult and inaccessible for many disabled writers at the best of times but especially now. Other disabled writers I know with books coming out this year or next had their launches delayed and book tours cancelled. The Disability Visibility Book Circle is my way of responding to the pandemic and helping other writers: the project offers one-time grants of $1000 to fifteen writers in the US who have been or will be published from January 1, 2020, through June 30, 2021. The funds will allow authors to organize their own online events, free and open to the public. I cannot wait to attend.

There's a tremendous amount of mutual aid and community organizing happening and this is my contribution, since I can't sew face masks or provide direct aid to neighbors in need. Creation, in the face of destruction and death, can come in big and small forms. We should welcome all of it.

"STEPPING ON A STAR," FROM *WE WEAR THE MASK: 15 TRUE STORIES OF PASSING IN AMERICA*
By Gabrielle Bellot

The first time a stranger propositioned me as a woman was in a room full of sculptures in a museum. He was a security guard at the National Gallery, far larger and taller than I was, and he had waited for the other tourists to leave the room before he began talking to me, then stepping closer, and closer. At the time, fewer than a handful of people in the world knew I was transgender, knew me as anything less than a forgettable cisgender male, and I had travelled to Washington, D.C., a place I had never been and had no family in, presenting as a woman. All of my ID still had an "M" for my sex and an old name that could not have been a woman's, and my voice was too filled with a deep rumble for anyone not to see I was a transwoman after a few words. I had travelled to this foreign city so that I could present as a woman for a few days without worrying about anyone I knew running into me—and to see if I could handle myself in an unfamiliar city, a friendless world. I was planning to come out as a queer trans woman the following month—and I knew that once I did that, once I said those words, like the spell of a witch, I would lose the ability to return to my home in the Caribbean, the Commonwealth of Dominica.

It was the week of Thanksgiving. Snow had begun to fall. I had walked to the museum in the long black dress, flowing brown coat, and Merlot lipstick of a lonely romantic, and although I knew I could already pass as a cisgender woman visually now if I wore makeup, months before I would begin taking hormones, I had not actually thought that going to the museum would be any different from how it had been in the past as a male. The streets and riding on the subway from the carnival atmosphere of Union Station seemed frightening, but I was still too unaccustomed to passing to realise how naïve I was. I had been to many museums presenting as a man before, and I had never once felt noticed by anyone. I had not been harassed as someone passing as a woman before. Today was when that changed.

The guard had seen me eating in the café in the museum from a distance, but I was so naïve at the time that I hadn't taken his glances for more than any other stranger's appraisals. It was only when I ended up in a room of sculptures with the guard again that I truly felt the terror of passing as a trans woman for the first time. He asked me if I was getting "nice" photos with my camera and if I had had a "nice" lunch, smiling widely and using the diminutive words of a casual patroniser. I was so afraid that my voice would give me away that I began to do something I would regret for many months of harassment later: I smiled back and mumbled rather than ignoring him. Finally, the guard came up to me and asked where I was from. I mumbled "Caribbean." He grinned and nodded, saying "yes, yes" and that he could see that and I was beautiful. He then told me to call him soon, his tongue flapping out as he said it, to have sex with him.

I was so scared that I lost my language. "Maybe," I said, afraid that "yes" or "no" would be too dangerous. Then I fled. I almost ran to the second floor, my heart a loud drum. Here was a man who was supposed to protect me trying to force himself upon me, a narrative I had seen in so many lurid cases of police officers abusing their authority. I imagined telling someone at the front desk, but then I immediately thought of the problems: the way I would not be treated as a woman because my voice would prevent me from passing as one, the way the guard, the authority figure, could perhaps simply deny I was telling the truth, the way pointing him out would likely necessitate coming into contact with him again. I began looking at every male guard, listening to their footsteps. The footfalls most of all. I began learning, without looking, when I was alone in a room— and learning, then, to move on rather than stay by myself. I had begun to learn, essentially, what it is like for so many woman, trans* or cis, to simply *be* in space, to be aware of where your body is and who is looking at it and what it feels like to be looked down upon, followed, chosen as a victim. I was terrified, feeling imprisoned by my voice and body. In the end, I left the museum early, half an hour before it closed, looking back as I walked through the light snow, hoping I would not see the guard walking after me.

I must have looked like a shipwreck victim in the museum after that incident, my eyes wide and flitting, filled with expectations of ghosts and footfalls.

I kept hearing that pounding, resounding sound.

All that afternoon, I tried to quiet the noise. Footfalls filled my head wherever I went. I felt my aloneness as a woman more strongly than ever. Later, it reminded me of Calvino. *If on a winter's night a traveller looks down in the gathering shadow*, she might begin to hear the sound of her own.

This was when my life changed, when passing stepped into my life like a shadow. When the footfalls began to follow me everywhere. It happened again everywhere I went: with a guard at the Smithsonian Museum of American Art, who made me take a photo of him on his own phone and I, too afraid to talk loudly, wordlessly said "yes." It happened again with a guard in the Peacock Room of the Freer Museum. It happened with man after man on the street. Once, I looked up at the night sky on my way back from the metro and a thought flitted through me: *this is like living on a new planet.* Soon, it was just a normal facet of my life, this harassment for being seen as a woman: sometimes comical, sometimes annoying, always a bit unnerving, sometimes terrifying.

Passing, suddenly, was always a step behind me.

I was born an only child in the United States to Dominican parents. We moved back when I was a child to Dominica, the place where most of my memories begin. The island had been named *Waitukubuli*, "Tall-Is-Her-Body," by the Kalinagos, and our best-known writers were Jean Rhys and Phyllis Shand Allfrey, and as a result I found myself in an island that had its words tied most to females while I did not feel free to use such language on myself.

Although the compass of all my memories points to my seeing myself as a girl, I did not, for a long time, understand what this really meant; what I remember best was the all-pervading dread of asking my parents to accept behaviours I had been taught did not correspond with my body: wearing makeup around our house, going out in a dress or girls' jeans, calling myself *she.* None of these, of course, *makes* anyone a man or woman, and there is a false-but-persistent proposition, often used to diminish the reality of trans people's experiences, that binary transgender people simply embrace conventionally gendered roles—when, in fact, we see ourselves as *being* women or men in a mind-body sense, unrelated to the objects or behaviours we like. But when you've been denied the conventional trappings of a gender, it is unsurprising to desire them strongly; something as simple as roll-on lip gloss or swishy dress—both contraband in my childhood—can become a brief portal to another world, a vision of ourselves embodying the experiences we never got to have, never got to take for granted later in life.

I constantly imagined worlds in which I had a female body. So I lived out these fantasies in brief secret moments. I waited for my parents to leave the home on some nights and then I would sneak off into the little grand palace of my mother's closet, trying on her clothes and her makeup and taking photos of myself, the latter a way to make it all seem real and material, for a bit longer. I stood on a balcony and gazed at the stars and the vast dark mountains that framed our home and I imagined, drifting off on the starship of my dreams, not needing to change when the rumble of my parents' vehicle on the dirt road began and when the dogs began to bark.

I tried to crush the girl inside me, hating her, hating myself because I could not understand why she was there, even as I did. In college in Florida I briefly assumed the mantle of "goth" partly as an excuse to wear makeup and "man-skirts" in public, as the subculture was known for breaking down the conventional barriers of male and female presentation. I dated a few women briefly and each time dreaded the secret I did not tell them, that I wanted to date them as a woman. It seemed ludicrous to me, like stepping on a star, or expecting the figurehead of a ship to speak, but it was something ludicrous that I couldn't get rid of—and, honestly, I didn't know who I would be if I *could* get rid of it. After all, it was me.

Not being able to show love as you are is a kind of living death, a stargazer's blindness.

I never dared present myself as a goth or anything similar in Dominica. In that island, like much of the Anglo-Caribbean, colonial-era anti-buggery laws, along with religious indoctrination, have created an atmosphere in which LGBTQIA individuals are generally neither well-understood nor respected if they express themselves openly, and my fear of being labelled gay—a *buller*, a *batty bwoy*, a *boggarah*, the *anti-man*, as we called gay and gender-non-conforming men—made me try to suppress the woman inside me for over twenty years. In many ways, passing racially is much easier in much of the Caribbean than passing as another gender, given the ways that race can sometimes be fluid for us, even as we have so many old assumptions about whiteness and blackness still in place. I tried to act masculine to throw anyone off my trail; I pretended to be homophobic as late as my early twenties, even as I knew being homophobic and acting masculine felt deeply wrong, even hypocritical, to me. More than once, I considered ending my life.

One memory always returns like the night. I was at college in Florida. I was in a dorm that housed four girls with a friend, a wonderful girl from Costa Rica. Suddenly, in walked her roommate with a gay male friend of hers and one of his friends. He was openly gay, and that night he was wearing a belt with rainbow studs, his tight black jeans partly hanging off his ass as he walked, his small grey hoodie slightly coming up above his underwear, showing his skin as he walked. He brought with him the odour of men in gyms and joked about smelling bad as he walked by. I looked away from him. While everyone chatted with him, I refused to join in. Later, my friend asked me what was wrong. I made up an image for myself then for her.

"I don't like gay people," I told her. "I think it's wrong."

Shortly after, I told her, with a kind of unhinged pride, that I was homophobic. It was an outlandish lie. I have always been attracted more to women than to anyone else, and masculinity has always repelled me in general, but I was still attracted to the idea of trying something with a man in theory. I am pansexual, attracted to anyone on the gender spectrum. But I would not admit that, and I would not admit my womanhood, either. I always remember the way I treated that gay student like the Other, for he represented something that scared me: not that I was a gay male, but that I would be seen as one if I let my sense of womanhood show. And so I Othered him. I Othered myself by Othering the queerness in him. I had left one country for college in another, and even in more liberal America, I was acting the way I had in Dominica. I hated myself but felt protected by this self-loathing, in a strange way, from people finding out. My hatred of myself was a lonely fortress to hide in. Of course, the mirrors in there always showed a woman in love with a woman, or, perhaps, with a man. You cannot suppress gender dysphoria, not really. It always came back, always tore down this absurd fortress, making me rebuild it, more laboriously, each time.

I began presenting as a woman on a trip to London with my best friend, as she had encouraged me to try it there in a city where virtually no one knew me. We had travelled together to London for a month to do research in the British Library for the novels we were writing. At the time we set down in London, it had never occurred to me to present as female there.

But seeing her dress up for nights out made me want to be able to do what she did. *Being* a woman is unrelated to clothes or makeup, obviously, but they represented heavily gendered parts of the social constructions of femininity I did happen to enjoy, just as my friend did. I wanted to be perceived as woman, like she was, when we went to places: not to cross-dress, but to literally become one, in every way. So I started with makeup, which seemed like the easiest way to begin to transform how I might be perceived. I wasted money on trips down the Tube to stations to walk in and out of makeup stores in fear. One day, I bit the bullet and went into a large Boots pharmacy to buy Dermablend foundation, Clinique lipstick, a nondescript eyeliner, and setting powder, where a bemused, initially hesitant Australian lady suggested products for me to try on at a mirror. The people walking by in the reflection as I tried on nude lipsticks unnerved me, but I stayed there for an hour, trying on things. I left with a bag of mass-produced treasures.

By coincidence, my friend asked me soon after, in a café in the British Library, if my parents knew that I wanted to be a woman.

I told her they did not. She told me what was obvious: that in this big city, I would have a chance to present as one and see what happened. This was my chance, she said. In some ways, I thought it would be my only chance to do so for a long time, if not forever.

And I began doing so, in small steps, towards the end of the trip. I went to see a play by Derek Walcott, *Omeros*, with a full face of makeup—not very expertly applied makeup, at that, but makeup that made me feel, suddenly, like I was breaking a boundary. I went to the British Library wearing a peacock-blue eyeshadow, at which point a man with an accent I thought was Nigerian, who worked behind the desk in one of the rooms, refused to help me when I asked him to retrieve a book I had ordered, even though he had helped me without problems on the days I had not worn makeup. I walked down Oxford Street and shopped. I got stared at on the London Tube by people who clearly knew I did not "pass" well at the time; and one sweet person on the train smiled at me when she sat across from me, and then began doing her makeup and glancing at me, and I remember feeling that, even if I looked a mess, here was someone smiling in a compassionate, accepting way. It was amazing, the way that something as simple as makeup, helped me feel like I could step towards what I wanted; a year later, after beginning to transition, I began to appreciate *not* wearing makeup as much as wearing it, and when I was finally able to "pass" without makeup, I felt a lovely sense of freedom. Makeup, once a partial bridge to a taboo place, had become what it was for so many cis women: an option, not a requirement. These obvious little insights mean a lot when you get to learn them later in life, when you blossom as you after a long period of being, in a sense, someone else.

But after the trip ended, I went back to feeling trapped in a place where many people knew me only as a male. I felt scared to go out presenting as female. It became agonising, this sense of entrapment. I came closer than I had ever before to killing myself, finally, with poison one lurid afternoon when I could no longer take having to pretend to be a "man" to everyone around me. When I finally came out to everyone as a queer transgender woman at twenty-seven in Tallahassee, where I was doing my graduate degree, it saved my life—even as it meant giving up something else, for I had already decided, months before I came out, that I would not return to Dominica until I could feel safe there as an openly transgender woman. I cried many, many nights at the things my mother said to me, things I knew mothers could say but never imagined mine would say, that I would be disowned, that I should forget I had a mother, that she was suicidal over me, that I was a failure and am abomination against God. It rang painfully in my ears.

It still does.

For Seneca, it is possible to turn off noise outside if you can silence it inside yourself. "There can be absolute bedlam without," he wrote in "On Noise," "so long as there is no commotion within." Living as a trans woman of colour, that has become my mantra: to live without screams, inside or outside, so I can keep smiling, hoping, dreaming.

But it is lovely, sometimes, to turn off the noise. It always shuts off, suddenly, when I am reminded that I am loved by someone else, that the compass of me does not point in all the wrong ways. It is a sudden shock, this silence in the night of the mind, and how lovely that feels, to be able to let go of the pain, knowing someone has loved you for you, trans or not, and all you can hear is the words that someone has said. Sometimes, the night is a grand palace, its halls filled with a din of noise, and you just need to find the right door to the right room, where someone you've searched for waits for you under the lamplight, and when you close the door, all the other noise vanishes away.

The words used to describe passing are not always well-defined. We often use words like "white" or "black" or "brown" or "man" or "woman"—all of which have been used, at different times of my life, to describe me—in simplistic ways that assume that all people who we call by such labels will more or less share basic characteristics. Although this is not a completely absurd assumption on some level, it is too reductive. After all, "black" can mean many things; one only need read Australian literature to see how the terms "blacks" and "blackfellas" are often applied to Australian aborigines, like in Patrick White's *Voss*, despite the fact that aboriginal people are often simply left out when people in, say, America use the term "Black" as a broad racial term for all persons of a certain darkness of skin. And some South-Asians, Polynesians, Maoris, and many other groups have also, of course, been called "black" or "brown" in certain contexts; Maori people have even been called Aryans, an extraordinary assertion that derives from the lunatic racialism of a nineteenth-century text called *The Aryan Maori*.

The same is true for simplistic assumptions about gender. If we are going to talk about passing, we need a language for passing—and that language must be precise. I have many problems with the idea of passing, but it is necessary that we talk about it accurately—or, at least, find language that can hold it.

The night is my translator, the time when language comes to me best.

I like thinking of identity in terms of fields of stars, constellations. For me, it is easy to call one field of stars "woman" and another "man," and then, from there, to see how my identity forms a constellation within the field of "woman," even as I have lived before in a different configuration of stars. For some of us, jumping between the fields is simply the norm. Some constellations branch between these two main fields, and others, off in a nearby inky elsewhere, do not really fit within either. There are many constellations in the star fields of "man" and "woman"; to be a transgender woman is to make up one of the configurations of womanhood, just as tall women and tiny women and women born without uteruses make up their own, even as what my configuration looks like may differ, in its own way, from what another trans woman's looks like, and vice versa. We will not, contrary to certain cis women's fears, erupt into supernovas and destroy the whole field, or turn into black holes and suck everyone into our space. We are women.

I know this, internally, intellectually—but it is easy to forget where you belong in the star fields when you are confronted, day after day, with the fear that you may not "pass" as a cisgender woman when you enter this restroom or walk down this city block or put on this woman's bathing suit, and suddenly you begin to wonder, as you have wondered so often before, if your position in that constellation is precarious, fixed only in the situations in which you are "passing," yet always in danger of becoming un-moored. You fear that your star will fade and that you will begin to see stars, very different stars, stars that come from a shock to the head, if the wrong person reads you as anything but the cisgender woman they thought you were at first. They will not fade—we are who we are, be we women or men or genderqueer or genderless—but the fear that they might, the fear that lives in the vast shadow of the idea of passing, is one of the most overwhelming I know, a fear that follows some of us down every well-lit hall. The fear of not passing is like a ghost of an old ruined house that does not want to be banished. I have avoided going to a doctor out of fear that I will not "pass" and that I will be ridiculed or denied service; I remember that when I fell hard on my third day of learning to snowboard, my arm driving so hard into the snow that I thought I had dislocated my shoulder, I did not want to have it checked out because I was afraid that a medical exam in a state I had never been in could be humiliating if I did not pass.

And it can be difficult, though it is necessary, to learn that "pass-ing" is not our goal if we identify as binary transgender women, as I do. We are women, no matter what we look like, even if not all of us can "pass" for one by the statistical norms of what cis-gender women look like. There is nothing inherently wrong with wishing to "pass" visually, aurally, or otherwise as a cis woman, or, though it is less likely, as a trans woman; but we do ourselves an intellectual disservice if we fail to realise that the language of "passing" implies both temporariness and trickery, and aiming to be *recognised* as women, regardless of what we look like, is a much loftier, if often more difficult, goal. And this recognition is not for cisgender people to give us, nor for transgender people to give us; it is for everyone to give us, ideally, yes, but most of all it is for you to give to yourself. It can be a sudden shock, like Woolf described in *Moments of Being*, to realise that you have accepted yourself as you, have come to love yourself, have come to learn you would let yourself into your home if you opened your door at a knock, and found yourself standing before you, a woman without reservations. If I can recognise myself as a woman—well, that's a good start to feeling more at home in the field I belong in. To finding words that point to me, and do not feel wrong, like looking in a mirror as a woman, and not seeing one looking back.

Every time I think I know the language, it becomes bigger, wider, stranger.

Passing is a thing with wings, fins, and ghost-light feet, a thing that follows me everywhere.

I have worried about my ability to pass at 7,000 feet near the open door of a tiny airplane, wondering if I will "pass" as a woman in the footage of the skydive I have asked to record. I have been chilled while learning to snowboard on the heights of a slope in Breckenridge with a group of strangers both from the grave mistake of wearing non-waterproof gloves and from my fear of my own coldness of body affecting my ability to hold a feminine voice. I have worried while planning to learn how to surf and to relearn the contours of scuba-diving because of fear that I will not pass in a wetsuit if some part of my image of assumed cis-womanhood does not hold, if some ignorant or genuinely trans-despising person sees a shape in my wetsuit that they think should not be there, and then they will say, *get out, you don't belong here!* To some cis people, such fears doubtless seem overblown, if not melodramatic.

But they are not hyperbolic, not the cries of a cult of victimhood. Rather, for many of us, they simply describe the contours of the world.

Sometimes, I have felt validated by passing. Sometimes, I am embarrassed to admit that the crude words a man has said to me as I walk by has made me smile internally, simply because he saw me as an attractive woman. Sometimes, the fact that men on online dating sites are shocked that I am trans when I tell them—invariably, they miss it in plain sight on my profile—makes me feel happy. Passing, like prettiness, is a privilege; passing, like prettiness, can also be a peril, if someone believes we are deceiving them.

I remember how I thought of passing the first time I let a man fuck me. How I thought of passing, even though he knew I was trans, had contacted me, indeed, because he wanted an experience with a trans woman. His marriage had collapsed into an impending divorce, and he wanted me as a kind of trans mistress, to see what might happen. I remember the conflicts: how I wanted to be fucked so badly, yet feared the very thing he wanted from me. How I did not want to be a mistress, yet wanted to be one in some perverse way. How, even though I had invited him into my home, I felt the need to look as feminine as possible when he opened the door, so he would not flee. And how I felt so happy, finally, when I realised that he wanted me simply for me, not for a version of me that "passed," how I felt like a queen stretched out on my bed with him atop me, a queen who was being treated like royalty by this gentle giant of a man, regardless of what genitalia she had or did not. I remember, then, how the noise left my head, and all I felt was joy.

I thought of passing, too, on a very different occasion. I thought of it the night burglars broke into my apartment, tearing through it like a brief tornado, strewing my clothes and student papers and drawers all over the floor. I had come to my home that night with no thought of being burglarised, only to find my window's screen flung onto the grass by my portico, my door left unlocked, my laptops and other electronics stolen. I thought of passing in the terror of opening doors and turning on lights and hoping no one was lying in wait, for I knew that if they thought me a cis woman, they might try to rape me, and if they found out I was not one because I had passed too well on the trips from my home they had perhaps been monitoring from the shadows or if I had not passed and they knew all along I was trans, well, if they knew either way, they might still rape me, but they might also beat the shit out of me not simply for being a woman, but for not being the kind of woman they could believe in, respect enough, if such an absurd term can apply in such a situation, to violate and leave behind without a fractured skull. It can happen to you as a cis woman or a trans woman, this violence, yet as a trans woman who can "pass" the spectre of punitive violence so often looms larger. You can begin to feel you are a new denizen of the deep sea, that place so like yet so unlike the night sky, under vast pressures on each side, and knowing that vast ghastly things lurk both in the dark and in what might at first seem like a welcoming bit of light.

And I thought of passing that same night of being burglarised when I called the police and had to try to keep my voice in the right range of pitch and forward resonance both on the phone and when the officer walked over to my door, so that I would not open myself to being accused of bringing punishment upon myself, as some police officers have told trans women who have complained of harassment before. Later that night, in my best friend's bed that she had made up for me so I could stay away from being alone in that violated space I had once thought was so secure, I began to lose my mind and thought of passing again, only this time in terms of how my body would be gendered if it were found floating in her apartment complex's swimming pool the next morning. I felt so defeated by being burglarised that, under the swinging lanterns of insomnia, I momentarily considered suicide by drowning, even looked it up on my phone to see how painful it might be, that peculiar and illogical millennial move, and I was held back, partly, by my knowledge that I would *not* pass in death, due to my genitalia.

Mainly, I wanted to live on to defeat my fears, to not give up a dream of helping others like me or of finding love. But I was also disappointed at realising how humiliated I would be in such a suicide: likely misgendered by the police, like so many other dead trans women of color, and perhaps I would have simply added to that all-too-common media narrative, that we are all teetering on the brink of suicide. I did not want either.

But it was a small eye-opener, the way that, even in imagining taking hold of Lady Death's hand, even in imagining passing *on*, I was still thinking about passing *in* this world.

I was still, even then, looking for the language of passing.

The language is hard to be sure of, but it fills the pages of so many books.

Is Don Quixote, lost in the labyrinths of his madness, not attempting to pass as a knight? Quixote, after all, is not unaware of his own identity, even as he wishes to believe, passionately, in his knighthood, at which point his self-sustaining fictions and his true madness may meet—but, really, even here, comically and tragically, we see the language of passing.

Many texts, of course, are more explicit in this language. It is hard not to bring up Nella Larsen's 1929 novel, *Passing*, which is one of the most sustained fictional accounts of racial passing, or Mark Twain's *Pudd'n'head Wilson*, in which a white and a "passably" white African-American child are switched at birth, with the white child growing up as a Negro servant and the black child being raised as a spoiled white male. The ghosts of passing fill the pages of so many books about American and European fears of miscegenation, whereby light-skinned mixed-race people, like myself, could be viewed as white or black, with the novels of Faulkner, like *Absalom, Absalom!* a prime example.

For obvious reasons, passing also appears in a lot of trans* literature. And in the latter, this is not always about trans* persons aiming to appear cis; indeed, there are some notable examples of cis characters "passing" for various reasons as trans*, like Ariel Schrag's *Adam*, in which a cis male passes as a trans man, or Rachel Gold's *Ellen*, in which a cis lesbian takes on the identity of a new transfeminine student to protect the latter from transphobic attacks.

Then, there are novels like Bernardine Evaristo's *Mr. Loverman*, in which two gay West-Indian men, now living in London, "pass" as heterosexual married men in order to avoid homophobia, as well as, partly, for the narrator to continue living in partial denial of embracing his homosexuality. This is another kind of passing, but a common, terrifying one: the desire to appear straight so as to avoid the hellfire indictments of homophobes. "Passing," in queer fiction, can appear on any angle of the compass, which is because the reality of passing is not a one-sided simplicity, but, rather, one in which both straight and non-straight, cis- and non-cis, are complicit and connected, whether all sides know it or not.

Passing is radical and mundane all at once.

But perhaps the most interesting texts are ones where passing is not about appearance but behaviour. Consider Percival Everett's *Erasure*, in which the protagonist, an African-American writer who writes postmodern novels, is not considered "black" enough to "pass" as a "real" African-American until he decides to adopt a fictional identity and write a deeply stereotypical novel about life in a ghetto for a black American man. In much colonial literature, this is a kind of fanatical obsession: the desire to pass not only in terms of race but also in terms of how "well" one can act like—that is to say, "pass" as—the colonising power, or, more broadly, as a social class that is perceived to have more power than one does. Take Mulk Raj Anand's *Untouchable*, in which a member of the Untouchable caste in India attempts to find his identity in a variety of ways, including by trying to appear more "British" by having a British field hockey stick, or how the black Jamaican woman, Hortense, in Andrea Levy's *Small Island*, wants desperately for much of the novel to be treated as—to pass as—a non-black Englishwoman.

And it is difficult to forget the complex historical realities of passing in events like the infamous Parsley Massacre of 1937, in which the Dominican Republic's dictator, Trujillo, ordered the death of vast numbers of Haitians then living on the borders of the Dominican Republic. During the lead-up to this horror, Afro-Haitians were, according to a legendary order from Trujillo, distinguished from Afro-Dominicans by how they pronounced the word "parsley," *perejil*, with those able to "pass" by pronouncing the word like the Dominicans having a greater chance of escaping. Passing, here, becomes woven to pronunciation, race and language braided into the so-often-salvific illusion-reality of being able to present, convincingly enough to the judge, as the expected thing.

Texts like these show how "passing," in some situations, is not only about how you look but how you act—something that binary transgender individuals perhaps know best of all, given the plethora of resources online that inform us "how to act like ladies" or "how to act like men." The assumption in all cases, be it through perceived race or gender, is that if you merely look like you belong in a certain group, you will be "read" or "outed" as someone who is merely trying to *pass* as a member of said group if you do not *also* follow the cultural norms expected of said group.

But we must remember, too, that "passing" is not the same as being, authentically, what we are. When I say I am transgender, this is not a whimsical choice on my part. All humans have a gender identity—that is, a sense of how our body and mind connect to each other in terms of maleness or femaleness. Most people do not think of these things, since they have no need to; their gender identity, like their sexual orientation if they are straight, is just something in the background, never in need of explanation or examination. But for those of us who are transgender, our gender identity often conflicts at some level with our bodies, and so what should have been something in the background becomes part of our foreground. This is something that, as with sexual orientation, science is slowly coming to better understand, through genetics, epigenetics, endocrinology, and neuroscience. Sexual orientation and gender identity, while different, are also similar; both are just there, things we just have, that most of us never need to think about, unless there is some conflict in our body or in how our identities relate to the norms of the society we live in.

People often misunderstand this. They think me saying "I am a woman" is equivalent to me identifying as anything else at all: a fox, an attack helicopter, a fantasy character, another race. This comparison is flawed. We know that transgender people have existed throughout human history, under a variety of names in various cultural contexts; we know, too, that many people in certain societies who were trans probably had no language for their identities if they lived sufficiently far back in time and so never left records of their persistent feelings out of fear or confusion. And we know that people *are* trans. It is not incredible or strange that, out of the vast word population, a small number might identify as another gender; it is a flipping of a switch, a mixing of wires. We know cisgender people of both genders; it is possible to just have the bodies switched, so to speak.

But identifying as something else, authentically, is problematic for many reasons. Rachel Dolezal, infamously, claimed that she "identified" as an African-American woman, when she was, in fact, white. In this case, there are a number of issues. "Transraciality," which some people adopted from the language of adoption for her case, has no history behind it; we simply do not have evidence of people who identify as other races like we do for transgender people. Moreover, the bigger issue is that "race," as a concept, is just that: a concept, a social construct, not something scientific. It is more accurate to speak of populations in science than race, per se, since individual populations of the same "race" can differ dramatically due to where they live. "Race," meaning attributes that all people of certain skin colours possess, is the province of debunked ideas about groups of people, which were often racist in nature; at best, "race" casts too wide a net over individual populations to be useful as a scientific idea. Transraciality, as a result, is not even plausible, since "race" does not really exist. Transraciality, in Dolezal's case, is more in the realm of *passing* than *being*— and I admittedly doubt that she truly identified as black, since her statements about being black clearly co-opted the then-popular language of transgender activism surrounding Caitlyn Jenner's then-recent transition.

And it should be clear, too, why identifying as something other than a human is not the same as being transgender. We cannot possibly know what it is like to be anything other than human, all the more so once we enter the realm of things that do not even exist, like dragons; we cannot know what it is like to be a bat, to paraphrase the philosopher Thomas Nagel in his famous essay on the subject from 1974, "What Is It Like to Be a Bat?" If we can give voice to identifying as a Siamese cat, we have proved, already, that we are not said cat just by the fact that we can give voice to it. I have no problem with anyone having strong emotional identifications with other animals or having a genuine love of another culture connected to a racial group; it just bothers me when people argue that identifying as a gender is equivalent to identifying as anything else. It isn't. Putting down trans people by arguing that we are no different than people who can identify as anything they wish is to miss the point: that being transgender is materially, scientifically, and philosophically different from identifying as another "race" or species or whatever else it may be, even if the ideas may seem superficially similar.

But all that means is that we have come a way in beginning to understand how gender identity may work. Ultimately, humanity is complex. And I like it being complex. I like people living their lives as whatever makes them feel happiest, if it does not harm anyone else. And if we can open our heart and mind to how complex the world and its languages for speaking about things are— well, if we can do that, we're far on our way, already, to being far better than many other people on this planet with us.

■   ■   ■

Sometimes, we *want* to pass as different things in different places.

I know it well, this desire to emphasise one space on the map of myself over another. In America, I often want my Caribbeanness to be clear, as the things that trouble me about trends in American ignorance make me feel ashamed, often, to have been born here. In Dominica, though I have never in fact solely called myself an American, I sometimes feel distant from the island and yearn to be back in America, for there is a claustrophobia in knowing you will be called "American" by many Dominicans for listening to rock, for skateboarding, for being an atheist, and even, if you are not beaten up, for being queer. I have been called "white" in Dominica as a result of my interests and the lightness of my skin, yet I invariably become "black" or, most frequently, that catch-all term, "Hispanic," when I enter the United States based on my appearance—my skin, my tight corkscrew curls of black hair, my full lips. And since I have never seen myself as white and cannot pass as white in a white-majority country, I am glad to not be seen as such—but I am always awaiting definition, it seems, due to my ethnic ambiguity.

It is of no surprise to me that when I was a child in Cincinnati before I moved to Dominica with my parents, I was singled out in a class by a white teacher with the only other non-white girl in the class, and I was told by the teacher, as white students surrounded us in a circle, that Fiona* and I were "different" from the white kids, an event that infuriated my mother when I informed her of it. Yet when I first went to Dominica, I was initially called a "white man" because of my light skin, perceived gender, and accent. I am multiracial, ultimately; I inescapably fit into multiple fields along the lines of race because I am perceived as multiple things.

I am most accustomed, however, to simply being what we call *shabine* in Dominica, St. Lucia, and other islands in the archipelago, a mixed-race person with light skin. For reasons that likely intersect with colonial notions about white skin equalling wealth

---

*Name changed for privacy.

and higher value than darker skin in many of our islands, *shabines* are frequently portrayed as the most desirable. The *shabine* cannot really pass as white or black by appearance, yet can pass as either more abstractly: as "white" in terms of societal privilege, and "black" in terms of being accepted as non-white by other non-white persons.

The *shabine* represents the binary of whiteness and blackness—and how anyone who believes we have abandoned casual racism in our islands, or outside of it, really, is severely misinformed.

Sometimes, it is petrifying, the way it feels that if I do not pass, I will pass, instead, onto the undiscovered country, like so many trans women of colour before me, if the wrong person reads the book of my being. But it is real, being me, being a trans woman, a woman—and I would not give that up for all the wishes an errant genie could grant, even if that genie could have me be born as a cis woman. After all, as much as that would make certain parts of me fit better together, it would also not be me; being trans is who and what I am, and I love it, hate it, and love it, and do not know what to make of it. As we travel, after all, our past changes, as we do in the present; the traveller into the future leaves behind a wake of self as tenuous as seafoam. And perhaps there is nothing that reveals this better—or worse, if such things frighten—than transition.

And people around us struggle as we do. Transition takes us all with it. The dissonant sounds of rejection from my mother still echo in me after we finally began to make up, and she, though still struggling, began to accept me as her daughter. Fittingly, perhaps, it was in the intermission of a concert we had gone to in Tallahassee when she first called me her daughter, when a stranger in the seat in front of them we had been speaking with asked for introductions. I teared up a little. A simple word, containing so much joy. Acceptance does not mean that all is well—after all, my parents would still tell me that I could not feasibly return home as a trans woman, due to the dangers and public shame they feared would result—but it means that we all grow as we learn more. We become bigger as our capacity for love does, even if our steps themselves are small.

We cannot stop talking about "passing." It is part of our past, present, future. But we should stop talking about it as if it is an ideal, or as if it is merely an ignorant form of idealisation. It is both, and it is neither, for it is too complex to be so constrained. I wish to be recognised as a multiracial woman—but recognition is not guaranteed, is, indeed, a privilege. I wish to work towards a world in which we can recognise people for who they truly are, but that is not a world in which passing will cease to exist, for passing is too ingrained into too many layers of history and culture. And the best we can do is to understand the nuances and importance of the language we use in each and every context, so that we do not uphold old supremacies—racial, sexual, gender-based—while merely adjusting the words we use.

On most days, I just want to be able to point to my constellation and think, *yes, that's me*, without hearing any footfalls, any noise, nothing but me and the calm of recognising myself for me.

CONCLUSION

I n the introduction to *Craft and Conscience*, I shared my motivations for writing this book. Here, I would like to conclude the book by sharing my hopes for you and your writing. I hope, first and foremost, that this book gives you—a person of conscience, who may have been hesitant to engage with social issues on the page—the confidence to push forward because the world needs more writers of conscience bringing the issues they are passionate about alive on the page. I hope the lessons and reflections I have offered are tangible tools to help guide your writing. Finally, I hope the rich array of essays you have read here convince you that there is no singular approach or voice when it comes to writing about social issues.

As a writer, you make decisions about how you craft your writing, who you want your ideal readers to be, how much context to provide on a crucial and complex issue, how to drive the narrative ever forward, whether you show up in your piece directly as a character or indirectly through your voice as the storyteller, and whether you believe you are the best storyteller for this story. Through *Craft and Conscience*, I seek to provide guidance and examples to help you make the best possible decisions as a writer of conscience.

I cannot promise that you will immediately change the minds of your readers or that your work will change entrenched policies and practices, but I assure you that if you approach writing about social issues guided by your conscience, your voice will join with those of a chorus of other writers of conscience, help-ing to, in time, manifest social change. Whenever I become dis-couraged by yet more injustices amidst the glacial pace of change and begin to doubt the significance of my role as a writer, I turn to the words of a writer I deeply admire both for their craft and conscience—Nobel Prize–winning author Toni Morrison: "This is *precisely* the time when artists go to work. There is no time for despair, no place for self-pity, no need for silence, no room for fear. We speak, we write, we do language. That is how civiliza-tions heal."[1]

If you are still hesitant because you fear all the "what if's"— *What if I write it and no one cares? What if I write it and people are critical of it and me? What if I don't have the qualifications to write about this issue because I'm not an expert? What if I'm an expert who's not sure how to write for an everyday audience?*—consider the conse-quences of not writing about the issue you care so deeply about. I'll pose the same questions to you now that I posed to myself years ago when I stood on the precipice of pursuing my own writing as-pirations, racked with self-doubt, in hopes that they will serve as a spark for you too: *What if you don't write about this issue you care so deeply about? What is lost to the world—and to yourself?*

It was these questions that haunted me, compelling me to push past all my rational and irrational doubts, including a strong case of imposter syndrome, to become a writer and tell the life story of Grammy-nominated Hindustani singer Lakshmi Shankar, who, despite being the most prominent Indian female singer in the movement to bring Indian music to the West, was overlooked by the cultural gatekeepers and history books. These questions helped me understand that my motivations for ensuring Shankar's life and musical legacy were remembered and for interrogating culture, race, gender, and their intersections were stronger than my fears and insecurities about being a writer.

I leave you with the insistent, inspiring words of brilliant play-wright Lorraine Hansberry, who in her "To Be Young, Gifted, and

Black" speech to winners of the Readers Digest/United Negro
College Fund creative writing contest on May 1, 1964, urged:

> Write if you will: but write about the world as it is and as you
> think it *ought* to be and must be—if there is to be a world. Write
> about all the things that men have written about since the be-
> ginning of writing and talking—but write to a *point*. Work hard
> at it, *care* about it.[2]

ACKNOWLEDGMENTS

This book, *Craft and Conscience*, grew out of the class I created and teach, Writing About Social Issues. This class, in turn, grew out of my close to fifteen years of working in social change and my close to ten years of writing about it. So, although this book is meant to be a guide for others in their writing lives, it contains so much of my own life and experiences as a writer translated into lessons and reflections.

The idea for this book was born soon after my daughter, Daya. I don't believe this is a coincidence, for with her arrival, I found much more inner confidence in myself as a mother and as a writer. With her in the world, working for social change and writing about it has taken on a new significance and urgency.

I wrote *Craft and Conscience* after several years of teaching my Writing About Social Issues class, and I continued to teach the class as I wrote the book. So my students remained my constant inspiration and focus throughout the writing process. Clichéd as it might be, I have learned so much from my students and continue to be inspired by their work and the passion they bring to the issues they care deeply about. I try to establish a tone of goodwill and understanding at the start of each class, and I've been touched time and again by the spirit of generosity and compassion they show to each other in the classroom—or in the virtual classroom, since the start of the pandemic. I want to thank Catapult for enthusiastically saying "yes" when I approached them about my idea for the Writing About Social Issues class and for their constant support, including working with me to provide a scholarship to a student for each class.

I'm so deeply thankful that I ran into Gayatri Patnaik at the elevators at a conference in Boston several years ago. Our conversation renewed my faith in my work and in publishing. I knew I wanted to work with Gayatri as my editor on this book and was thrilled that she felt the same way. Gayatri's support and editorial acumen has been invaluable. But beyond this, I've constantly felt that she believes in the necessity of *Craft and Conscience* as much as I do. Thank you also to the entire Beacon Press team for all their help and dedication in making this book the best it can be and getting it out into the world. This includes Helene Atwan, Ruthie Block, Perpetua Charles, Beth Collins, Emily Dolbear, Sanj Kharbanda, Susan Lumenello, Melissa Nasson, Louis Roe, Jill Dougan, Alyssa Hassan, and the entire Beacon Press family. Beacon Press has a history of publishing books by writers, thinkers, and activists of conscience I so admire, and it is an honor to be in their company.

Thank you also to my agent, Lucy Cleland of Kneerim & Williams, for believing in me as a writer and in this book.

There are so many writers whose writing on social issues I admire especially those who champion these issues off the page. I'm particularly grateful to those who agreed to lend their brilliant words to *Craft and Conscience*. I'm still in disbelief that the words of prolific and prescient writers George Orwell and James Baldwin, two of the twentieth century's greatest writers of conscience, are included. I'm also overjoyed that *Craft and Conscience* includes the work of these remarkable writers of conscience of our time: Gaiutra Bahadur, Gabrielle Bellot, Garnette Cadogan, Crystal Z Campbell, Alexander Chee, Nicole Chung, Jaquira Díaz, Roxanne Dunbar-Ortiz, Yashica Dutt, Kaitlyn Greenidge, Lauren Michele Jackson, Imani Perry, and Alice Wong. Thank you so much to each of these writers for believing in this book by being part of it.

I'm also thankful to visual artists Crystal Z Campbell and Andrew Esiebo for lending their incredible images to *Craft and Conscience*, helping us see the world more clearly.

I'm thankful for my community of writing mentors and fellow writers. Ten years ago, when I jumped into writing full-time with little more than my passion, I never dreamt that I would be embraced and count so many writers I love and admire as mentors and friends. I especially want to thank Mira Jacob for penning the foreword and the late Valerie Boyd for her early belief in this book's key concepts. I admire them as much for their writing as for modeling being good literary citizens, in every sense.

I worked in social change for close to fifteen years, from local government to philanthropy, from community development to public health to racial justice. Working on these social issues shaped me and my writing. I'm thankful for these experiences and for colleagues I worked alongside, for whom the issue was not just a job but a purpose. Nowhere was this more true than during my time as marketing and communications director at Race Forward.

I want to thank the friends who love me as much on days I write and publish a piece as on days where I haven't written a word. Their friendship through life's ups and downs and in particular these last two years of mothering during a pandemic has been a boon, whether we were giggling or grieving (sometimes both). I especially want to thank: Carmen Mejia, Garnette Cadogan, Sonya Choudhury, Sunita Dutta, Swati Khurana, Nidhi Kohli, Shamala Pasupathy, Sheetal Khanna-Ravich, and Trina Saha.

Finally, I want to thank my family for their continued support and encouragement. In particular, I'd like to thank my husband, Om Prakash Arora. For the first year of the pandemic, we didn't have childcare. I loved getting to witness and experience my child's blossoming so closely, but it was definitely challenging trying to balance parenting and working. I'm thankful to Om for his commitment to finding and keeping this balance. Consequently, I'm more thankful than ever to have found an amazing caretaker for my child in Diane Nappi. In truth, it shouldn't take a pandemic to draw attention to the challenges faced by working families and in particular, working mothers, but I'm glad these issues are being discussed and championed more widely. I hope it's a first step to meaningful change.

RECOMMENDED
RESOURCES

A s you continue on your journey to writing with conscience, I want to offer some resources including books, outlets, and organizations that might provide some guidance. This list is by no means exhaustive, but I hope it is helpful.

BOOKS ON CRAFT

Appropriate: A Provocation, by Paisley Rekdal*
Craft in the Real World: Rethinking Fiction Writing and Workshopping, by Matthew Salesses*
Critical Creative Writing: Essential Readings on the Writer's Craft, edited by Janelle Adsit
Emerging: Contemporary Readings for Writers, edited by Barclay Barrios
Let Me Tell You What I Mean, by Joan Didion*
On Writing: A Memoir of the Craft, by Stephen King
The Byline Bible: Get Published in 5 Weeks, by Susan Shapiro
The Situation and the Story: The Art of Personal Narrative, by Vivian Gornick
Vulnerable Subjects: Ethics and Life Writing, by G. Thomas Couser*
Why I Write, by George Orwell*
Writing the Other: A Practical Approach, by Nisi Shawl and Cynthia Ward
Writing to Persuade: How to Bring People Over to Your Side, by Trish Hall*

LITERARY AND JOURNALISTIC OUTLETS

Apogee Journal
*The Atlantic**

*Referenced in *Craft and Conscience*

Catapult*
Colorlines (published by Race Forward)*
Disability Visibility Project
Epicenter-NYC*
The Guardian*
Guernica*
Longreads*
Los Angeles Review of Books*
The Margins (Asian American Writers' Workshop)
The New Yorker
NPR
Off Assignment
The Offing
On Being
Orion
PEN America
Rewire
The Rumpus*
Smithsonian
Stanford Social Innovation Review

ORGANIZATIONS
Catapult
Disability Visibility Project
Narrative Initiative
Nieman Storyboard
OpEd Project*
PEN America (PEN World Voices Festival)
Poynter
Race Forward (Facing Race Conference)*
The Shipman Agency
Solutions Journalism Network*
Tin House
Unicorn Authors Club Changemakers Authors Cohort
VONA (Voices of Our Nations Arts Foundation)

CULTURAL SENSITIVITY RESOURCES

Black Editors & Proofreaders*
Conscious Style Guide*
Disability Visibility LLC
Editors of Color Database*
Minorities in Publishing (podcast)
People of Color in Publishing*
Writing Diversely*
Writing with Color*

ABOUT KAVITA DAS,
AUTHOR

Kavita Das worked in social change for close to fifteen years, addressing issues ranging from community and housing inequities to public health disparities and racial injustice. Although Kavita remains committed to social justice issues, she left the social change sector to become a full-time writer and to write the life story of Grammy-nominated Hindustani singer Lakshmi Shankar in her first book, *Poignant Song: The Life and Music of Lakshmi Shankar* (Harper Collins India, June 2019).

At the root of both her writing and social change work is Kavita's desire to provoke thought and engender change by recognizing and revealing the true ways in which culture, race, and gender intersect, especially when it comes to societal inequities. She has been a regular contributor to *NBC News Asian America*, *Los Angeles Review of Books*, and *The Rumpus*. In addition, her work has been published in *Poets & Writers*, *Catapult*, *LitHub*, *Tin House*, *Longreads*, the *Kenyon Review*, the *Washington Post*, *The Atlantic*, CNN, *Guernica*, *McSweeney's*, *Fast Company*, *Quartz*, *Colorlines*, *Teen Vogue*, *Romper*, *WIRED*, and elsewhere. She was nominated for a 2016 Pushcart Prize, and her full writing portfolio can be found at kavitadas.com.

Kavita Das created the popular "Writing About Social Issues" nonfiction course, which inspired *Craft and Conscience*, has taught at the New School and continues to teach at *Catapult*, along with being a frequent guest lecturer. Her essays on social issues have been included in two creative-writing textbooks. She received a BA in Growth and Structure of Cities from Bryn Mawr College and an MBA in marketing from University of North Carolina at Chapel Hill. A native New Yorker, Kavita and her husband, Om, try to keep up with their toddler, Daya, and Harper, their hound. Connect with her at kavitadas.com or on Twitter @kavitamix.

ABOUT MIRA JACOB,
FOREWORD WRITER

M ira Jacob is a novelist, a memoirist, an illustrator, and a cultural critic. Her graphic memoir *Good Talk: A Memoir in Conversations* was shortlisted for the National Book Critics Circle Award, longlisted for the PEN Open Book Award, and named a *New York Times* Notable Book as well as a best book of the year by *Time, Esquire, Publishers Weekly,* and *Library Journal.* It is currently in development as a television series with Film 44. Her novel *The Sleepwalker's Guide to Dancing* was a Barnes & Noble Discover New Writers pick, shortlisted for India's Tata First Literature Award, longlisted for the Brooklyn Eagles Literary Prize, and named one of the best books of 2014 by *Kirkus Reviews,* the *Boston Globe, Goodreads, Bustle,* and *The Millions.* Mira Jacob is currently a visiting professor in the MFA Creative Writing program at the New School and a founding faculty member of the MFA program at Randolph College.

ABOUT THE
CONTRIBUTORS

GAIUTRA BAHADUR is the author of *Coolie Woman: The Odyssey of Indenture*, a personal history of indenture shortlisted for the Orwell Prize, the British literary prize for artful political writing, in 2014. She teaches writing and journalism at Rutgers University-Newark. She's a contributor to the *New York Times Book Review*, the *New York Review of Books*, the *New Republic*, *The Nation*, and *The Guardian*, among other publications. The recipient of literary residencies at MacDowell and the Rockefeller Foundation Bellagio Center in Italy, she is a two-time winner of the New Jersey State Council on the Arts Award for prose.

JAMES BALDWIN (1924–1987), one of America's foremost writers, was a novelist, an essayist, a playwright, a poet, and a social critic. His writing explores palpable yet unspoken intricacies of racial, sexual, and class distinctions in Western societies, most notably in mid-twentieth-century America. A native of Harlem, New York, he lived periodically in exile in the south of France and in Turkey. Baldwin is the author of several novels, books of non-fiction, and poetry including *Notes of a Native Son*, *Go Tell It on the Mountain*, *Giovanni's Room*, *Tell Me How Long the Train's Been Gone*, *If Beale Street Could Talk*, *The Fire Next Time*, *The Evidence of Things Not Seen*, and *Jimmy's Blues and Other Poems*.

GABRIELLE BELLOT is a staff writer for *Literary Hub* and a contributing editor at *Catapult*, where she also serves as head instructor. Her work has appeared in the *New York Times*, *The Atlantic*, the *New Yorker*, the *New York Review of Books*, the *Paris Review Daily*, *Guernica*, *The Guardian*, *Shondaland*, *VICE*, and many other places. She holds both an MFA and PhD in English from Florida State University. She grew up in the Commonwealth of Dominica and now lives in Queens, New York.

GARNETTE CADOGAN is the Tunney Lee Distinguished Lecturer in Urbanism at the School of Architecture and Planning at the Massachusetts Institute of Technology.

CRYSTAL Z CAMPBELL is a multidisciplinary artist, experimental filmmaker, and writer of Black, Filipino, and Chinese descent. Campbell finds complexity in public secrets—fragments of information known by many but untold or unspoken. Honors and awards include a Guggenheim Fellowship in Fine Arts, a Harvard Radcliffe Fellowship, the Pollock-Krasner Award, MAP Fund, MacDowell, Rijksakademie, Whitney ISP, and Skowhegan. Exhibitions or screenings have been included at the Drawing Center, ICA-Philadelphia, and the San Francisco Museum of Modern Art. Campbell's writing is featured in two artist books (VSW Press), *World Literature Today*, *Monday Journal*, and *Hyperallergic*. Founder of archiveacts.com, Campbell is currently a University at Buffalo Center for Diversity Innovation Distinguished Visiting Scholar who lives and works in New York and Oklahoma.

ALEXANDER CHEE is the author of the novels *Edinburgh* and *The Queen of the Night*, and the essay collection *How to Write an Autobiographical Novel*. A contributing editor at the *New Republic* and an editor at large at *VQR*, Chee is a 2021 United States Artists Fellow, a 2021 Guggenheim Fellow in Nonfiction, and the recipient of a Whiting Award, a NEA Fellowship, an MCCA Fellowship, the Randy Shilts Prize in gay nonfiction, the Paul Engle Prize, and the Lambda Editor's Choice Prize. He is an associate professor of English and creative writing at Dartmouth College.

NICOLE CHUNG is the author of the national bestseller *All You Can Ever Know*. Named a Best Book of the Year by NPR, the *Washington Post*, the *Boston Globe*, *Time*, and *Library Journal*, *All You Can Ever Know* was a finalist for the National Book Critics Circle Award, a semifinalist for the PEN Open Book Award, and an Indies Choice Honor Book. Chung is a contributing writer and editor at *The Atlantic*, and her work has also appeared in the *New York Times*, the *New York Times Magazine*, *GQ*, *Time*, and *The Guardian*.

JAQUIRA DÍAZ was born in Puerto Rico and raised in Miami. She is the author of *Ordinary Girls: A Memoir*, winner of a Whiting Award, a Florida Book Awards Gold Medal, and a Lambda Literary Awards finalist. *Ordinary Girls* was an Indies Introduce Selection, a Barnes & Noble Discover Great New Writers Notable Selection, an Indie Next Pick, and a Library Reads pick. Her work appears in *The Guardian*, *Time Magazine*, *T: The New York Times Style Magazine*, and elsewhere. She is the recipient of two Pushcart Prizes, an Elizabeth George Foundation grant, and fellowships from the MacDowell Colony, the *Kenyon Review*, and the Wisconsin Institute for Creative Writing.

ROXANNE DUNBAR-ORTIZ grew up in rural Oklahoma in a tenant farming family. She has been active in the international Indigenous movement for more than four decades and is known for her lifelong commitment to national and international social justice issues. Dunbar-Ortiz, the winner of the 2017 Lannan Cultural Freedom Prize, is the author or editor of many books, including *An Indigenous Peoples' History of the United States*, a recipient of the 2015 American Book Award. Her most recent book is *Not "A Nation of Immigrants": Settler Colonialism, White Supremacy, and a History of Erasure and Exclusion*. She lives in San Francisco. Connect with her at reddirtsite.com or on Twitter @rdunbaro.

YASHICA DUTT is a leading anti-caste expert, a journalist, and the author of the memoir *Coming Out as Dalit*, which has been lauded critically and embraced by readers. It was awarded the 2020 Sahitya Akademi Yuva Puraskar (India's National Academy of Letters' Young Writers Award) and is currently taught at several universities across the United States.

ANDREW ESIEBO, born in Nigeria, is an award-winning visual storyteller who explores themes such as sexuality, gender politics, football, popular culture, migration, religion, and spirituality. His works have been exhibited and published across the globe. They are in several private and public art collections around the world.

KAITLYN GREENIDGE is the author of the novels *Libertie* and *We Love You, Charlie Freeman*. She is the recipient of fellowships from the Whiting Foundation, the National Endowment for the Arts, the Radcliffe Institute for Advanced Study, the Lewis Center for the Arts at Princeton University, and the Guggenheim Foundation. Greenidge is currently features director at *Harper's Bazaar* as well as a contributing writer at the *New York Times*.

LAUREN MICHELE JACKSON is an assistant professor of English at Northwestern University and a contributing writer at the *New Yorker*. She is the author of the essay collection *White Negroes: When Cornrows Were in Vogue . . . and Other Thoughts on Cultural Appropriation*. Her writing about race and culture has appeared in *The Atlantic*, the *New Yorker*, the *Paris Review*, *Essence*, the *New Republic*, *Teen Vogue*, *Rolling Stone*, and *New York* magazine. She lives in Chicago. Connect with her at laurjackson.com and on Twitter @proseb4bros.

GEORGE ORWELL (1903–1950) was a British novelist, essayist, social critic, and one of the most influential writers of the twentieth century. As the author of the novels *Animal Farm* and *Nineteen Eighty-Four*, and nonfiction works including *Down and Out in Paris and London*, *The Road to Wigan Pier*, and *Homage to Catalonia*, Orwell addressed pressing sociopolitical issues of his time, including the immorality and perils of imperialism, fascism, and poverty.

IMANI PERRY is the Hughes-Rogers Professor of African American Studies at Princeton University, where she also teaches in the Programs in Law and Public Affairs and in Gender and Sexuality Studies. She earned her PhD in American Studies from Harvard University, a JD from Harvard Law School, an LLM from Georgetown University Law Center, and a BA from Yale College in literature and American studies. She is a native of Birmingham, Alabama, and spent much of her youth in Chicago, Illinois, and Cambridge, Massachusetts. Perry is the author of several award-winning books, including *Breathe: A Letter to My Sons* and *Looking for Lorraine: The Radiant and Radical Life of Lorraine Hansberry*. She lives outside Philadelphia. Connect with her on Twitter @imaniperry.

ALICE WONG is a disabled activist, writer, media maker, and consultant. She is the founder and director of the Disability Visibility Project, an online community dedicated to creating, sharing, and amplifying disability media and culture created in 2014. Alice is the editor of *Disability Visibility: First-Person Stories from the Twenty-First Century*, an anthology of essays by disabled people, and *Disability Visibility: 17 First-Person Stories for Today*, an adapted version of the anthology for young readers. Her memoir, *Year of the Tiger*, is forthcoming (Vintage Books, 2022). You can find her on Twitter @SFdirewolf.

■

NOTES

CHAPTER 1: WHY WE WRITE

1. Christian Wallace, "The Resurrection of Bass Reeves," *Texas Monthly*, July 2021, https://www.texasmonthly.com/being-texan/the-resurrection -of-bass-reeves.

2. *Merriam-Webster*, https://www.merriam-webster.com/dictionary/social; *Merriam-Webster*, https://www.merriam-webster.com/dictionary/issue; *Merriam-Webster*, https://www.merriam-webster.com/dictionary/social%20 conscience.

3. US Sentencing Commission, *Differences in Federal Sentencing Practices*, https://www.ussc.gov/sites/default/files/pdf/research-and-publications /backgrounders/rg_differences-series.pdf, accessed January 27, 2022.

4. Joan Didion, *Let Me Tell You What I Mean* (New York: Alfred A. Knopf, 2021), 49.

5. Didion, *Let Me Tell You What I Mean*, 57.

6. Chimamanda Ngozi Adichie, "The Danger of a Single Story," TED Global Talk, July 2009, https://www.ted.com/talks/chimamanda_ngozi _adichie_the_danger_of_a_single_story/transcript.

7. Adichie, "The Danger of a Single Story."

8. Adichie, "The Danger of a Single Story."

9. Christiane Amanpour, "Remarks at International Press Freedom Awards," transcription, Poynter, November 2016, https://www.poynter.org /newsletters/2016/christiane-amanpours-speech-on-press-freedom-fake -news-and-the-state-of-journalism-under-donald-trump.

10. Amanpour, "Remarks at International Press Freedom Awards."

11. James Baldwin, preface, *Notes of a Native Son* (Boston: Beacon Press, 1984), xx.

12. Baldwin, preface, *Notes of a Native Son*, xix.

13. Baldwin, preface, *Notes of a Native Son*, xix.

14. John Romano, "James Baldwin Writing and Talking," *New York Times*, September 23, 1979.

15. Romano, "James Baldwin Writing and Talking."

16. Romano, "James Baldwin Writing and Talking."

17. Romano, "James Baldwin Writing and Talking."

18. Toni Morrison, "Remarks to the Ohio Arts Council," 1981.

CHAPTER 3: DIVING IN DEEP OR CASTING WIDE

1. Epigraph: Willie Johns, "A Seminole Perspective on Ponce de León and Florida History," *Forum Magazine* (Florida Humanities Council), Fall 2012, http://indiancountrytodaymedianetwork.com/2013/04/08/seminole-perspective -ponce-de-leon-and-florida-history-148672 (accessed September 24, 2013).

2. The full refrain of Woody Guthrie's most popular song: "This land is your land / This land is my land / From California to the New York island / From the redwood forest to the Gulf Stream waters / This land was made for you and me."

3. Henry Crow Dog, testimony at the 1974 Sioux Treaty hearing, in Dunbar-Ortiz, *Great Sioux Nation*, 54.

4. David A. Chang, *The Color of the Land: Race, Nation, and the Politics of Landownership in Oklahoma, 1832–1929* (Chapel Hill: University of North Carolina Press, 2010), 7.

5. Patrick Wolfe, "Settler Colonialism and the Elimination of the Native," *Journal of Genocide Research 8*, no. 4 (2006): 387.

6. See Blake Watson, *Buying America from the Indians: "Johnson v. McIntosh" and the History of Native Land Rights* (Norman: University of Oklahoma Press, 2012), and Lindsey G. Robertson, *Conquest by Law: How the Discovery of America Dispossessed Indigenous Peoples of Their Lands* (New York: Oxford University Press, 2005). For a list and description of each papal bull, see *The Doctrine of Discovery*, http://www.doctrineofdiscovery.org (accessed November 5, 2013).

7. Robert Williams, *The American Indian in Western Legal Thought: The Discourses of Conquest* (New York: Oxford University Press, 1992), 59.

8. George R. Stewart, *Names on the Land: A Historical Account of Place-Naming in the United States* (New York: New York Review Books, 2008), 169–73, 233, 302.

9. Bernard Sheehan, "Indian-White Relations in Early America," *William and Mary Quarterly 3*, no. 26 (1969): 267–96.

10. Leo Killsback, "Indigenous Perceptions of Time: Decolonizing Theory, World History, and the Fates of Human Societies," *American Indian Culture and Research Journal 37*, no. 1 (2013): 131.

11. Frederick Jackson Turner, *The Frontier in American History* (New York: Henry Holt, 1920), 127.

12. "Convention on the Prevention and Punishment of the Crime of Genocide, Paris, 9 December 1948," Audiovisual Library of International Law, http://untreaty.un.org/cod/avl/ha/cppcg/cppcg.html (accessed December 6, 2012). See also Josef L. Kunz, "The United Nations Convention on Genocide," *American Journal of International Law 43*, no. 4 (October 1949).

13. Jean M. O'Brien, *Firsting and Lasting: Writing Indians Out of Existence in New England* (Minneapolis: University of Minnesota Press, 2010).

14. Quoted in Edward Lazarus, *Black Hills/White Justice: The Sioux Nation versus the United States, 1775 to the Present* (New York: HarperCollins, 1991), 39; John F. Marszalek, *Sherman: A Soldier's Passion for Order* (Carbondale: Southern Illinois University Press, 2007), 379.

15. Wolfe, "Settler Colonialism," 393.

16. 18 U.S.C.§1151 (2001).

17. Walter R. Echo-Hawk, *In the Courts of the Conqueror* (Golden, CO: Fulcrum, 2010), 77–78.

18. "Tribes," US Department of the Interior website, http://www.doi.gov/tribes/index.cfm (accessed September 24, 2013); "Indian Reservation," *New World Encyclopedia*, http://www.newworldencyclopedia.org/entry/Indian_reservation (accessed September 24, 2013). See also Klaus Frantz, *Indian Reservations in the United States: Territory, Sovereignty, and Socioeconomic Change* (Chicago: University of Chicago, 1999).

19. Matthew 6:34.

20. Ralph Waldo Emerson, *The Speaker: A Quarterly Magazine of Successful Readings* 7: 337.

21. Toni Cade Bambara, *Those Bones Are Not My Child: A Novel* (New York: Knopf Doubleday, 2009).

CHAPTER 5: STAKING A CLAIM:

1. Jose Antonio Vargas, "My Life as an Undocumented Immigrant," *New York Times Magazine*, June 22, 2011, https://www.nytimes.com/2011/06/26/magazine/my-life-as-an-undocumented-immigrant.html.

2. Jose Antonio Vargas, "Undocumented in Trump's America," *New York Times*, November 19, 2016, https://www.nytimes.com/2016/11/20/opinion/sunday/undocumented-in-trumps-america.html.

3. Kathleen Kingsbury, "Why the New York Times Is Retiring the Term 'Op-Ed,'" *New York Times*, April 26, 2021, https://www.nytimes.com/2021/04/26/opinion/nyt-opinion-oped-redesign.html.

4. Kingsbury, "Why the New York Times Is Retiring the Term 'Op-Ed.'"

5. OpEd Project, "About" page, https://www.theopedproject.org/mission.

6. OpEd Project, "Structure," https://www.theopedproject.org/oped-basics#structure.

7. OpEdProject, "Questions to Ask Yourself When Writing," https://www.theopedproject.org/resources#questionstoask.

8. Trish Hall, *Writing to Persuade: How to Bring People Over to Your Side* (New York: Liveright Publishing, 2019), 28.

9. Hall, *Writing to Persuade* 167–70.

10. Hall, *Writing to Persuade* 175.

11. Hall, *Writing to Persuade* 175.
12. Hall, *Writing to Persuade* 177.
13. Hall, *Writing to Persuade* 180.
14. Hall, *Writing to Persuade* 183–84.

CHAPTER 6: ARE YOU THE RIGHT STORYTELLER FOR THIS STORY?

1. Matthew Salesses, *Craft in the Real World: Rethinking Fiction Writing and Workshopping* (New York: Catapult, 2021), xv.
2. Salesses, *Craft in the Real World*, xv.
3. Salesses, *Craft in the Real World*, 30.
4. Salesses, *Craft in the Real World*, xiii.
5. Salesses, *Craft in the Real World*, xiii.
6. Salesses, *Craft in the Real World*, xiii.
7. Salesses, *Craft in the Real World*, 29.
8. Paisley Rekdal, *Appropriate: A Provocation* (New York: W. W. Norton, 2021), 19.
9. Rekdal, *Appropriate*, 3–4.
10. Rekdal, *Appropriate*, 14.
11. Rekdal, *Appropriate*, 16.
12. Rekdal, *Appropriate*, 55.
13. Rekdal, *Appropriate*, 56 and 194–95.
14. Rekdal, *Appropriate*, 3–4.
15. All epigraphs are from Charles W. Chesnutt, *The Marrow of Tradition* (1901), ed. Werner Sollors (New York: W. W. Norton, 2012).
16. Langston Hughes, "Note on Commercial Theatre," in *The Norton Anthology of American Literature*, 9th ed., ed. Robert S. Levine, vol. 2 (New York: W. W. Norton, 2017).
17. Hughes, "Note on Commercial Theatre."
18. Adam Bernard, "Grandmaster Caz Interview," RapReviews.com, March 7, 2007, http://www.rapreviews.com/interview/caz2007.html.
19. "Cultural Appropriation: A Roundtable," *Artforum*, Summer 2017.
20. Lauren Berlant, "Cruel Optimism," in *The Affect Theory Reader*, ed. Melissa Gregg and Gregory J. Seigworth (Durham, NC: Duke University Press, 2010).
21. William Darity Jr. et al., *What We Get Wrong About Closing the Racial Wealth Gap* (Durham, NC: Samuel DuBois Cook Center on Social Equity/ Insight Center for Community Economic Development, 2018).
22. Chuck Collins et al., *The Ever-Growing Gap: Without Change, African-American and Latino Families Won't Match White Wealth for Centuries* (Washington, DC: Institute for Policy Studies, 2016).
23. Walter Benn Michaels, "Nobody's Story: The Myth of Cultural Appropriation," *Chronicle of Higher Education*, July 7, 2017, https://www.chronicle.com/article/The-Myth-of-Cultural/240464.

CHAPTER 7: RIPPLE EFFECTS OF MAKING WAVES

1. Masha Gessen, "Why Are Some Journalists Afraid of 'Moral Clarity'?," *New Yorker*, June 24, 2020, https://www.newyorker.com/news/our-columnists/why-are-some-journalists-afraid-of-moral-clarity.

2. Gessen, "Why Are Some Journalists Afraid of 'Moral Clarity'?"

3. Gessen, "Why Are Some Journalists Afraid of 'Moral Clarity'?"

4. Website of the Solutions Journalism Network (SJN); "Our Impact" page, https://www.solutionsjournalism.org/.

5. Website of the Solutions Journalism Network (SJN); "Our Impact" page.

6. Website of the Solutions Journalism Network (SJN); "Our Impact" page.

7. Website of the Solutions Journalism Network (SJN); "Our Impact" page.

8. Mathew Ingram, "Advocates Are Becoming Journalists. Is That a Good Thing?," *Columbia Journalism Review*, June 15, 2018 https://www.cjr.org/analysis/advocates-journalism.php.

9. Ingram, "Advocates Are Becoming Journalists."

10. Ingram, "Advocates Are Becoming Journalists."

11. Mia Sato, "How a Tiny Media Company Is Helping People Get Vaccinated," *MIT Technology Review*, April 21, 2021, https://www.technologyreview.com/2021/04/21/1023212/epicenter-is-a-vaccine-matchmaker-in-new-york-city.

12. Sato, "How a Tiny Media Company Is Helping People Get Vaccinated."

13. Sato, "How a Tiny Media Company Is Helping People Get Vaccinated."

CONCLUSION

1. Toni Morrison, "No Place for Self-Pity, No Room for Fear," *Nation*, March 23, 2015, https://www.thenation.com/article/archive/no-place-self-pity-no-room-fear/.

2. Lorraine Hansberry, Speech to the Winners of the Readers Digest/United Negro College Fund Creative Writing Contest: "Young, Gifted, and Black," New York City, May 1, 1964, https://www.lhlt.org/quotes?tid=5.

CREDITS

"Why I Write" from *Why I Write*, by George Orwell, was first published in 1946.

"Autobiographical Notes" from *Notes of a Native Son*, by James Baldwin, was first published in 1955.

"Ellaji and Lakshmiji," by Kavita Das, was first published in *Catapult* in March 2020.

"Tramp," by Kavita Das, was first published in *The Rumpus* in January 2013.

"Jyoti's Rainbow," by Kavita Das, was first published in *Guernica* in June 2015.

"Black and Blue," by Garnette Cadogan, was first published in the inaugural issue of *Freeman's* in 2015.

"Football, Free on the Streets," by Garnette Cadogan, was first published in the *New York Review of Books* in July 2018.

"Red Ink of Revisionist History," by Kavita Das, was first published in the *Los Angeles Review of Books* in August 2017.

"Selective Perception of Disinformation," by Kavita Das, was first published in the *Kenyon Review, Resistance, Change, Survival Issue* in October 2017.

"Introduction: This Land," from *An Indigenous Peoples' History of the United States*, by Roxanne Dunbar-Ortiz, was first published in 2014.

An excerpt from "Fear," in *Breathe: A Letter to My Sons*, by Imani Perry, was first published in 2019.

"How Could I Write About Women Whose Existence Is Barely Acknowledged?," by Gaiutra Bahadur, was first published in *The Guardian* in June 2016.

"COVID-19 Vaccine: What White Conservatives Can Learn from Black Americans," by Kavita Das, was first published in *Colorlines* in June 2021.

"A Virulent Privilege," by Kavita Das, was first published in *Nat. Brut* in 2017.

"La Otra," from Jaquira Díaz's memoir *Ordinary Girls*, as adapted in *Longreads* in June 2018.

"The School-to-Prison Pipeline Is Getting Worse for Black and Brown Girls," by Jaquira Díaz, was first published in *The Guardian* in March 2019.

"99 Years After the Tulsa Race Massacre, an Artist Reflects," by Crystal Z Campbell, was first published in *Hyperallergic* in June 2020.

"The Anti-Vaxxer Threat amid a Pandemic," by Kavita Das, was first published in *Newsday* in April 2020.

"Tolerance Has a Fatal Flaw. This Is the Solution," by Kavita Das, was first published in *CNN Opinion* in June 2020.

"Stories of Transracial Adoptees Must Be Heard—Even Uncomfortable Ones," by Nicole Chung, was first published in *The Guardian* in April 2019.

"The Specter of Caste in Silicon Valley," by Yashica Dutt, was first published in the *New York Times* in July 2020.

"Introduction: Appropriation and American Mythmaking" and "Conclusion: Business as Usual" from *White Negroes: When Cornrows Were in Vogue . . . and Other Thoughts on Cultural Appropriation*, by Lauren Michele Jackson, were published in 2019.

"Who Gets to Write What?," by Kaitlyn Greenidge, was first published in the *New York Times* in September 2016.

"How to Unlearn Everything: When It Comes to Writing the 'Other,' What Questions Are We Not Asking?," by Alexander Chee, was first published in *New York* magazine in October 2019.

"Who Gets to Write About Whom: Examining Authority, Authenticity, and Appropriation in Biography," by Kavita Das, was first published in the *Los Angeles Review of Books* in July 2018.

"Writers Shouldn't Romanticize Rejection," by Kavita Das, was first published by *The Atlantic* in November 2015.

"Recovering My Fifth Sense," by Kavita Das, was first published in *Longreads* in January 2018.

"There Is No One Way," by Alice Wong, was originally commissioned by SFMOMA's Open Space platform and published as part of the series *Six Degrees of Separation* in May 2020. This piece is adapted from the original.

"Stepping on a Star," adapted from *We Wear the Mask: 15 True Stories of Passing in America*, by Gabrielle Bellot, was published in 2017.

PERMISSIONS